The invention of Spain

Cultural relations
between Britain and Spain,
1770–1870

Manchester University Press

The invention of Spain
Cultural relations between Britain and Spain, 1770–1870

David Howarth

Manchester University Press
Manchester and New York

distributed exclusively in the USA by Palgrave

Copyright © David Howarth 2007

The right of David Howarth to be identified as the author of this work has been asserted by him in accordance with the Copyright, Designs and Patents Act 1988.

Published by Manchester University Press
Oxford Road, Manchester M13 9NR, UK
and Room 400, 175 Fifth Avenue, New York, NY 10010, USA
www.manchesteruniversitypress.co.uk

Distributed in the United States exclusively by
Palgrave Macmillan, 175 Fifth Avenue,
New York, NY 10010, USA

Distributed in Canada exclusively by
UBC Press, University of British Columbia, 2029 West Mall,
Vancouver, BC, Canada V6T 1Z2

British Library Cataloguing-in-Publication Data is available

Library of Congress Cataloging-in-Publication Data is available

ISBN 978 0 7190 6563 7 paperback

First published by Manchester University Press in hardback 2007

This paperback edition first published 2011

The publisher has no responsibility for the persistence or accuracy of URLs for any external or third-party internet websites referred to in this book, and does not guarantee that any content on such websites is, or will remain, accurate or appropriate.

Printed by Lightning Source

Contents

List of figures	*page* vii
Preface	ix
Acknowledgements	xiii
Chronology	xv
Abbreviations	xix
1 The decline of Spain	1
2 Politics	29
3 Religion	59
4 Historians	89
5 The Spanish School	120
6 Collectors	155
7 Picturing Spain	188
Select bibliography	229
Index	232

Figures

1 Sir Henry Raeburn, *Dr William Robertson*, University of Edinburgh   *page* 2
2 Antonio Chatelain, *Richard Ford*, National Portrait Gallery, London   36
3 J.F. Lewis, *Zumalacarregui and the Christina Spy*, By permission of the Board of Trustees, The Victoria and Albert Museum   55
4 Herbert Watkins, *Cardinal Nicholas Wiseman*, National Portrait Gallery, London   60
5 (?)Joseph Slater, *Joseph Blanco White*, National Portrait Gallery   61
6 *Served with a Writ*, *Punch*, 1850   77
7 Francis Williamson, *Sir William Stirling Maxwell, 9th Bt*, National Portrait Gallery, London   91
8 Sir George Reid, *James Anthony Froude*, National Portrait Gallery, London   105
9 Ludwig Passani, *Sir Austen Henry Layard*, National Portrait Gallery, London   145
10 David Roberts, *Chapel of the Nunnery of the Virgin at Carmona*, National Library of Scotland   195
11 David Roberts, *The Tower of the Comares, The Alhambra, Granada*, National Library of Scotland   199
12 David Roberts, *Chapel of Ferdinand and Isabella, Granada*, National Library of Scotland   202
13 David Roberts, *Part of the High Altar during Mass and the Great candle in the Chancel of Seville Cathedral*, The National Library   205
14 David Roberts, *Correo de los Moros, Granada*, National Library of Scotland   207
15 J.F. Lewis, *The Celebration of Mass in a Moorish Chapel in Cordova Cathedral*, The Property of Mr Francis Ford. Photograph Survey, Courtauld Institute of Art   209

16 J.F. Lewis, *Murillo Painting the Virgin in a Franciscan Monastery*, Reproduced by courtesy of The David Daniels Fund, The Minneapolis Institute of Fine Arts   211
17 Sir John Everett Millais Bt, *The Escape of a Heretic, 1559*, Museo de Arte de Ponce, The Luis A Ferré Foundation Inc., Ponce, Puerto Rico   215
18 Sir David Wilkie, *The Confessional*, *The Art Journal*, 1866   217
19 John Phillip, *The Early Career of Murillo, 1634* Christie's Images Ltd, 2006; Private Collection   219
20 Alfred Elmore, *The Emperor Charles V at the Convent of Yuste*, Reproduced by courtesy of Royal Holloway College, University of London   222
21 John Phillip, *Buying the Tickets*, Reproduced by courtesy of McManus Galleries, Dundee City Council Leisure and Arts   224
22 John Phillip, *Reading the Numbers*, Reproduced by courtesy of Aberdeen Art Gallery and Museums Collection   225

Preface

In *The Invention of Spain* I have tried to chart ways in which Spain and its history impinged on Britain from the age of the Enlightenment to the decline of the Victorian era. But I have also been interested in seeing the dialogue between Spain and Britain more broadly. The argument of this book is that for all the interest Spain provoked intermittently in Britain, the British never really understood the Peninsula on its own terms. Between 1808 and 1812 there was a massive emotional investment in the country because of the common cause against Bonapartism – a kind of mutual respect and sentimental belief that united the Briton and the Spaniard. Prior to that, ostensibly Britain and Spain had been enemies, but historic attraction and common sympathy made observers claim that these combatants, when they faced one another at the battle of Trafalgar, behaved with a marked degree of mutual chivalry which was different in kind from how the British and French responded in the theatre of war.

Great struggles played out in Spain during the Napoleonic occupation and its aftermath, together with the horrors of the Carlist Wars, provoked impassioned debate within Britain as to the virtues and defects of a conservative or liberal form of government. Lord Holland, torch-bearer for the radical politics of the liberal Charles James Fox, saw the Peninsula as a greenhouse where nostrums which the British would not accept for themselves could flourish in a hotter environment. For a Tory such as Wellington, postwar engagement with Spain had rather less to do with the country itself than with resistance to France. Many Victorians saw the Spanish as possessing an instinctive respect for tradition, and so the Spaniard as racial type was recruited by Tories as a bulwark in Europe against the rabid spread of Jacobinism, that dangerous legacy of the French Revolution.

In Britain, religious issues were passionately felt, from the failure to grant emancipation to Catholics in 1800 until the re-establishment of a Catholic hierarchy half a century later in 1850. The peculiar brand of Catholicism which was Spanish was a lurid aspect of the great debate in

Britain about granting freedom of worship. Emancipation was eventually accomplished, but only in the face of a demonisation of Catholicism based not just on the Vatican but – to an extent not previously acknowledged – also upon the theatre of worship played out in the churches of Spain. Emancipation was the only battle Wellington ever lost. The acceptance by the British of a Catholic hierarchy in Britain after 1850 was a victory won by Nicholas Wiseman, whose upbringing and culture had been profoundly Spanish. The interest of the British in Spanish religiosity was morbid, inseparable from the fears men had as to the reappearance of a proscribed faith in Britain.

British imagination and British prejudices often occluded a real understanding of a country declared by Voltaire in 1760 to be (for the European sensibility) as distant as Africa. Voltaire was delivering himself of his views on Spain at the same time as Samuel Johnson was holding forth in the London coffee houses. Johnson, the dominant figure in eighteenth-century English letters, appears to have been largely indifferent to Spain – but he was certainly actively hostile to Scotland. Once, in conversation with Boswell as to the best British historians, he dismissed the efforts of William Robertson, the Edinburgh clergyman and academic. Like a gale of wind, Johnson blew down the pretensions of Robertson as historian of Spain at its most golden as he took his interlocutor to task:

> BOSWELL. Will you not admit the superiority of Robertson, in whose history we find such penetration, such painting?
>
> JOHNSON. Sir, you must consider how that penetration and that painting are employed. It is not history, it is imagination. He who describes what he never saw, draws from fancy. Robertson paints minds, as Sir Joshua [Reynolds] paints faces, in a history-piece; he imagines an heroic countenance. You must look upon Robertson's work as romance, and try it by that standard. History it is not.[1]

Much is made of Robertson in what follows. To the Georgian and Victorian mind, Spain was romance, invention. Others besides Johnson, writers who could not have known his views, also described Robertson's genius as pictorial. They did not go so far as to compare him with Sir Joshua Reynolds and his heroics, but – had they thought about the parallel – they too would have seen the fitness of Johnson's analogy. Reynolds was in the habit of addressing an annual lecture to the students of the Royal Academy and, on those august occasions, habitually also told his audience of the need to transcend reality in pursuit of an elevated image. Now, it is precisely the degree of invention in Robertson's account of the Emperor Charles V which interests me: how – through moulding his conception of the kingdom of Spain – Robertson was revealing as much about his own society as about how he imagined life had once been in

Spain. Taking the broader chronological view, it would appear that much of the best writing by historians of Spain was offered to its readership as literature, not history: Sir William Stirling Maxwell's *Cloister life of Charles V* is more like a play in three acts than a sober account of 'what happened'. The indefatigable Victorian James Anthony Froude once declared that his ambition in writing his twelve-volume history of Tudor England, a work in which Spain featured prominently, had better approximate to a novel than to anything else, if it was to succeed.

Many who formed the sensibility of the Enlightenment, the Regency and the Victorian periods never set foot on Spanish soil. Arguably Britain's greatest painter, J.M.W. Turner, was wild about the Alps but ignored the Pyrenees. His great apologist John Ruskin, for all his Spanish connections, and it may be recalled his money came from sherry, was an ungrateful son. Ruskin shunned the romance of Seville for melancholic and aqueous Venice. Sir David Wilkie, a fashionable but overrated British painter, tried and failed to copy the secrets of Spanish facture onto canvas. It was only after the mid-point of the nineteenth century that a serious and scholarly study of Spanish architecture appeared – George Edmund Street's book on the gothic in Spain. But then, Street's researches hardly represented disinterested scholarship. He used his book as a missile to lob at opponents in the war over building preservation in Britain.

In literature Byron was much taken with Spain, and Disraeli enjoyed finding copy for his novels in the louche and perfumed interiors of Seville. Other writers periodically worked up a Spanish theme, but the most successful authors on Spain were American: Washington Irving and William Hickling Prescott. Spain did not provide that rich a vein of ore for the British literary mind.

Such Spanish artists as the British did warm to were often appreciated because they looked like something else – works by the Venetians or Flemish artists such as Van Dyck. The one exception was Velázquez, but he was a complicated case. The two most percipient British critics of Spanish art, Richard Ford and Sir William Stirling Maxwell, were devoted to him; or rather, it would be more accurate to say to what they imagined him to be. It was all a bit like Don Quixote's Dulcinea. As the knight kept a fantasy of his heart's desire in his deluded imagination, so what Victorian enthusiasts took to be the work of the great Spanish master remains an intriguing misconception in the history of connoisseurship.

As far as public institutions were concerned – that is to say, the 'national' gallery promiscuously open to all – Spanish painting was far better appreciated in France than in Britain. This was in part due to the creation on behalf of Louis-Philippe, of *Le Musée espagnol* at the Louvre in the 1830s. Whereas France had helped itself to Spanish paintings during the French occupation of 1808–1812, Britain had no such chance of rich Spanish pickings. Britain had been the beneficiary of France's troubles after the Revolution and the execution of the French royal family.

Wonderful Italian pictures had come to London from Paris but, hardly surprising, Spanish paintings were not among those consignments. The net effect was to reinforce the British prejudice in favour of Italian art. Thereafter it was a long struggle for the British connoisseur to begin to appreciate the 'Spanishness' of Spanish art. The later chapters of this book are as much concerned with the effort the British had to exert in coming to terms with Spanish material culture as they are in recording who had what when. London never did a brisk trade in Spanish painting – with the sole exception of an interlude in the mid-nineteenth century when the great French Hispanic collections were dispersed. The first acquisition by the National Gallery in London of a picture by Goya, to many now the pre-eminent artist of Spain, post-dates the chronological parameters of this book by some twenty years.*The Invention of Spain* reflects a British face in a Spanish mirror. What follows reveals more about Britain than about Spain, in an unusually tumultuous century. Spain was much in the air in the Augustan and Victorian periods, a point made by the English antiquary Richard Gough when he wrote to the Scots historian George Paton in February 1779: 'The Kingdome of Spain is at present a favourite object of Recherche with our people and I trust both nations will be benefited by it'.[2] Spain – or at least Hispanic Studies – is today, if not a favourite 'object of research', then at least a thriving aspect of university undergraduate curricula in Britain. Sadly, other languages and their cultures appear to be in precipitate retreat but not, it appears, Spanish and its offshoots. I trust the appearance of this book is timely, therefore, and that it will be of interest as cultural history.

Notes

1 R.D. Rust (ed.), *The Complete Works of Washington Irving*, 27 vols (Boston: Twayne, 1978), vol. xvii, 'Oliver Goldsmith: A Biography', p. 143.
2 Richard Gough to George Paton, 15 February 1779, N.L.S. Adv. Ms. 2956 (1), fol. 44v.

Acknowledgements

I would like to thank the following for help: Tom Bean, Claudia Heide, Paul Seabright and Nick Tromans, who read all or part of the manuscript. Their corrections and suggestions have been invaluable. In addition I have received much encouragement from my colleagues at Edinburgh University: Jeremy Robbins and Richard Thomson. Others have helped in so many important ways: Alan and Olivia Bell, Iain Brown, Viccy Coltman, Sir John Elliott, Robert Ferguson, Antonio Giménez Cruz, the late Sir Brinsley Ford, Frances Harris, James Holloway, Alex Howarth, Christina Hussell, Lowell Libson, Christopher Lloyd, Hilary MacCartney, Tim and Catherine Myles, Richard and Gill Rusbridger, Nick and Frances Stadlen, Crystal Webster, Bob and Hilary Williams, and Amaia Zulaika-Carmichael.

I owe a particular debt to The Leverhulme Trust and the Arts and Humanities Research Board who together, but at different critical moments, gave me extended leave from teaching, thus providing means to work in libraries and archives. I am most grateful also to the President and Fellows of St John's College, Oxford, who awarded me a visiting Long Vacation scholarship. This enabled me to undertake extended work in the Bodleian Library. I am much in debt to the staff of the Glasgow City Archives and Special Collections for their patience and assistance over several years. There are, however, two people without whose support and generosity with information and ideas this book could not have been written. They are Tom Bean and Nigel Glendinning.

I am particularly grateful to the following for permission to quote from manuscripts in their possession: the Earl of Clarendon, Sir Hew Hamilton Dalrymple, Mr D. Maxwell MacDonald and Oliver Russell.

Chronology of main events, 1516–1898

Politics in Spain	Politics in Britain	Cultural events
16th century 1516–1556 Charles V (abdicated) 1556–1598 Philip II	1554 Marriage of Philip of Spain and Mary Tudor in Winchester Cathedral 1588 Spanish Armada	1598–1664 Zurbarán 1599–1660 Velázquez Building of the Escorial 1563–1584
17th century 1621–1665 Philip IV	1623 Charles I in Madrid	1618–1682 Murillo
18th century 1759–1788 Charles III, King of Spain 1771–1779 Lord Grantham, Minister in Madrid	1701–1713 War of Spanish Succession 1756–1763 Seven Years War	1746–1828 Goya Anton Raffael Mengs in Madrid in 1760s and again 1775/6 1759 William Robertson *History of Scotland* 1769 Robertson *History of the Reign of the Emperor Charles V* 1776 Adam Smith *An Enquiry into the Nature and Causes of the Wealth of Nations* 1776–1788 Edward Gibbon *Decline and Fall of the Roman Empire* 1777 Robertson *History of America*
19th century 1808: Abdication of Charles IV French invasion of Spain Madrid occupied by Murat Joseph Buonaparte king of Spain Convention of Cintra 1809 English army in Portugal Sir John Moore killed at Corunna		

Chronology

Politics in Spain	Politics in Britain	Cultural events
1812 Wellington drives French out of Spain Constitution of Cádiz 1813 Ferdinand VII (1808–1833) returns to throne. Repudiates Constitution of Cádiz and reigns as a reactionary. 1820 Liberal Revolt in Spain 1820–1823 *Trienio* – three years of liberal constitutional government in Spain 1823 'The Ten Thousand Sons of St Louis' (French army) ousts *liberales* and restores Ferdinand VII 1831 General Torrijos attempts to raise Andalucía in revolt. Is executed together with English supporters 1833 Ferdinand VII dies 1833–1840 first Carlist War 1833–1868 Isabella II; Mariá Cristina as regent 1833–1839 George Villiers British Minister in Madrid 1870 General Prim assassinated	1825 Canning recognises the independence of Spanish colonies in South America 1827 Catholic Emancipation 1835 Evans recruits British Expeditionary Force to fight for *Cristinos* 1850 Cardinal Wiseman issues his letter *From out of the Flaminian Gate* re-establishes the Catholic hierarchy in England	1812 Wellington receives gift of Spanish paintings from grateful nation. This forms the basis of the Apsley House collection. Includes Velázquez *Water-Carrier of Seville* 1814 Goya paints *Ferdinand VII and his Family* 1814 Scott's *Waverley*, his first historical novel Ferdinand VII presents Velázquez *Tela Real* to Sir Henry Wellesley, British minister at Madrid. Bought by National Gallery in 1846 1819 Prado Museum Madrid founded 1819 Lord Byron *Don Juan* 1822 Joseph Blanco White *Doblado's Letters from Spain* 1824 National Gallery London founded 1823–1832 Southey *History of the Peninsular War* 1825 White's *Evidence Against Catholicism* 1826 Washington Irving moves to Madrid 1827–1828 Wilkie in Spain paints *Maid of Saragossa* 1828 Irving *Life of Columbus* 1829 Irving *Conquest of Granada* 1830–1833 Richard Ford lives in Andalucía (Seville and Granada) and travels extensively through Spain 1833 David Roberts and John Frederick Lewis painting in Andalucía 1838 *Le Musée espagnol* opens in Paris 1842 Owen Jones and Pascual de Gayangos *Plans Sections and Elevations of the Alhambra* Borrow *The Bible in Spain*

Politics in Spain	Politics in Britain	Cultural events
		1845 Richard Ford *A Handbook for Travellers in Spain*
		1848 William Stirling *Annals of the Artists of Spain*
		1840s Charles Clifford photographs Spain
		1851 Owen Jones exhibits an Alhambra room at the Great Exhibition
		1853 National Gallery buys Zurbarán *S.Francis in Meditation*
		1856 Owen Jones *Grammar of Ornament*
		1856–1870 James Anthony Froude *History of England* (12 vols)
		1857 Manchester Art Treasures Exhibition
		1865 George Edmund Street *Some Account of Gothic Architecture in Spain*
		1869–1877 Sir Austen Henry Layard, British Minister in Madrid. With Sir Henry Cole arranges for casts of Spanish sculpture and architecture to be sent to the South Kensington Museum. Plans to cover the interior of the dome of St Paul's Cathedral with *azulejos*
		1898 National Gallery London buys its first Goyas

Abbreviations

BL	British Library
BL Add. Ms.	British Library Additional Manuscripts
Bod. Lib.	Bodleian Library, Oxford
MLG	Stirling Maxwell of Pollok Records, Glasgow City Archives and Special Collections
NLS	National Library of Scotland
NRA (S)	National Register of Archives Scotland

For Francis and Nick

1
The decline of Spain

The most ambitious book in English on the place of Spain in early modern Europe has the sonorous title *The history of the reign of the Emperor Charles V: with a view of the progress of society in Europe, from the subversion of the Roman Empire, to the beginning of the sixteenth century*. It was written by William Robertson, a Scots clergyman and university principal (Figure 1). His *Charles V* appeared in three volumes in 1769. Edward Gibbon, one of the most celebrated stylist of all English historians, paid fulsome tribute when writing to Robertson's son with condolences after the death of his father in the summer of 1793. Gibbon acknowledged how he had looked to him to encourage his own writing: 'I have always revered Dr Robertson as the first historian of the British school, and the praise which associates me, at whatsoever distance, to his name and honour will ever be the most grateful to my ear. Instead of the jealousy which sometimes adheres even to superior merit I have invariably found him disposed to encourage my labours, and to cherish my reputation.'[1]

The affable Robertson was the most prominent figure of the Scottish Enlightenment, although David Hume and Adam Smith had better minds – but they were more private men. Between 1750 and 1790, Robertson was the keystone of an arch which spanned the two universities of Glasgow and Edinburgh. Robertson, Smith and Hume dominated an interlude of intellectual enquiry more distinguished than any in the cultural history of Scotland. The central paradox for that country is how it was that immediately after the decisive defeat of national aspiration at Culloden in 1746, for the first and only time in its history, Scotland became international.

Smith left Edinburgh for Glasgow and Hume migrated to London, while Robertson by contrast spent his whole life in or near the Scottish capital. There he became a public figure whose views were courted by the Hanoverians. At the time of the 'Forty Five, Robertson had already been ordained a minister of the Church of Scotland, but that had seemed no

1 Sir Henry Raeburn, *Dr William Robertson*

impediment to his deserting a flock at Gladsmuir in East Lothian to volunteer against the Jacobites. Thereafter, Robertson became both head of Edinburgh University and the dominant influence in the Church of Scotland. Between 1762 and 1792 Robertson enjoyed the office of Principal; his friend and biographer Dugald Stewart noted how during those thirty-one years the University Senate delivered unanimous agreement on every issue. In addition to commanding the affairs of a large university, in 1763 Robertson was also made Moderator of the Church of Scotland, an office which could only be held for one year. However, for nearly two decades he acted as the dominant force in the nation's ecclesiastical life; a restraining and calming presence, he made it his business to reconcile wayward presbyteries who were inclined to be cantankerous and disrespectful of the decisions of the Church establishment. Instinctively consensual, Robertson sided with the powers that be. A talent for promoting compromise made him valued by the Hanoverian regime during the difficult years after the final defeat of the Stuart cause.

Robertson was enviably prolific as an academic: he would have done well in any current university's Research Assessment Exercise. He had his first major success with his *History of Scotland*, published in Edinburgh in 1759. This was followed ten years later by the most influential of his books, *The History of the Reign of Charles V* (1769). This chapter is concerned with how that once famous but now neglected book was a major influence in moulding a British conception of Spain. So too the subject of the decline and fall of Spain features prominently in Adam Smith's still more celebrated *The Wealth of Nations*. Intriguingly, the most illuminating writing on Spain to appear in eighteenth-century Britain was the achievement of the Scottish Enlightenment. How it was that all this came from the pens of progressive Protestant writers is the present subject of enquiry. Scotsmen, no sooner subjugated by English imperialism, became drawn to a study of a still greater 'tyranny' – that of Spain, an empire upon which it was said the sun never set. Scots traditionally allied themselves with France, the inveterate enemy of Spain. It was England not Scotland that had the historic ties with Iberia: the English alliance with Portugal was its oldest and one about which English politicians could wax sentimental when it suited them, while the English themselves had been deeply committed to the War of the Spanish Succession (1701–1713). In that protracted affair, the two sides were commanded by British generals.

Part of the explanation is that those Scotsmen who wrote about Spain saw themselves as North Britons; members of an island race, and who wished to look at Spain because they needed to understand the nascent imperial power which Great Britain had become by 1750. This quest for Spain was as much a journey of self-discovery as it was an attempt to understand a body politic which, two hundred years before, had been an empire larger than that of ancient Rome; an empire whose earlier and separate decline was being traced by Gibbon in London while Robertson and Smith busied themselves north of the border with a more recent dissolution.

Robertson took time to choose the subject of Charles V, and two of his most distinguished admirers counselled him against it. Neither David Hume nor Horace Walpole felt that the subject would have that mass readership which had been captivated by Robertson's *The History of Scotland*. Both were eager to press their own themes on the mellifluous historian: Walpole wanted Robertson to write of Greece, while Hume suggested 'Henry the Fourth of France'. Robertson's friend and biographer Dugald Stewart revealed that neither idea appealed, whereas the subject of Charles V: 'attracted his curiosity to two of the greatest and most interesting subjects of speculation in the history of human affairs; –

the enterprises of modern ambition in the Western World, and the traces of ancient wisdom and arts existing in the East'.[2]

Robertson was also the first major British writer of any influence to offer a sympathetic view of the place of Islam in the Mediterranean basin, though hardly, it has to be said, the first person in British public life to show marked sympathy for aspects of Islamic culture. Toward the end of the seventeenth century, Sir Christopher Wren had been sufficiently intrigued by 'Saracenic' architecture, a term inchoate enough to include Moorish architecture within it, to provide a variation on that theme for Tom Tower, the entrance to Christ Church, the grandest of the Oxford Colleges. A century or so later, Sir William Chambers erected a classicised version of the Alhambra in Kew Gardens. Such examples represented only the beginnings of a sustained if somewhat superficial interest in Moorish design. The whimsy of Chambers' design for Kew makes it perhaps surprising that such buildings were not described as *Islamick* rather as Walpole's Strawberry Hill, just down the river, was recognised as *Gothick*. As it was, it took another thirty years or so before a term became current in English architectural writing which attempted to define the bizarre eclecticism to be found in William Porden's remodelling of the Duke of Westminster's house at Eaton Hall, Cheshire (1804–1812). The famous diarist and commentator on late Georgian culture, Joseph Faringdon, remarked of how a friend had enthused to him about Eaton which Faringdon recorded was 'in a style of architecture called Morisco Gothic'[3], that is, a hybrid style which demonstrated about as much understanding of Islam as a *chinoiserie* tea caddy did to Confucian China. Nevertheless, there was even then sympathy within Britain for the 'other'. Recently much has been written about the attitude of the West toward the Moslem world, and many of those who have surveyed this clash of cultures have marked out a dusty and arid road.[4] The Occident has been seen as largely hostile and contemptuous of Islamic culture. However, Robertson represented something of a gilded spine amidst a shelf of dark leather. His interest in Islam was of real importance in developing sympathy for non-Western civilisations. To some extent it was due to the popularity and influence of Robertson's history that the kingdom of *Al-Andalus* became the first Islamic culture to be appreciated in the more developed European nations. This was by virtue of its geographical proximity, and its status as a hybrid of European and Islamic elements.

Stewart, who knew Robertson well but wrote his appreciation at the beginning of the nineteenth century, was anxious for his readership to understand that if the Enlightenment was to apply the nostrums of theory to practical politics, it had needed to understand that there was an unbroken continuity between the world of the early sixteenth century and the age which had succeeded the Seven Years War, a global conflict which had lasted from 1756 to 1763 and ended with the Treaty of Paris. Thereafter Britain became master in Canada and India, an intruder into Central

America with the acquisition of the islands of Tobago, St Vincent, Dominica and Grenada, and manipulator of Spain whom she forced to give up Florida in exchange for Havana. British representatives in Paris, gathered for the peace, worked to insure that Britain would replace Spain as the world's dominant colonial power, while historians in Edinburgh worked to promote understanding of how Britain could learn to sustain international responsibilities where the Spaniards had failed.

When *Charles V* was published in 1769, everyone read it. Admired in Moscow by Catherine the Great and studied by Jefferson in Monticello, it was appreciated for the felicity of its style, the universalism of its themes, and the timeless relevance of its argument. Stewart suggests how it was received both as a work of political theory and disinterested history: 'In truth, this *Dissertation*, under the unassuming title of an Introduction to the History of Charles V, may be regarded as an introduction to the History of Modern Europe. It is invaluable, in this respect, to the historical student; and it suggests, in every page, matter of speculation to the politician and the philosopher.'[5]

So much for Stewart as to the relevance of Robertson for both the scholar and the man of business. But it is necessary to begin at the beginning. The title page reveals the instinctual optimism which Robertson shared with his Enlightenment *confrères*. Robertson chose the word 'progress' to describe the unfolding of history as it could be observed within the context of his account of the place of Charles V in early modern Europe. Much, it might be thought, turns on the use of the word 'progress'. It is so suggestive because although Robertson's book offers an interpretation of Charles V as a heroic failure, his exegetical, providential text is a profoundly constructive account, as forward-looking as it is retrospective. The central thesis of Robertson has to do with Charles's attempt to create a balance of power in Europe set against centrifugal forces. To sustain his argument, Robertson extended his gaze. What might be assumed from its title to be a biography of Charles V is actually an overview of Europe. Taking his inspiration from what he saw to have been the huge ambition of his subject, Robertson seems to have had Charles's motto steadily before him: *Ne plus ultra*. For Robertson no less than for his hero, dominion stretches to the ends of the civilised world as the reader travels from Aleppo to Augsburg, from the Crusades to the Council of Trent.

But there was something else besides universalism which holds a key to understanding the tremendous success of *Charles V*, a success which is to be gauged from the appearance of a 10th edition by 1802; just over thirty years after the first appearance of the book. Robertson's place as a historian of European stature had as much to do with presentation as content. Although Robertson lacked Gibbon's mordant humour and suggestive cynicism, he was a stylist of great elegance if marked superfluity: read in the drawing room for pleasure, in the study for instruction. But then

Robertson is not Gibbon and today he is fit only for academics. It was, after all, of him that Samuel Johnson was thinking when he argued with his biographer James Boswell about British historians. Johnson recalled the view of an old college tutor when he and Boswell were setting to over the relative merits of Goldsmith, Hume, Robertson and Lord Lyttleton. Johnson declared: 'I would say to Robertson, what an old tutor of a college said to one of his pupils, "Read over your compositions, and whenever you meet with a passage which you think is particularly fine, strike it out!"'[6]

Robertson is remembered now as a historian, but in his own lifetime public men who read him – and most did – were as interested in how he managed the religious life of Scotland as they were in what he had to say about the Inquisition and the bearing which the history of Spain might have on current problems. Thus, late in Robertson's life William Wilberforce wrote to recruit him for his campaign against slavery, wanting to know whether Robertson's understanding of how the Catholic Church had conducted itself in South America might be useful for his thinking about Africa:

> The subject which is the occasion of my troubling you with this letter, that of the Slave Trade, is one on which I am persuaded our sentiments coincide and in calling forth your good offices in such a cause I trust you will think that whilst I incur, I also bestow an obligation. Let me add also, that I should be extremely thankful for any intelligence respecting the institutions of the Jesuits in Paraguay which it has long struck me might prove a most useful subject of investigation to anyone who would form a plan for the civilization of Africa [7]

Robertson's position as the commanding voice in Presbyterian Scotland required intelligence and courage. It was a role he had exercised in Edinburgh during the anti-Catholic Gordon riots in London of 1780; just the year before, his own house in Edinburgh had been sacked because he had persuaded the Assembly to throw out a remonstrance against removing civil penalties against Catholics. Here it is as well to recall that *Charles V* had been preceded by his *History of Scotland* (1759). Both revealed what might be termed the author's 'professional' interest in the history of religious bigotry and the damage it had done historically in different societies. The *History of Scotland* had been as much an exhortation to compatriots to recognise what they had been, discover who they were and aspire to what they might become as it was a history of events centred upon the period from the Reformation to the Union of 1707. The *History of Scotland* was a political pamphlet, albeit in a distinctly ambitious and extended form. Never in the history of Scottish letters has anything quite so subversive been produced, and never so significant a challenge to the inflammatory issue of self-identity couched in such beguiling prose. One recent commentator summarised this with powerful clarity: 'Robertson questioned the accepted antiquity of the Scottish kingdom; raised major doubts about this small nation's proud historic tradition of embattled independence; interrogated the values of its distinctive Reformed Church; and undermined the very notion of an authentic history of freedom within Scotland prior to incorporating Union with England in 1707.'[8]

Through *The History of Scotland*, Robertson set out the parameters of how a settlement could be reached between countries whose internecine warfare the author had always deplored. The challenge of the *History of Scotland* for Robertson was to grind a lens to see how to prevent another disaster for his country of the sort which had ended at Culloden. Robertson was never tempted to use his work as a siege engine to lay against the walls of English imperialism. So it was that by declining to urge a recall to arms, Robertson ingratiated himself with government in London who were reassured to identify what Johnson always thought a rarity – a Scotsman of international stature who was an eminently reasonable man. Robertson's *History of Scotland* blends analysis and admonition to deliver a homily on the need for countries to dispose of their difficulties by promoting the virtues of a balanced constitution and a respect for difference. To the extent that the *History of Scotland* does this, there is an important philosophical connection between Robertson's account of his own country, and the altogether more alien prospect of Spain; even though ten years separate the appearance of the respective books. Having provided prescriptions for harmonious union between the crowns of Scotland and England, it was perhaps predictable that Robertson should have been drawn to the Emperor Charles V, a man whose mission had been to build on the work of Ferdinand and Isabella who had united the country, by binding together the constituent parts of what had now become under Charles himself an empire. Charles V attempted this by trying to obtain submissive cooperation from nations with quite distinct cultural antecedents. Robertson was a patriot certainly, but one who saw the survival of his country in terms of how successful it could be in rising above the partisan. Much analysis in *The History of Scotland* is devoted to understanding how the dynamics of crown, aristocracy and people produced the peculiar history and current profile of the nation, something he was to consider again in his dissection of the kingdom of Spain. Robertson championed the Union as the 'decisive deliverance of Scottish society from aristocratic oppression' just as he would be intrigued by how Spain had achieved its greatness because the Spanish city balanced the conflicting interests of crown and aristocracy. Robertson's fixed belief in what he saw as the flourishing social condition of the city in early modern Spain meant that for him there had been a context in which the commoner could exercise freedom and – through the Cortes, or Spanish parliament – express his viewpoint. Although Robertson never pauses to tell the reader how the Cortes worked, who belonged to it and what its powers were, in no way did this impede him from pointing up the difference with the situation as it had prevailed in Scotland. Although at no point in Robertson's *Charles V* is the contrast between Spain and Scotland spelled out, the different role of the city in each was something Robertson pondered. The place of the city in the emergence of the Scottish nation is summarised by a modern commentator: '[a] mountainous land lacking good overland communications, Scotland provided a refractory baronage with secure regional power-bases from which to flout the limited authority of the monarch. Nor were the powers of the barons checked by the emergence of cities in which legal values might have developed'.[9]

This contrasts markedly with the understanding which Robertson acquired of the place of the city in Spain. The basic argument of Robertson's *History of the reign of Charles V* was that Charles had a vision of European peace which could have transcended nationalities, reconciled Christians, and provided a bulwark against the infidel. The mantra which echoes throughout is 'the balance of power in Europe'. Although Robertson is critical of how often Charles V was ready to go to war, he reserves his most damning strictures for the tireless appetite for fighting which Francis I of France had all too frequently displayed. With Charles V warfare was conducted for altogether more expansive reasons which had to do with a European vision and not, as in the case of Francis I, the pursuit of a partial and narrow nationalism. Here it might be added that a partial and narrow nationalism was exactly what Robertson had wished to educate his readership to avoid when he had published his *History of Scotland*. According to Robertson, Charles V's vision of a Europe held together by balance and counter-balance, was split open upon the rock of Valois intransigence. It is argued that after years of effort to come to an accommodation with the king of France, Charles V gave up in disgust and retired to his melancholy retreat, the monastery at Yuste. For generations thereafter, Yuste was to become a shrine to the historians of Imperial Spain no less attractive than Santiago remains to the Catholic observant.

There is, then, a common thread which connects the *History of Scotland* with *The History of Charles V*. Just as England and Scotland were born to war as the sparks fly up, so too for Robertson, Spain and France were inveterate enemies. But although Robertson may have deplored the enormous waste of European nations turning upon each other, rather than as they should have been upon their common enemy the infidel, societies had an ineluctable tendency toward progress. The agenda of *Charles V* was to compose a moral exegesis for Robertson's own age. As an enlightened thinker, Robertson subscribed to the belief that through the study of history, it was both possible and indeed requisite to extrapolate lessons and learn from the mistakes of the past. What Charles had failed to achieve for Europe in 1550 was for Robertson a goal worthy of a civilised society which based its conduct on the assumption of progress and the application of reason. Accordingly, although Robertson felt that Charles had failed in his attempt to create a balance of power, what the Emperor had wanted could be achieved by Robertson's own generation. Just as Robertson had offered a history of the relations between Scotland and England as a powerful argument to demonstrate the need for the two countries to settle their differences without recourse to further bloodshed, so the future of Europe – as it emerged from the disruption of the Seven Years War (1763) – was that balance of power which had always eluded Charles V. Robertson had pressing reasons to consider Spain. He was a Scottish patriot whose cosmopolitan education made it abundantly clear that a narrow form of nationalism represented the road to obscurity. But he was also an Enlightenment thinker dependent upon correspondents from Edinburgh to Naples. Robertson was ambitious to extrapolate what was most progressive and valuable about the past and apply it to the challenges of his own society. The attempt by Charles V to create a pan-nationalist empire had a pressing relevance to Robertson as he observed the political contours of Europe in his own day. Such, then, are the reasons why the most distinguished account of Golden Age Spain to appear in eighteenth-century Europe came to be written by the unlikely figure of a Scots cleric. What does Robertson say about Spain, however, when it appeared to be at the height of its powers?

The dominance of Spain or, rather, the illusion of Spain's abiding dominance is something which Robertson remarks upon as a feature of the mid-eighteenth century intellectual landscape. Those in Britain wishing to understand how the nation to which they belonged had arrived at the state it was in *c.*1770 were bound to address themselves both to the earlier dominance of Spain in Europe and, as a corollary, to its decline and fall. Toward the end of the third and final volume of *Charles V*, Robertson writes of how

> Nothing can give a more striking idea of the ascendant which it [Spain] had acquired, and of the terror which it had inspired, than that after its vigour was spent with extraordinary exertions of its strength, after Spain was become only the shadow of a great name, and its monarchs were sunk in debility and dotage, the house of Austria still continued to be formidable. The nations of Europe had so often felt its superior power, and had been so constantly employed in guarding against it, that the dread of it became a kind of political habit, the influence of which remained when the causes, which had formed it, ceased to exist.[10]

Robertson saw Charles V as a man of tenacious purpose who overshadowed the impetuosity of Francis I and the swollen vanity of Henry VIII. He believed that a close scrutiny of the actions and policies of Charles V was a more valuable exercise than studies of Charles's English and French rivals. For Robertson, Charles had a vision more penetrating and sagacious than any promoted by either Francis I or Henry VIII, indeed a far better chance of realising his aims because of the extent of his territory, the superiority of Spanish arms, and the influx of New World wealth. Furthermore, Robertson clearly thought that his own age looked out over a continent which had essentially the same political landscape as Europe of two hundred years earlier. The fact that the contours were the same was in important ways a direct consequence of Charles V's policies. Central to Robertson's thesis is his belief that Charles was the potter at the wheel:

> The nations of Europe in that age, as in the present, were like one great family ... It was during his reign and in consequence of the perpetual efforts to which his enterprizing ambition roused him, that the different kingdoms of Europe acquired internal vigour; that they discerned the resources of which they were possessed; that they came both to feel their own strength, and to know how to render it formidable to others. It was during his reign, too, that the different kingdoms of Europe, which in former times seemed frequently to act as if they had been single and disjoined, became so thoroughly acquainted, and so intimately connected with each other, as to form one great political system, in which each took a station, wherein it has remained since that time with less variation than could have been expected after the events of two active centuries.[11]

Here perhaps most eloquently, Robertson records his belief that a study of Charles V holds the key for political economists who wished to understand how Europe looked in the last quarter of the eighteenth century. Benighted and priest-ridden Spain had to be studied if Europe was to be understood in the age of Rationalism.

There are a multitude of ways in which Robertson's great study shaped the approaches of later historians. But of particular interest is Robertson's essentially sympathetic account of the place of Islam in Mediterranean civilisation. Given the extensive afterlife of Robertson's publications, his concession that during the Middle Ages the Moslem world was a more civilised society than the Christian may be what helped to make people think creatively about the place of the Spanish caliphate in Iberian history. Paralleling Gibbon's cynicism, Robertson writes of the great and destructive initiative of the Crusades, of how they represented '[the] only common enterprize in which the European nations ever engaged, and which they all undertook with equal ardour, [and it] remains a singular monument of human folly.'[12] But while Robertson remarks on the rapacity of the Crusades and the destructive effect of their temporary conquests, there is also much about the meeting of East and West which is regarded as positive. The encounter between Christian Europe and Islam would also be noted separately by Adam Smith as central to the progress of civilisation in Europe. Robertson saw the Crusaders' contact with the Caliphate as wholly to the advantage of a barbarous European rabble: 'It was not possible for the Crusaders to travel through so many countries, and to behold their various customs and institutions, without acquiring information and improvement. Their views enlarged; their prejudices wore off; new ideas crowded into their minds; and they must have been sensible, on many occasions, of the rusticity of their own manners, when compared with those of a more polished people.'[13]

Robertson traces the effects of the Crusaders' contacts with the superior civilisation of the East by arguing that before long, the Crusaders themselves acquired a taste for the arts, ' a love of elegance and splendour', which these spiritual mercenaries introduced into Europe on their return from the Middle East. However, the superiority which Europe enjoyed over the rest of the globe by Robertson's lifetime were attributable to something else– the appearance in Europe in the late Middle Ages of autonomous cities and the growth of the city state, themselves the product of that increase in commercial intercourse which was a direct consequence of the meeting of East and West during the Crusades.

Robertson thought that the political health of a nation depended less on any promises enshrined in written constitutions than on the state of its trade, discernible from the relative vigour of cities. Interestingly, Robertson then went on to identify what he called the 'feudal government' of Spain at the accession of Charles V to the Spanish crown as 'in a state more favourable to liberty than in any other of the great European kingdoms'. Robertson saw the city in Spain at the dawn of early modern Europe, as if it were a gene holding the key to future growth. Urban settlements in Spain, so Robertson believed, were the most advanced then existing in Europe, a view which is something of a fixed belief throughout the book but which latter-day economic historians would find hard to accept. According to Robertson, Spanish cities had the most developed and sophisticated patterns of trade, and it was their mercantile status which he identified as the critical element leading to the safeguarding of the rights of individuals and the checks and balances from which contemporaries benefited. For Robertson, cities are that element of society which is best equipped and most inclined 'to mitigate the rigour of the feudal institutions, and to introduce a more liberal and equal form of government ... ever ready to act as the guardians of the public freedom and independence'[14]

Many aspects of *Charles V* helped to shape the Victorian approach to Spain, but perhaps its most abiding contribution had to do with the significance of the rise of the city in medieval Castile. It was due to the relative vigour of the city there that the *Cortes*, or Parliament, became an independent force significantly sooner than its equivalent in England. At no point does Robertson offer a comparative chronology between the different systems of government which he describes as having arisen in Spain and England respectively. It is partly because of these broad and somewhat inchoate generalisations – to which at times it might be thought Robertson was addicted – that his views as to the comparative importance of representative institutions in the two countries represented something of a contentious claim. It was, however, a bold argument subscribed to by later historians; until it came to be modified by the great nineteenth-century Spanish antiquarian Pascual de Gayangos, whose scrutiny of original documents made him take a more sober view of the real nature of the Cortes.[15]

Robertson felt that what had given rise to the pre-eminence of the Spanish city in early modern Europe was the knock-on effect of that promotion of trade which had been stimulated by the Crusades. In the Middle Ages, Spain had been peculiarly well qualified to take advantage of commercial exchange between the Christian and the Moslem worlds because of the Caliphate of Córdoba established in southern Spain in 756 and obliterated as a Islamic enclave with its capture by Ferdinand III of Castile in 1232. Paradoxically, however, it was the very existence of Moslem Spain, and the threat that it represented to the outlying Christian community, which also helped account for the greatness of the Spanish city. Robertson explains it thus:

> As the Spanish cities were populous, many of the inhabitants were of a rank superior to those who resided in towns in other countries of Europe. That cause, which contributed chiefly to their population, affected equally persons of every condition, who flocked thither promiscuously, in order to find shelter there, or in hopes of making a stand there against the enemy, with greater advantage than in any other station. The persons elected as their representatives in the Cortes by the cities, or promoted to offices of trust and dignity in the government of the community, were often, as will appear from transactions which I shall hereafter relate, of such considerable rank in the kingdom, as reflected lustre on their constituents, and on the stations wherein they were placed.[16]

Robertson thought Spain and its empire central to an understanding of mid-eighteenth-century Europe. But Robertson was a powerfully ambitious man who perceived the need not only to promote but also to protect his reputation by proclaiming his methodology. By contrast, the earl of Clarendon, the pre-eminent historian of seventeenth-century England and eyewitness and chronicler of its Civil War, writing just over a century before Robertson, had felt no need to refer to documents to lend authority to his interpretation of his own times: he was quite untroubled as to any theoretical debate as to how facts were best garnered and history written most authoritatively. His approach was in marked contrast to that of Robertson. Through absence from the drama of personal involvement, Robertson was not writing a memoir, as could be thought had been the case with Clarendon. As well, Robertson was writing on an European scale whereas Clarendon confined himself to the British Isles. These differences may then account in part for the concern Robertson shows to make abundantly clear his strenuous efforts to acquire the facts from people who were closer to his subject than he.[17] Such preparatory papers as have survived – and they are in the National Library of Scotland, consisting in part as slips of paper with brief jottings, but also some much longer and carefully considered letters – indicate that Robertson cultivated those who had direct experience of the places in which he was interested. He corresponded with Thomas Robinson, 2nd Baron Grantham (1738–1786), who together with his predecessor, Sir Benjamin Keene (d.1757), were of all British ambassadors to Spain those with the broadest sympathy for its culture.[18] In Spain Keene served longer than any other representative, with two periods of office in 1724–1739 and 1749–1757. However, Grantham too was a remarkable observer of the country between 1771 and 1779, when he was nurturing British interests. In Spain, Grantham demonstrated a quite exceptional enthusiasm for its culture. Both Grantham and his chaplain, Robert Waddilove, made strenuous efforts to supply material unavailable to Robertson in Edinburgh, some of it best described as ethnography. Waddilove may have been chosen by Grantham because he was deeply interested in material culture, and painting especially; he made extensive notes of pictures he could identify in the Escorial as having come from the collection of Charles I of England and, in 1796, published a translation in two volumes of Anton Raphael Mengs's *Essay on Painting*.

Among the Robertson memoranda is a long letter from Grantham, actually a short essay, so prolix that its author felt the need of an apology. It was sent from the Escorial on 31 October 1776. Grantham begins by acknowledging how much he is indebted to Waddilove who he considers much better equipped to 'unravel to search and to judge' what might be germane to Robertson's purposes. Grantham then reveals himself to have been only the first of a long line of Hispanicists who were to find the difficulties of conducting primary research in Spain almost insurmountable. What was a solo by Grantham was to become a part song by the middle of the nineteenth century when the Spanish royal archives at Simancas began to be mined for what would become the monumental histories of the Golden Age. By then, everyone complained of the huge difficulties of finding anything. Grantham's anticipation of these frustrations was evident enough when he responded to Robertson's request for material: 'It is in this Country extremely difficult to persuade anybody that Enquiries of the kind, which you wished to be made, are directed to general and liberal purposes not to some particular View, and that they may be literary, not political Pursuits. It is besides very difficult to gain access to Repositories in which valuable Materials are supposed to exist and much more so to unravel whether they exist or not.'

Grantham then suggests that the *Conquistadores* deliberately exaggerated the sophistication and level of cultural life which they met from the native races whom they encountered in the New World. This they did, Grantham believed, because their achievement would thereby seem to be still more glorious. Grantham's remarks came as a result of his close scrutiny of deposits which had recently been put on display by the government in Madrid. Here he wrote what constitutes an early and unusual attempt to draw inferences from the culture of remote peoples:

> From what I have seen, I do not scruple to pronounce that they have ever been in a very infant state in that part of the world, which contradicts the relations sent and brought by the first spoilers of the Riches of America. But various Causes have contributed to the misrepresentations made by them: their Ignorance, their Surprize at the Quantity and Purity of a Metal so intrinsically valuable, the usual style of Spanish Narrative, and perhaps an Intention in the Conquerors of enhancing the merit of their own Achievements, by representing them as effected against polished and civilized Nations, all cooperated to form the exaggerated Accounts of the Wonders of a New World ... In the Armoury of the Palace which is very well taken care of, there are Suits of Armour which are called Montezuma's. They are composed of thin Lacquered Copper Plates and I think are evidently Eastern, the forms of the Silver Ornaments upon them representing Dragons and confirm me in this Opinion, and are infinitely superior in Point of workmanship to any thing American which I have seen. I say nothing of the great Facility with which the present Indians practise the Imitative Arts with some degree of success; as it does not apply to the Question before us, my superficial Observations upon which, if at all founded, tend to shew that the Indian Nations never were so much polished, as might be expected from their Numbers, and therefore that a great degree of Caution is to be thrown into the Credit due to the first accounts which describe them as highly cultivated[19]

Grantham's detailed response to Robertson, derived from artefacts displayed in the *Armería Real* in Madrid and in other ethnographic collections, anticipates that later pioneer of Hispanic studies, William Stirling. Stirling's work was remarkable because his historical research would never be confined merely to the state letter or the palace portrait. Stirling would rule nothing out: furniture, embroideries, metal work, frontispieces, coats of arms, all could be as illuminating as a letter of Pizarro or the tomb of Cardinal Ximénez. Indeed his first visit to the *Armería Real* in 1842 was something of an epiphany. Then he would remark how he thought its contents the finest collection of relics in existence. Of interest for understanding British historical consciousness about Spain was Robertson's last publication, the *History of India* (1791). This was devoted to a more arcane theme than any attempted before. Robertson was interested in how much the ancients knew of India. Abstruse though such a subject may have seemed, there was a certain logic here. Much of Robertson's writing from his *Scotland* of 1759 onward had touched on the relationship between a dominant and a dependent state. After *Charles V*, Robertson had moved on to consider the Spanish presence in America. That interest had produced the *History of America*. This was to have been followed up with a history of the British in America. But then abruptly, Robertson had felt himself obliged to lay that project on one side; declining to press ahead 'on account of the *ferment* which then agitated our North American Colonies'.[20] Nevertheless, the status of colonies and imperial expansion was something that had a bearing on India no less than it was having in America, and once had had on Spain. Robertson strove to promote toleration and understanding of difference. Accordingly it made very good sense to acquaint his readership with the antiquity of Indian civilisation as Britain stood on the threshold of rulership over that subcontinent. The extent to which all Robertson's histories were both accounts of the past but also prescriptions for the future is affirmed by the concluding remarks of the *History of India*, when Robertson expresses the hope that his account: 'of the early and high civilization of India, and of the wonderful progress of its inhabitants in elegant arts and useful science, shall be received as just and well established, it may have some influence upon the behaviour of Europeans towards that people'.[21]

Such sentiments were entirely characteristic of the Enlightenment to which all things seemed possible. In preparation for publication on India, Robertson sent parts of his manuscript round Edinburgh, soliciting responses. One came from Robertson's old friend Hugh Blair who concurred with Robertson who had emphasised how important commerce was as a handmaid to culture, something Robertson had felt ever since he had deplored the absence of Scottish cities and underscored the significance of the city in the rise of Spanish hegemony. Blair wrote to Robertson after reading about India:

> On Governments I should think, the freer and more general intercourse occasioned by Commerce must have tended to lessen the severe despotism which prevailed in the Middle Ages. It certainly had the effect to raise Cities, and private Citizens, into more consequence; and by diffusing wealth more equally, to break and lessen the powers of Aristocracy. If it did not alter the political form of any Governments, yet by its gradual effect on manners it tempered the spirits of Government. Perhaps there might be ground for some observations of this kind, in favour of the Connexion between extended trade and liberty; which is always a popular subject.[22]

Interestingly enough John Robinson, a secretary of the Treasury, told Robertson that what he said in his *History of India* about Alexander the Great had radically changed his understanding. Hitherto Robinson confessed to having held to the common view that Alexander had been a great conqueror *tout court*. However, now he had come to understand that he had been 'a great Wise politician, and a great commercial Man, beyond the bold daring Hero and great general, hot headed, violent, and debauched.'[23]

Now Robertson and Adam Smith concurred in the priority each gave to commerce in explaining the development of civilisations, whether those had arisen out of Macedonian Greece or Castilian Spain. The special place given by Robertson to the Spanish city in the painful birth of consensual government in Europe has already been noted. What, however, did Adam Smith himself make of Spain in that most enduring and famous work of economics: *The Wealth of Nations*? The book appeared in 1776 – the year in which the British government was overtaken by the crisis of the American Revolution.

There was a multitude of ways in which Robertson and Smith were connected in the small world of Enlightenment Edinburgh. One of the intriguing questions about the genesis of Robertson's *Charles V* is the extent to which its emphasis upon commerce as a stimulant to the growth of civilised societies may have been influenced by arguments Robertson had heard Smith put forward in lectures. It is a question difficult to answer because Smith was a reluctant and dilatory correspondent who destroyed many papers just before his death. As it is, such letters as have survived are not helpful. What we can be much more certain about, however, is how Smith shared with Robertson a belief in the value of studying Spain in order to understand how Britain had arrived at where it was and where it might be going.

Smith's *Enquiry into the Causes of The Wealth of Nations* (1776) was published thirteen years after the end in 1763 of what is described by its author as the most expensive conflict Britain had ever been engaged in, that is to say the Seven Years War. *The Wealth of Nations* appeared at the very moment when relations with Britain's American colonies reached a crisis-point. If *The Wealth of Nations* is to be correctly situated, then it is important to be aware that it was composed with the experience of one global conflict in mind and the anticipation of another. War was a nexus which partly explains the amount of attention paid in Smith's book to the history and predicament of the Spanish empire, itself historically engaged in perennial warfare and located in the Americas as a substantial part of the British empire had become. Of course *The Wealth of Nations* would not still stand as the most influential book ever written on economics were it not for the fact that it set out to be a disinterested and historical account of international trade and commerce. Nevertheless Smith was also urgently committed to what might be termed a partisan and admonitory agenda addressed specifically to Britain and its empire in 1776. As a patriot writing at a time when academics sometimes had remarkable influence on politics, Smith wished to demonstrate how Britain could avoid mistakes by telling a cautionary tale about the decline and fall of Spanish greatness:

> Though the system of laws which is connected with the bounty, has exactly the same tendency with the police of Spain and Portugal; to lower somewhat the value of the precious metals in the country where it takes place; yet Great Britain is certainly one of the richest countries in Europe, while Spain and Portugal are perhaps among the most beggarly. This difference of situation, however, may easily be accounted for from two different causes. First, the tax

in Spain, the prohibition in Portugal of exporting gold and silver, and the vigilant police which watches over the execution of those laws, must, in two very poor countries, which between them import annually upwards of six millions sterling, operate, not only more directly but much more forcibly in reducing the value of those metals there, than the corn laws can do in Great Britain. And, secondly, this bad policy is not in those countries counter-balanced by the general liberty and security of the people. Industry is there neither free nor secure, and the civil and ecclesiastical governments of both Spain and Portugal, are such as would alone be sufficient to perpetuate their present state of poverty, even though their regulations of commerce were as wise as the greater part of them are absurd and foolish.[24]

However, it would be quite wrong to think of Smith as the first Briton to take an interest in Spain and its consumptive economy. A century before Smith occluded himself in his manse in Kirkcaldy to think about these things, John Locke had observed the disaster which New World gold had visited upon metropolitan Spain. In *Some Considerations of the Consequences of the Lowering of Interest and the Raising the Value of Money* (1691), he had concluded that '[it] is death in Spain to export money and yet they, who furnish all the world with gold and silver, have least of it among themselves. Trade fetches it away from that lazy and indigent people, notwithstanding all their artificial and forced contrivances to keep it there.'[25]

In *Two Treatises of Government* (1690), Locke remarks rather more economically how 'Spain seems as poor as the American wilderness'.[26] Americans, and some of those Britons who influenced Americans, also looked to learn from Spanish practices. David Hume and the euphoniously named Mordecai Postlethwayt, both of whose writings were of considerable interest to the Founding Fathers, scrutinised the Spanish empire. Eighteenth-century rationalists were generally of the fixed view that the soil of the Spanish West Indies, as that of metropolitan Spain itself, was impoverishing paradoxically because it was superabundantly fertile. In parallel with this observation was Hume's enquiry as to the fate of bullion once it was unloaded in metropolitan Spain. Spain was beggared by gold because it did so little to encourage home manufacturing for export with consequent circulation of currency and goods:[27]

> What other reason, indeed, is there, why all nations, at present, gain in their trade with SPAIN and PORTUGAL; but because it is impossible to heap up money, more than any fluid, beyond its proper level? The sovereigns of these countries have shown, that they wanted not inclination to keep their gold and silver to themselves, had it been in any degree practicable.
>
> But as any body of water may be raised above the level of the surrounding element, if the former has no communication with the la[t]ter; so in money, if the communication be cut off, by any material or physical impediment (for all laws alone are ineffectual) there may, in such a case, be a very great inequality of money.[28]

The centrality of agriculture in the Spanish economy certainly helped to shape the mind of Alexander Hamilton, the financial genius behind the American Revolution. His effective campaign to break the hold that land banks had on his compatriots, and his success in financing the Revolution through the introduction of paper banks and loans, was in part a reaction to his understanding of the disastrous hold land as a unit of economic value had had in the Old World and its dependencies, a hold which was nowhere stronger than in the Spanish mind. Hamilton wrote a *Report on Manufactures* in which he set out to explain why trade and commerce produced a livelier nation than one of agricultural labourers such as existed in Spain:

> but the artisan can with difficulty effect the same object, without exerting himself pretty equally with all those, who are engaged in the same pursuit. And if it may likewise be assumed as a fact, that manufactures open a wider field to exertions of ingenuity than agriculture, it would not be a strained conjecture, that the labour employed in the former, being at once more *constant*, more uniform and more ingenious, than that which is employed in the latter, will be found at the same time more productive.[29]

Adam Smith's *An Enquiry into the Nature and Causes of the Wealth of Nations*, like *Charles V*, was in part a manifesto dedicated to pointing out how imperial responsibilities can encourage and enhance economic power. However, Smith was also aware that triumph in one continent had to be considered against immanent crisis in another: in 1763 Britain had emerged from The Seven Years War as the dominant colonial power, but just over a decade later was in danger of losing what was its greatest potential asset. In 1776 *The Wealth of Nations* was sold out in a matter of weeks. It is because Smith sensed the crisis facing Britain in America that what he has to say about Spain is connected with his views on that continent. This is for two reasons – historically, Spain had had the earliest and geographically the biggest commitment to American colonisation but, more urgently, Smith believed that Britain might yet extricate itself from its American colonial crisis if it could learn from Spain's mistakes.

Smith was intrigued by a number of remarkable paradoxes which seemed to be connected to the Spanish empire. Perhaps the central riddle was to understand how Spain had become beggared by the fabulous riches of Peru – riches, according to Smith, which provided 'a revenue too, of a nature to excite in human avidity the most extravagant expectations of still greater riches'.[30] Something else which evidently intrigued him was how Spanish colonies, potentially 'the richest and most fertile in the world', had come to be 'less populous and thriving than those of almost any other European nation'.[31] Finally, Smith asks himself, how is it that Spain which was a manufacturing nation before it acquired any colonies has altogether ceased to be so at the time of writing – something all the more extraordinary given that as the first at the table, it had been able to help itself to the best food? In trying to answer these questions, Smith made a major contribution to developing an interest in Spain not only in late eighteenth-century Britain but in Europe at large, a contribution in the field of economic history which complemented and then surpassed what Robertson had already given the world in the sphere of politics and history.

Smith tries to answer the question as to why, despite all the potential of Spanish America, Spain was made sick by her dependants. This he does by comparing how Spain had managed its responsibilities in South America with the conduct of the British in their New World colonies. Immediately after declaring that the Spanish colonies are considered the least robust of those of any European power, Smith contrasts their palsied state with those of the British, declaring '[but] there are no colonies of which the progress has been more rapid than that of the English in North America'.[32] Despite the fact that most of the British possessions in North America are certainly inferior to those of Spain in terms of fertility, and probably too to those of the French, nevertheless, British settlements have flourished. How then does Smith explain the marked contrast between the manifest failure of Spanish colonies and the burgeoning of British dependencies? Smith begins by suggesting that this is because the British administrators have discouraged 'engrossing' – the accumulation of land by absentee proprietors which remains idle and uncultivated. Although this abuse is present within the British system 'it has been more restrained in the English colonies than in any other'.[33] Other critical difference between English colonies and those of European nations in America is that in some colonies, and here Smith cites Pennsylvania, there is no right of primogeniture. Tax differentials between the English and Spanish regimes are in Smith's view also critical to the failure of the one system and the success of the other. Smith writes of how 'the labour of the English colonies is not only likely to afford a greater and more valuable product, but, in consequence of the moderation of their taxes, a greater proportion of this produce belongs to themselves, which they may store up and employ in putting into motion a still greater quantity of labour'.[34]

Although Smith makes no attempt at comparative ethnography, he accords some significance to the role of consumption and public display. Perhaps betraying loyalty to his Presbyterian origins, Smith's personal feelings make a rare appearance when he betrays a degree of repugnance in the face of Spanish colonial ceremony. He expresses disapprobation while contriving to rope together Peruvian viceroys and mendicant friars. He points out that the sums spent upon the reception of a new viceroy of Peru 'have frequently been enormous' and what is still more pernicious, the ceremonies themselves introduce among the colonists 'the habit of vanity and expence upon all occasions'.[35] Here Smith is either less charitable or indulgent than Robertson, whose views of the role of the Jesuits in South America are surprising for their generosity. Robertson was happy to acknowledge the part the order had played in mitigating some at least of the horrors of the *conquistadores*.

What really set the Spanish and the English colonies on different courses, however, was how the respective metropolitan countries came to handle trade between a colony and the mother country. This touches on the real heart of Smith's argument and it has to do with monopolies. Smith begins by conceding that at first there was little material difference in policy toward colonial trade among any of the European nations: 'Every European nation has endeavoured more or less to monopolize to itself the commerce of its colonies'. The point is that 'the manner in which this monopoly has been exercised in different nations has been very different'.[36] Here Smith begins by wagging his finger not at the Spanish, but at their historical enemies the Dutch. This arises in the context of his disapproval of how the Dutch had elected to engage in trade with their colonies through the instrument of what Smith describes as 'exclusive companies' – in the case of the Dutch, *De Westindische Compagnie* which was founded in 1621 and granted the monopoly of trade between America, Africa and Holland. Smith roundly condemns this policy: 'Of all the expedients which can well be contrived to stunt the natural growth of a new colony, that of an exclusive company is undoubtedly the most effectual. This, however, has been the policy of Holland'.[37]

Smith then turns to Spain to begin with the point that the Spaniards had not done as the Dutch were to do later. Rather, from 1503, the Spanish crown had opted to direct all imports through the *Casa de Contratación* in Seville. Effectively this meant that whatever was brought to Europe from Spain's colonies had to pass through that one Spanish port. This might be thought in some senses a preferable system to the Dutch, but Smith believed that there were a number of problems, most conspicuously that since everything had to come through Seville, this had encouraged such a concentration of traders that a cartel was the inevitable consequence: 'The profit of those merchants would be almost equally exorbitant and oppressive. The colonies would be ill supplied, and would be obliged to buy very dear, and to sell very cheap.'[38] Such a system benefited neither the colonies nor indeed the metropolitan country.

By contrast, the system adopted in Britain was vastly superior because trade with the colonies was conducted from anywhere in the mother country. That militated against a 'general combination' and 'their competition is sufficient to hinder them from making very exorbitant profits'. Smith's objection to exorbitant profit in general seems to have been threefold. First, large profits rotted the mercantile class because it encouraged them to sink their money into idle luxuries. Smith's choice of the word 'idle' is less negative than it sounds, since he meant merely that the spending of savings on luxuries was less productive than other uses of capital. It was a case of utilising profits just as a doctor might encourage flow of oxygen by prescribing exercise, so for Smith, capital should never be idle but should circulate so as to encourage trade and expand growth. Smith's second objection was that the spending habits of those at the top of the mercantile pyramid had a profound influence on consumption generally. Thus the extravagance of the few has a disproportionate effect on the health of a national trade. The excessive profits of a cluster of nabobs forces the colonies to sell very cheap and buy very dear, with far-reaching ramifications for the political and social stability of the colonies themselves. Third, that nation is best which is most liberal in its commercial laws. Smith therefore goes out of his way to praise Britain for allowing people to trade to America from any or all of its ports. Whereas Europeans insisted that all colonial exports were to be directed through metropolitan ports, Britain reserves to itself a limited inventory of produce – the so-called enumerated commodities – which have to reach Europe via Britain. Otherwise non-enumerated goods may be exported directly to other countries 'provided it is in British or Plantation ships, of which the owners and three-fourths of the mariners are British subjects'.[39]

Smith also sought to provide an explanation as to why Spain and Portugal's accession of colonies, the most fertile on the surface of the globe, had bankrupted the once prosperous kingdoms of the Iberian peninsula. The problem had begun, as has been noted above, with the insistence by Spain on canalising trade through Seville and the *Casa de Contratación*. From this, other poisons had flowed down that narrow channel. Psychologically, Spaniards had never been able to free themselves from the paralysing misconception that they should hoard bullion as it arrived from the New World. This they did because they could not accommodate themselves to the realisation that 'gold and silver' was merely a token of exchange – certainly the most efficient the world has employed, but one which nevertheless always remains just that and, as such, something which should properly be used in active exchange, not part of what Smith describes as 'the dead stock of society'. Had Spanish merchants exported gold and silver in exchange for goods, a mechanism would have developed to transform the Spanish economy:

> The gold and silver which would go abroad would not go abroad for nothing, but would bring back an equal value of goods of some kind or another. Those goods could not be all matters of mere luxury and expence, to be consumed by idle people who produce nothing in return for their consumption. As the real wealth and revenue of idle people would not be augmented by this extraordinary exportation of gold and silver, so neither would their consumption be much augmented by it. Those goods, would, probably, the greater part of them, and certainly some part of them, consist in materials, tools, and provisions, for the employment and maintenance of industrious people, who would reproduce, with a profit, the full value of their consumption. A part of the dead stock of society would thus be turned into active stock, and would put into motion a greater quantity of industry than had been employed before. The annual produce of their land and labour would immediately be

augmented a little, and in a few years would, probably, be augmented a great deal; their industry being thus relieved from one of the most oppressive burdens which it at present labours under.[40]

For Smith, Spain was atrophied. The price of gold and silver which could be obtained legally in the Peninsula was 'degraded'. This was because supply far exceeded demand and, despite the best efforts of the authorities, smuggling of gold and silver was one of the few flourishing industries of the 'beggarly' countries of Spain and Portugal. Spain was in a weak position for trading with other European countries because it had very feeble and restricted industries which could offer little which was attractive to foreigners. Spanish industry was thoroughly anaemic because the continuous infusion of bullion discouraged the rich from putting their wealth to active use by investing in new enterprise. However, there was also the disastrous Spanish taxation system, of which the most notorious was identified by Smith as the *alcabala* ('sales tax').

The problem of the *alcabala* in Smith's view was that it was not only a tax on the profits of merchants, but was repeated at every stage in the sale of goods. As Smith pointed out, the levying of the tax required a multitude of revenue officers 'sufficient to guard the transportation of goods, not only from one province to another but from one shop to another'.[41] The *alcabala* severely depressed agriculture too, because it was levied on produce. Besides bedevilling trade between two men living in the same city, the *alcabala* also clamped a ball and chain upon anyone who tried to move goods from one end of the country to another, as the merchant was required to pay levies on the highroads. Furthermore, the Spanish government did its best to discourage exports by what Smith called 'improper taxes upon exportation'.

But the truth is, neither was Smith fully informed about the *alcabala* nor did he have a balanced view of Spain under the enlightened Charles III. It would seem that Smith concentrated his analysis on the atrophied state of the Spanish economy as it manifested itself in Castile while he assumed that the taxation system in Aragon was uniform and uniformly oppressive, which was not the case. He regarded the *alcabala* as a more significant impediment to economic growth than it really was, while not taking into account how tax was collected – which often caused it to remain static when prices were rising. With regard to Castile, here Smith may have extrapolated views of the old power base of the Habsburgs and applied them to the Peninsula at large. He was perhaps influenced by the collective wisdom of the British which would be articulated later by Joseph Townsend in his *Journey through Spain in the years 1786 and 1787* (1791). Of Castile and its decayed wool towns, Townsend was to write of how they were: 'skeletons of towns once populous and crammed with factories, workshops and stalls, now full of churches, convents and hospitals ... destitute of commerce, supported by the church'.[42]

Castile was in serious and irreversible economic decline. Here certainly were chronic problems, among others a system of land cultivation which was grossly inefficient and conducive to massive erosion. Such manufacturing as existed in central Spain relied upon old staples which indeed may have been borne down by a restrictive taxation system as Smith claimed was applicable to all Spain. However, there were nascent industries in the peripheral areas of the Peninsula which manifested real signs of change and dynamism. Valencia was on equal terms with Lyons in silk production, though falling behind in the nineteenth century. Catalonia could boast the biggest concentration of dyers and weavers outside Lancashire. Such was the sense of economic optimism along the Mediterranean littoral that the directors of the Bank of San Carlos could report in positive terms of 'the progress of our industry, the multiplicity of modern factories in Catalonia, the growth of agriculture, and the increase in the demand for its products'.[43]

As is now well known, at the outset of his reign Charles III had tried to reduce tax burdens and increase stimulus to production. Charles too was to have some very able ministers (of which perhaps the most notable was the Spaniard of Irish extraction, Richard Wall). They had done much to improve the economy of Spain just as Necker was making real progress with French finance during the *ancien régime* in France. Unhappily, progress in both countries was then halted by the French revolution and the French invasion of Spain respectively. Smith possessed one of the great analytical minds of the Enlightenment but this did not prevent him from foisting prejudices upon what he wrongly perceived to have been a uniformly moribund economy. He needed to shape his discourse in such a way as to provide an appropriate moral tale for the enlightenment of his own countrymen. Thus even this supposedly limpid and detached genius of political economy was hardly dispassionate about Spain. The Peninsula was required to supply an appropriate cautionary tale to a burgeoning British economy. Accordingly, the picture was made darker than it need have been. But Smith's account was also a great deal more theoretical than it should have been. Like the American historian W.H. Prescott who wrote about Spain during the Victorian era, Smith never set foot in the country. There was a certain aridity which Smith shared with Prescott, a marked contrast from the robust pragmatism of those British prison reformers who visited Spain to see things for themselves and to learn at first hand what Charles III's reformist ministers were trying to achieve. More important than technical questions of Spain's taxation and revenue system was the paramount issue of justice, or as Smith believed, the absence of judicial impartiality. This was still more critical than the multitude of oppressive taxes designed to increase revenue but which actually reduced what came into the public purse. Smith draws a sharp contrast between what he understood to be the system prevailing in Spain and that of Britain. For Smith the failure of the Spanish courts to act impartially was 'above all' the cause of the chronic debility of the Spanish economy even under the relatively enlightened Charles III.

The problem in Spain was what is described in *The Wealth of Nations* as irregular and partial justice. This protected the rich and powerful debtor, making the industrious part of the nation afraid to prepare goods for the consumption of 'those haughty and great men' or the Spanish grandees whom Smith criticises elsewhere when, as colonial governors, they set a standard of opulence and extravagance which can only damage the societies whose best interests they are ostensibly there to protect. The situation prevailing in Spain could not be in more marked contrast to that in Britain where' that equal and impartial administration of justice which renders the rights of the meanest British subject respectable to the greatest, and which, by securing to every man the fruits of his own industry, give the greatest and most effectual encouragement to every sort of industry'.[44]

The last sense in which Smith draws a fundamental distinction between how Spain historically had managed its economy and how Britain was doing so, concerns what is termed 'the practice of funding'. What Smith meant by this was servicing the National Debt or what is currently known as Government Borrowing. Smith pointed out that Spain is heavily and damagingly in debt – indeed had been 'deeply in debt' before the end of the sixteenth century, 'about a hundred years before England owed a shilling'.[45] Here we are presented with something of a puzzle. Spain glittered with gold, yet Smith states that it did not pay its debts. Why so? It is a paradox that is not addressed in *The Wealth of Nations*. In this instance we have to guess at what Smith may have been thinking. The tradition which had long existed in Spain of engrossing, combined with Spain's historic debts which were of an antiquity hoarier than those of any other country in Europe, induced imprisonment of bullion. According to Smith, the value of gold and silver was degraded 'below what it is in most other countries', and so perhaps it was felt by Spaniards that servicing national debt would have been a greater haemorrhage for Spain than for other states. The sheer quantity of bullion which would have had to leave the country reinforced a historic Spanish paranoia about releasing precious metals. Perhaps, too, vestigial memories played their part. The Spanish treasure fleet, so often attacked like a stag savaged by dogs, had laboured for centuries to bring gold and silver safely into harbour in Seville. Such apparent wealth secured under constant duress was something to hoard, not cast out again on the metaphorical waters of economic probity and growth. And so it was that Spain came to be manacled in gold and silver. When many in Spain laboured under the massive misapprehension that specie had an absolute instead of a notional value, while being under no illusion of how palsied the economy was, it was emotionally difficult to use reserves to pay off debts. Spain's unwillingness to employ metals as capital investment in the promotion of industries was of course quite another and still more disastrous inhibition.

The impolitic raising of loans in Spain when internal taxation cannot meet expenses Smith condemns, though he acknowledges that this pernicious practice which started in the Republics of Genoa and Venice has spread like a contagion throughout Europe. Here as so often, Smith is addressing his readership not just as an academic economist but also as a lobbyist intent upon addressing the particular ministry then at the head of British politics. Smith wishes to use the lessons of history to avoid mistakes. This he does by pointing out that unlike Spain and Holland which are much enfeebled by their national debts, Britain as yet is not. However, in order to persuade government to avoid the temptation of raising loans at exorbitant rates of interest on the international money market, Smith resorts to a rhetorical question: 'Is it likely that in Great Britain alone a practice, which has brought either weakness or desolation into every other country, should prove altogether innocent?'[46] He then declares that the system of taxation established in those different countries is inferior to that in England, largely because thus far England has not burdened itself with huge public debts. Despite having just financed a notably expensive war, it has emerged financially unscathed from that because 'the frugality and good conduct of individuals seem to have been able, by saving and accumulation, to repair all the breaches which the waste and extravagance of government had made in the general capital of society'.[47]

Although Smith concludes that the economy of England at the end of the Seven Years War was flourishing – so that the nation seemed to support with ease a burden of which half a century earlier nobody believed it capable – politicians would be very rash to conclude that it should follow the path of the Dutch and the Spaniards. Indeed, 'Let us not, however, upon this account [of Britain's capacity to fund an international war] rashly conclude that she is capable of supporting any burden; nor even be too confident that she could support, without great distress, a burden a little greater than what has already been laid upon her.'[48]

Smith was a political economist. He formulated theories about money and how it worked, but he also sought to educate his political masters as to their responsibilities in fostering the wealth of the nation. Wealth had to be concentrated and encouraged within those units of society which the human race had defined over millennia as states – the two, wealth and society, were as inseparable as hands and pendulum. Smith wrote his masterpiece to reveal the mechanisms by which trade could best be conducted and promoted, and to identify the dangers which beset his country which ten years before his book appeared found itself in charge of a hugely expanded world empire. Thus Smith not only contributed to a debate as to the propriety or otherwise of public debt, he looked unblinkingly at the threat presented to Great Britain by the revolt of the American colonies. It is inferred that Britain as a colonial power must do better than Spain had done. Smith suggested ways in which an impasse can be resolved after he summarised the essential issue in one sentence: 'The parliament of Great Britain insists upon taxing the colonies; and they refused to be taxed by a parliament in which they are not represented'.[49]

Smith located the solution to America in the far recesses of history, the 'declension of the Roman republick' when Rome itself had detached its erstwhile allies from the league which they had formed against it on being refused all the privileges of Roman citizenship. This Rome had done by granting those privileges to her former allies 'one by one, and in proportion as they detached themselves from the general confederacy'. So it followed that full representation and equal rights must now be granted to each American colony in proportion to 'what it contributed to the publick revenue of the empire'.[50] By so doing, the colonists, whose upbringing and culture should naturally incline them to see the inhabitants of the mother country as their brothers and sisters, not only would be bound to the metropolitan power, but also would develop a stake and ambition in the deliberations of Westminster: 'Instead of piddling for the little prizes which are to be found in what may be called the paltry raffle of colony faction; they might then hope, from the presumption which men naturally have in their own ability and good fortune, to draw some of the prizes which sometimes come from the wheel of the great state lottery of British politicks.'[51]

Nothing demonstrates how relevant *The Wealth of Nations* was to the imperial crisis of the 1770s than the prescience of its author as to the future greatness of America. It was essential to resolve that conflict before Britain lost its greatest potential asset: 'From shopkeeper, tradesmen, and attornies, they [Americans] are become statesmen and legislators, and are employed in contriving a new form of government for an extensive empire, which, they flatter themselves, will become, and which, indeed, seems very likely to become, one of the greatest and most formidable that ever was in the world.'[52]

The amount of attention Smith gave to Spain in *The Wealth of Nations* must not be exaggerated. Nevertheless, how he considered its history as a means to prognosis helped to stimulate what might be termed a library interest in a country which virtually no civilised Briton dreamt of actually going to see. Adam Smith allowed Britons to see their Empire as the logical successor to those which had begun with Rome and, until the unlooked-for rise of the British version (according to the conventional wisdom of eighteenth-century historians), had shown promise of being extinguished with the death of Philip II at the Escorial on 13 September 1598.

The purpose of this chapter has been to suggest that an engagement with Imperial Spain by two of the most distinguished and influential writers of the Scottish Enlightenment was an eloquent example of cultural displacement. The quest was undertaken because the Austrian Habsburgs had drawn up the parameters of early modern Europe – nations emerged, systems evolved, religions protested, thinkers reacted, all to restrictions Spain had first imposed and then tried to sustain. Robertson and Smith crowded round their subject like Rembrandt's anatomists. They performed a post-mortem upon the corpse of Spain to understand the workings of politics, economics and religion. These two friends being votaries of progress, it seemed at first improbable that they should have chosen to acquaint themselves with failure on such an imperial scale. But they were united in looking to a future for Britain, having consulted a Spanish past.

Notes

1 Gibbon to Robertson, Sheffield Place, 26 July 1793, NLS, Ms. 3944, fol. 151r, v.
2 J. Smitten (ed.), *The Works of William Robertson*, 12 vols (London: Routledge/Thoemmes, 1996), XII, *Miscellaneous Works and Commentaries: Dugald Stewart, 'Account of the Life and Writings of William Robertson, D.D.'*, p. 133.
3 Tonia Raquejo, 'The "Arab Cathedrals": Moorish Architecture as Seen by British Travellers', *Burlington Magazine* (August 1986), p. 563.
4 For instance Edward Said's *Orientalism* (London: Routledge & Kegan Paul, 1978).
5 Stewart, *'Account'*, p. 147.
6 Rust, *Goldsmith*, pp. 143–4.
7 William Wilberforce to Robertson, London, 25 January 1788, NLS Ms. 3943, fols 230–1.
8 Colin Kidd, 'The Ideological Significance of Robertson's History of Scotland', in Stewart J. Brown (ed.), *William Robertson and the Expansion of Empire* (Cambridge: Cambridge University Press, 1997), p. 123.
9 Ibid., p. 131.
10 Smitten, vol. VI, *Charles V*, vol. IV, p. 310.
11 Ibid., pp. 304–5.
12 Smitten, vol. III, *Charles V*, vol. I, p. 30.
13 Ibid., p. 31.
14 Smitten, vol. IV, *Charles V*, vol. II, p. 210.
15 Review of Acts of the Cortes [Colección de Cortes, publicada por la Real Academia de la Historia, Madrid 1840], *The Athenaeum*, 679 (31 October 1840), pp. 863–4.
16 Smitten, vol. III, *Charles V*, vol. I, p. 189.
17 For Robertson's complicated response to self-generated primary material see Bruce P. Lenman, 'From Savage to Scot', p. 202 in Brown, *Robertson*.
18 Nigel Glendinning, Enriqueta Harris, Francis Russell, 'Lord Grantham and the Taste for Velázquez: 'The Electric Eel of the Day', *Burlington Magazine* (October 1999), pp. 598–605.
19 Grantham to Robertson, 'Escorial', 31 October 1776, NLS Ms 3942, fols 283–290v.
20 Stewart, *Account*, p. 114.
21 Smitten, X, *An Historical Disquisition Concerning The Knowledge Which the Ancients Had of India*, pp. 331–2.
22 Hugh Blair to Robertson, Restalrig, 24 May 1790, NLS Ms. 3944, fol. 20v.
23 John Robinson to Robertson, Syon Hill, 18 June 1791, NLS Ms. 3944, fol. 58r.
24 R.H. Campbell, A.S. Skinner and W.B. Todd (eds), *An Enquiry into the Causes of the Wealth of Nations*, 2 vols (Oxford: Clarendon, 1976), p. 541, IV. v. b. 45.
25 Peter McNamara, 'Political Economy and Statesmanship: Adam Smith and Alexander Hamilton', Ph.D., University of Michigan, Ann Arbor, 1991, p. 131.

26 Ibid.
27 For an explanation of the contemporary paradox of how states with abundant resource wealth perform less well than their resource-poor counterparts see Michael L. Ross, 'The Political Economy of the Resource Curse', *World Politics* 51 (January 1999), pp. 297–322 and also his 'Does Oil Hinder Democracy?', *World Politics*, 53 (April 2001), pp. 325–61.
28 Eugene F. Miller (ed.), *David Hume: Essays Moral, Political and Literary* (Indianapolis: Liberty, 1985), Essay V, 'Of the Balance of Trade', pp. 312–13.
29 Harold C. Syrett (ed.), *The Papers of Alexander Hamilton*, 27 vols (New York and London, 1966), 10, p. 242.
30 Campbell et al., *Wealth of Nations*, p. 567, IV. vii. b. 7.
31 Ibid., p. 568, IV. vii. b. 7.
32 Ibid., p. 571, IV. vii. b. 15.
33 Ibid., p. 572, IV. vii b. 18.
34 Ibid., p. 573, IV.vii. b. 20.
35 Ibid., p. 574, IV.vii. b. 20.
36 Ibid., p. 575, IV. vii. b. 21.
37 Ibid., p. 575, IV. vii. b. 22.
38 Ibid., p. 575, IV. vii. b. 22.
39 Ibid., p. 577, IV.vii. b. 25.
40 Ibid., p. 513, IV. v. a. 19.
41 Ibid., p. 899, V. ii. k. 67.
42 Raymond Carr, *Spain 1808–1939* (Oxford: Clarendon, 1966), p. 32.
43 Ibid., p. 22.
44 Campbell et al., *Wealth of Nations*, p. 610, IV, vii. c. 54.
45 Ibid., p. 928, V. iii. 57.
46 Ibid.
47 Ibid., p. 929, V. iii. 58.
48 Ibid.,
49 Ibid., p. 622, IV. vii. c. 75.
50 Ibid.
51 Ibid., pp. 622–3, IV. vii. c. 75.
52 Ibid., p. 623, IV. vii. c. 75.

2
Politics

Spain and Britain seem to have had utterly different political trajectories during the course of the nineteenth century, but it is the purpose of this chapter to suggest that the politics of the Peninsula impinged upon Britain to a larger extent than has been realised. During the Napoleonic domination of Europe, Britain remained free while Spain became occupied. The Spanish *Cortes* which met at Cádiz in 1810 failed in its attempt to transform Spain into a regime with an abiding commitment to liberalism. Lack of focus and splits within the ranks of the *liberales* themselves, tensions associated with the genesis of the 1812 Constitution and its aftermath, all contributed to harming the cause of enlightenment within metropolitan Spain. Here was an irony, however, since the 1812 Cádiz Constitution – referred to at the time within Spain by its supporters as the 'sacred codex' – was to become the foundation for the classic liberal constitutions of Latin Europe as they sprouted across that continent during the 1820s. Ferdinand VII had returned to the throne in 1813 and shortly afterward repudiated the *liberales*; sending a first wave of Spaniards into exile – many to Britain. For the next six years Ferdinand lived from hand to mouth politically until 1820 when a rising sympathetic to the aspirations of constitutional monarchy was led by the army under Rafael Riego (1785–1823), soldier and liberal martyr. This further interlude in constitutional monarchy for Spain – the *trienio* – was in turn suppressed by the intervention of the European powers led by a French army; the so-called *Ten Thousand Sons of St Louis* who crossed the Spanish border in April 1823, reached Madrid, released Ferdinand from palace arrest and squeezed him back into his throne. Ferdinand died ten years later as Britain emerged from challenges to social stability induced by postwar depression and agrarian unrest. The death of Ferdinand, in 1833, came a year after Britain started down the long road of political accountability which had been marked with the passage of the 1832 Great Reform Bill. Just a year after the passing of that famous act in Britain, in Spain the full fury of civil war was unleashed. It was caused by a dispute as to which claimant had the better right to the Spanish throne. Much to everyone's amazement – not least his own – at the end of his life, Ferdinand found himself with an heir in the person of his infant daughter Isabella II who was duly crowned Queen after her father's death. However, her claim was disputed by Ferdinand's brother Don Carlos who argued, and here there was a case to be answered, that Spanish law had specifically excluded females from the accession. Accordingly, Don Carlos raised an army and proceeded to hold much of the north of Spain against the infant queen. The fiercest fighting of a terrible civil war took place in 1837, the same year which saw Britain witness the peaceful accession of Victoria, during whose reign of more than sixty years the country acquired an empire with some claims to rival the one over which Philip of Spain had presided some 250 years before. In 1870 Spain's strong man General Prim, whose talents and force of character seemed to promise longed-for stability, was assassinated. That year the British Parliament passed Forster's Education Act which laid the basis for universal education in Britain. In 1898, four hundred years exactly since the sun had set, if not on the Spanish empire, then on Philip II, Spain lost the final tattered remnants of its former colonial glory.

It was not a question of the British applying political nostrums learned from Spain, which achieved nothing politically from the death of Charles III in 1788 until the death of Franco in 1975. Rather, it was Spain's heroic failures which seem to have provided a constant source of debate, indeed inspiration, at moments of internal crisis and anxiety in Britain. Whether the *liberales* could ever have achieved anything permanent for Spain out of Cádiz in 1812 must be doubtful. Nevertheless the Spanish interlude was not forgotten. It was an experiment which in part inspired the independence movement in Italy, and its vision was carried over the south Atlantic and into the nascent republics of the old Spanish empire. Naiveté, weakness, chaos and disillusionment all may have played their part in the failure of constitutional monarchy in Spain in 1812 but, nevertheless, the three years of constitutional government between 1820 and 1823 remained a landmark in Spanish politics – and was as well something long remembered throughout Europe. For Marx, what had gone on in Cádiz 'was a genuine and original offering of Spanish intellectual life, regenerating the ancient and national institutions, introducing the measures of reform loudly demanded by the most celebrated authors and statesmen of the eighteenth century, making inevitable concessions to popular prejudice'.[1]

Marx was not the only significant figure to have marked out such an interlude in Spanish liberalism. Lord John Russell, Prime Minister of Britain (1846–1852, 1865–1866), as an impressionable young man was taken round Spain by its greatest English apologists, Lord and Lady Holland. Russell witnessed Vitoria, Wellington's greatest Peninsula victory, but he was also present at Cádiz during the evolution of the 1812

Constitution. What Russell observed there, by way of impassioned debates as to the nature of political accountability, was a good tutelage for the critical part he later played in ensuring that Wellington and the ultra-conservatives were not able to sabotage the Reform Bill of 1832.

Spain was present in Britain not just in speech but in print. The most powerful influence on intellectual thought in the United Kingdom throughout the nineteenth century was not the newspaper but the periodical review. It was for this reason that the publication in 1808 of the notorious 'Don Cevallos' article in the *Edinburgh Review* had had momentous consequences. Written by Lord Brougham and Francis Jeffrey, it was supposed to have been a dispassionate overview of Spanish politics.[2] But Tories thought quite otherwise, seeing sentiments expressed in the article as pure Jacobinism. It created outrage. Walter Scott cancelled his subscription, Sydney Smith reported how men fumigated their shelves, while one Edinburgh aristocrat opened his front door and cast the whole run out into the street. What would turn out to be the principal organ of Tories for the whole of the nineteenth century, *The Quarterly Review*, was founded to counter what its proprietors felt were the pernicious views of the *Edinburgh*. Spain vicariously gave birth to the *Quarterly*.

The revolt in the Peninsula which had occasioned the notorious 'Don Cevallos' furore met at the intersection of politics and history. Coleridge was convinced that it was the way in which Spain was trying to counter the French invasion which provoked in England a new examination of political principles. The poet-philosopher claimed that 'it was not till the Spanish insurrection that Englishmen of all parties recurred, in toto, to the old English principles, and spoke of their Hampdens, Sidneys, and Miltons, with the old enthusiasm'.[3] Evidently then a famous Romantic poet felt that the fortunes of the Iberian Peninsula excited public men. What is certain, however, is that the pre-eminent apologist in Britain for all things Spanish was Henry Vassall Fox, 3rd Baron Holland (1773–1840). Holland was a friend and admirer of the Spanish patriot, reformer and political thinker Gaspar Melchior de Jovellanos (1744–1811). A lawyer by training, Jovellanos had defied the royal favourite and lover of the Queen, Manuel Godoy. For this he was exiled for six years to Majorca. But the revolution of 1808 had enabled him to re-establish contact with the Hollands and reaffirm his admiration for England; an admiration which had extended to a translation of *Paradise Lost*. Jovellanos gave up after Book 1, doubtless exhausted by the effort to uncoil Milton's serpentine lines.

During the period of the French wars, Holland identified Jovellanos as Spain's best hope for a new age of constitutionalism: the bust of the Spanish patriot carved by Angel Monasterio in 1809 came to reside prominently in his London house.[4] That was a mark of special distinction, since Lord and Lady Holland were not noted patrons of the arts, though they took a greater interest than they have been credited with. The

Hollands were pre-eminent in promoting a political utopia. This they did by espousing the principles of the tutelary deity at Holland House, Charles James Fox (1749–1806), Holland's uncle. Fox had led the Whigs in the long years when Pitt the Younger dominated British politics; bequeathing to his nephew a quixotic but unattainable legacy based upon the naive assumption that politics was susceptible to rationalisation. Given that Fox had spent years as Leader of the Opposition, had never been Prime Minister, and only served briefly in office, his nephew and disciple showed a rare moment of realism in reckoning that Britain was not perhaps the best place to promote such advanced Whig ideals as Fox had espoused for so many years. Spain not Britain was to be the promised land. What drew the Hollands to Jovellanos and the Spanish *liberales* was their perception that they entertained principles which had been worked out 'by those of true philosophy and of the most accredited patriotism, such as Cicero and Mr Fox'.[5] And so it came about that for nearly half a century, from the first visit of the Hollands to the Peninsula in 1793 until the death of Holland himself in 1840, the liberals of Spain were subjected to a kind of political imperialism of such a condescending degree as would only be matched some fifty years later, and in the religious sphere, with the despatch of the Victorian missionary to the Hotentotts of Africa.

These overbearing attitudes were tolerated, however, by those Spaniards who had foregathered at Cádiz in 1810. Spanish pride was assuaged partly by an understanding that the Hollands were prepared to sacrifice much for Spain and, no less importantly, the *Junta* of Seville recognised that their predicament was too desperate to resent the reams of bossy admonishment dispatched on a regular basis from the library of Holland House. Indeed it was not Spaniards but members of the British Establishment who resented that bizarre combination of sympathy and condescension which made up the peculiar attitudes the Hollands had toward the Peninsula. Lord Auckland was outraged by discovering that the Hollands, with their West Kensington philosopher John Allen in tow, were progressing round Spain in the middle of the war. Auckland attributed this insanity to 'a sort of Spanish fever, which still holds possession of him [Holland] ... disgraceful to our political and military character'.[6]

It is the purpose of this chapter to consider that 'Spanish fever' in the light of the struggle between good and evil which was how so many in Britain thought of the battle with Napoleon. But although for Holland much of the pressing urgency of Spain had to do with not only its future, but a future political order for constitutional government at large, the Peninsula provoked new interest in the history of England. Many of the arguments about the future of Spain, whether conducted by Whig or Tory, were cast in the mould of Stuart thought. Landseer painted Allen, librarian at Holland House, pouring over books with a bronze Cromwell perching above like some malevolent corvine. That bronze provoked diabolical thoughts about Spanish ecclesiastics in Blanco White, a notorious renegade Spanish priest of Irish extraction, whose lurid accounts of religious ecstasy in Spanish conventual houses did more to establish negative views about Iberia than anything else. White broke off a famous account of his former confessor to describe the physical appearance of his erstwhile spiritual director: 'His countenance, besides, was very striking. It must be an interesting face to physiognomists, and perhaps, to phrenologists, that an excellent bust of Cromwell, which I had frequently before my eyes during two years of my residence in this country, forcibly reminded me of my old spiritual leader.'[7]

The most earnest moral commitment to Spain in print came not from Lord Holland, however, but from William Wordsworth (1770–1850), the renegade Jacobin. Famously, Wordsworth had welcomed the French Revolution but had then turned against all that it stood for when France invaded Switzerland. Wordsworth shared with his friend and fellow Lakeland poet Robert Southey (1774–1843) a deep interest in the progress of French arms in Europe. Both too felt a profound sense of shame when, in 1808, the British general Sir Hew Dalrymple had allowed a defeated army to march back into France. Both Wordsworth and Southey were so moved by what they saw as a profoundly misguided and dishonourable act that they collaborated together on a pamphlet denouncing the Convention of Cintra (1808), the treaty which had allowed the French to escape and the war to be prolonged. Density of sentence, latinised vocabulary, frequent Miltonic assonance, all suggested that Wordsworth's study at Grasmere, where his denunciation of Cintra was composed between the autumn of 1808 and the spring of 1809, might have had a bust of the republican poet; just as Allen's in London was then presided over by Cromwell.

Wordsworth was always partial to moral earnestness, but nothing seems to have shocked him quite so much as the conduct of the British at Cintra, just as no document is more revealing of what Iberia was supposed to do for Britain than Wordsworth's pamphlet. It appeared under date 20 May 1809, and with the pompous title *Concerning the relations of Great Britain, Spain and Portugal, to each other, and to the common enemy, at this crisis; and specifically as affected by the Convention of Cintra.*

The Wordsworth tract reveals more vividly even than Southey's three-volume *History of the Peninsular War*, which would appear between 1823–32, the peculiarly self-referential way with which the British looked upon Spain and Portugal. The issue as to why Britain had not already gone to the aid of Austria and Prussia, given that all Europe faced 'the common enemy', is raised early on. It is because Spain possessed an 'innate heroism of temperament' which, implicitly, Prussia and Austria did not. But then Wordsworth goes further; he crosses the Atlantic. Spain, it is declared, has an instinctive sense of the value of independence and a nobility of temperament which is unique. Here English admirers of a romanticised Iberia were taking rhetoric out of the mouth of Spain's apologists. For example, Jovellanos mounted a Burkean defence of what he described as 'the ancient and venerable constitution of Spain'. For Wordsworth too, even the Americans and the Dutch, both of whom historically had a will to independence, do not have 'the moral excellencies which will allow them to understand the nature of liberty' which the Spaniards possess innately[8]

Spain appealed so powerfully to Wordsworth because it was a country romantically ablaze. As we pick out shapes in a fire, so those who came near and looked at Spain in 1808 saw their own spectres in the flames. For Wordsworth, turning as he then was against progress, the Spanish were described in a way which would have been unrecognisable to British soldiers or diplomats in the field in May 1809: 'Was there ever – since the earliest actions of men which have been transmitted by affectionate tradition or recorded by faithful history, or sung to the impassioned harp of poetry – was there ever a people who presented themselves to the reason and the imagination, as under more holy influences than the dwellers upon the Southern Peninsula.'[9]

Wordsworth, like his contemporaries in Britain, made frequent reference to episodes in Spanish history – to the 'ancient stories of Numantia or Saguntum', or the deeds of Pelayo and El Cid. The former were legendary sieges associated with Hannibal and Scipio, and Wordsworth affirms by association the heroism and timeless significance of these to the 1809 siege of Saragossa which had ended in honourable defeat for Spain while the Cintra pamphlet was being composed. In immortalising the heroism of an Aragonese city, poet was anticipating painter: Sir David Wilkie was to create his Spanish masterpiece *The Defence of Saragossa* from the same epic romance. Wilkie's is a vision of the triumvirate which saved the honour of the city – General Palafox, a local Augustinian friar Father Consolazion, and the maiden Agostina – on a canvas which would be acquired for George IV.

Wordsworth compares France's attempt to subjugate Spain with the fate of the Welsh and the Scots, areas of the United Kingdom which still sustained in the early nineteenth century an unbroken balladic tradition which told of the romance of the Middle Ages. It is claimed that as a result of the forced incorporation of the one nation and the voluntary union of the other, 'a thousand interchanges of amity' have occurred. But there is also a rueful confession that something Blakean and heroic was lost in those processes:

> yet the flashing eye, and the agitated voice, and all the tender recollections, with which the names of Prince Llewellin and William Wallace are to this day pronounced by the fire-side and the public road, attest that these substantial blessings have not been purchased without the relinquishment of something most salutary to the moral nature of Man; else the remembrances would not cleave so faithfully to their abiding-place in the human heart. But if these affections be of general interest, they are of especial interest in Spain; whose

history, written and traditional, is pre-eminently stored with the sustaining food of such affections; and in no country are they more justly and generally prized, or more feelingly cherished.[10]

Robertson approved the Jesuits as Wordsworth conceded the efficacy of religion in Spain for the fight against a godless tyrant. He infiltrated the idea that the religion of a Spaniard was a present help as he carefully sanitised Spanish Catholicism. He compared the spirit of the defenders of Saragossa with the rectitude of Sir Thomas Fairfax's 'godly men' – that is, the parliamentary soldiers who under Fairfax's command had decisively routed Charles I's army at Marston Moor in 1644. The Spanish foot soldier has become an honorary roundhead, and so by an unlikely process of assimilation, it is declared that '[t]here is (I cannot refrain from observing) in the Catholic religion, and in the character of its priesthood especially, a source of animation and fortitude in desperate struggles – which may be relied upon as one of the best hopes of the cause'.[11]

Wordsworth's righteous indignation had as much to do with what was amiss with Britain as it had with anything in the Peninsula. Wordsworth held up Spain as a mirror to the ills of Britain and the evils of France. Something of his old radical credentials was still there, however, in what was said about the response of His Majesty's Government to the petition moved at the Guildhall by the City of London on 4 October 1808. The City had declared that the Convention of Cintra was humiliating and degrading to Britain and injurious to its allies. The Government had responded by claiming that the petition was inadmissable; there was no legal means by which the Crown could be required to respond. Here Wordsworth suggested how melancholy it was that in denying a petition as a means of expressing a grievance, an attempt has been made to tear out of the venerable crown of the British Sovereign what was a gem in the turban of the Emperor of Morocco: what was allowed in a tyranny like Morocco was denied to the British whose duty it was to show the world how to conduct its affairs.

Wordsworth, like many British writers involved with Spain, recruited the country as an ally in battles which were fought out in the mind of the writer. As a Tory, Wordsworth had developed a deep loathing for the values of the French Enlightenment and the *philosophes*. Wordsworth approved the integrity of Spain in the face of progress, but with a shrillness which betrayed anxiety about aspects of economic and social change in Europe which threatened what he described as 'the throne of imagination'. He declared that 'no flight of infidel harpies' had descended on Spain because a Spanish understanding was too strong to give way to the 'pellets' of logic which in France Condillac 'ha[d] cast in the foundry of national vanity'. As for the 'reveries' of Rousseau and the 'flippancies' of Voltaire, these were plants which simply will not naturalise in the country of Calderón and Cervantes.[12]

But there were dangers not confined to books. Part of what had to be cherished about Spain was exactly what Adam Smith had deplored as being absent – a modern economic infrastructure. Manufactures and commerce which Smith did his best to promote for the nascent British industrial economy, Wordsworth noticed with relief, were a great deal less developed in Spain than elsewhere. Madrid, Wordsworth informed his readership, was a small city and not industrialised. Paris by contrast was overgrown and disproportionate: 'sickening and bowing down by its corrupt humours, the frame of the body politic'. Here Wordsworth anticipates Richard Ford, a fellow Tory and the most gifted of all English travel writers on Spain (Figure 2). Ford in his writings on the Peninsula of some

2 Antonio Chatelain, *Richard Ford*

thirty-five years later would roll like a dog in filth; so offensive and ubiquitous was the anti-Gallican smell of the first edition of his *A Handbook for Travellers in Spain* (1845) that it was withdrawn lest its distribution were to bring down a firestorm.

Before then, however, Wordsworth describes the virtues of Spain and Spaniards, by recourse variously to the incorruptible world of Plutarch, the heroics of Sir Philip Sidney, and the millenarian vision of Cromwell. The inappropriateness of these parallels to circumstances in Spain in the age of Ferdinand VII is a measure of that British tendency to paint the country in their own colours.

Wordsworth's friend Robert Southey was no exception to this habit of seeing Britain and its ills in a Spanish glass. He was clear that the national humiliation which was Cintra rocked Britain to its foundations. He discussed it all in his monumental *History of the Peninsular War*. Although that book was soon to be superseded by the account of the campaign written by Sir Charles Napier which had benefited from access to documents Wellington had refused Southey, the offering by Southey, written by a diehard Tory, influential contributor to the reviews, and Poet-Laureate, was not without considerable influence. Napier may have had the papers but Southey had the pulpit. He saw what had happened in the Peninsula as admonitory and exemplary. According to him, at the time the Convention had been signed nothing else could be talked of, nothing else could be thought of, as men were kept awake at night, 'like a misdeed or a misfortune of their own'.[13] It seems unlikely that anyone could have become more indignant about how the British had treated their Iberian allies in 1808 than Wordsworth, but somehow Southey managed it. His *Peninsular War*, which was to be published in separate volumes over several years, had begun to appear fourteen years after *The Convention of Cintra* by Wordsworth – epitaph to a struggle which Southey, like Wordsworth before him, believed was the greatest conflict in history. Southey saw the fighting in Iberia in these transcendental terms because the enemy had been 'more formidable than that of Rome in its height of empire, of Zingis, or of Timour'. French arms were powerful but what made them almost irresistible was that a military colossus was directed by the 'will of an individual the most ambitious of the human race'.[14]

Southey reverts repeatedly to the idea that the commitment Britain made to Iberia was as much for the good of Britain as for those it was going to rescue. The battles against Napoleon constituted no common war but, rather, they were the clearest case history afforded of the fight of good against evil. Accordingly, it had been a war waged for England and Europe as well as for Spain and Portugal. The Peninsular War was for the preservation not only of liberty, but of literature and, indeed, for the domestic morals and happiness of England and Spain. So clear-cut were the issues that the expulsion of the French was for 'the vital welfare of the human race'.

Southey was guilty of accepting an illusion commonly held in England which might be termed 'the Spanish fallacy'. What conservatives in Britain longed for at home they saw in the Peninsula – a fantasy which found in Spain a social harmony such as the Victorians would come to believe had once existed in England in the Middle Ages. The more ignorant and illiterate the 'meanest peasant' in Spain might be, the better. It was the illiterate but true-hearted Spaniard, both man and woman, who constituted a far more effective fighting force than the regular Spanish soldiery which, when gathered into an army, 'resembled the trunk of a tree, of which the termites have eaten out the timber, and only the bark remains'.[15] Southey declared that everyone in Spain knew that the country had once been prosperous and powerful and, being familiar with the names of its heroes, all were able to speak of the past with a feeling 'which was the best omen for those who were to come'.[16] It was a naive if condescending view which was tenacious and licensed by what was perceived as that which the Spanish owed the British for having saved them from disaster during the Peninsular War. Long after Southey had stopped passing judgements on Spain, George Borrow, author of *The Bible in Spain*, reported an argument he had had with a young Spanish officer at a *posada*. There he had felt compelled to expound a history lesson by telling his adversary how Britain had expended millions of pounds and an ocean of blood in extricating Spain from the predicament in which it had found itself with the invasion of the French. This abiding sense that the Spanish and Portuguese owed the British an unpayable debt often went with a belief in the virtues of the illiterate, worthy of Rousseau at his most idealistic:

> I would sooner talk of the lower class, not only of Madrid but of all Spain. The Spaniard of the lower class has much more interest for me, whether *manolo*, labourer, or muleteer. He is not a common being; he is an extraordinary man. He has not, it is true, the amiability and generosity of the Russian *mujik*, who will give his only rouble rather than the stranger shall want; nor his placid courage, which renders him insensible to fear, and at the command of his Tsar sends him singing to certain death. There is more hardness and less self-devotion in the disposition of the Spaniard; he possesses, however, a spirit of proud independence which it is impossible not to admire. He is ignorant, of course; but it is singular that I have invariably found amongst the low and slightly-educated classes far more liberality of sentiment than amongst the upper. It has long been the fashion to talk of the bigotry of the Spaniards, and their mean jealousy of foreigners. This is true to a certain extent; but it chiefly holds good with respect to the upper classes. If foreign valour or talent has never received its proper meed in Spain, the great body of the Spaniards are certainly not at fault. I have heard Wellington calumniated in this proud scene of his triumphs, but never by the old soldiers of Aragon and the Asturias, who assisted to vanquish the French at Salamanca and the Pyrenees. I have heard the manner of riding of an English jockey criticised, but it was by the idiotic heir of Medina Celi, and not by a picador of the Madrilenean bull-ring.[17]

But before Borrow delivered himself of all this, hardly less broad prejudices had been aired by Southey, an influential writer whose contributions to Tory periodicals encouraged, as they nurtured, the views of those who perceived themselves to be threatened. Southey composed his history of the Peninsular War in the aftermath of the Congress of Vienna of 1815. The purpose of the Congress had been to re-establish the *status quo ante*, as if events since 1789 had never happened. At home, Southey's backdrop was a violent canvas. The demand for wholesale political change was orchestrated by William Cobbett, the leading journalist of the time and originally a ploughman. In 1802 he had first published the *Weekly Political Register* which, when in 1816 its price was reduced to 2d, obtained a circulation of 50,000 a week. Cobbett used the paper to advocate annual parliaments and universal suffrage. The end of the Continental war produced acute agrarian unrest in Britain. Luddism revived from 1816 and so a renewal of the destruction of agricultural machinery. London shivered as Manchester rocked. Following the Spa Fields riots of December 1816, a London crowd mobbed the Regent on his return from the opening of Parliament and, in early March 1817, *Habeas Corpus* was suspended as the Government prepared itself for revolution. In the summer of 1819, the magistrates of Manchester sent in the yeomanry to arrest 'Orator' Hunt in St Peter's Fields when addressing a crowd estimated by some at as much as 100,000. The authorities panicked and ordered the 15th Hussars to charge in what became known as the Peterloo Massacre. Five of the crowd were killed and many injured. It was an engagement which would not be stitched onto the regimental colours. Owing to events in Manchester, the Government, believing that 'every meeting for Radical Reform is an overt act of treasonable conspiracy against the King and the Government', passed the Six Acts.[18] These represented, in theory at least, a very serious infringement of the liberty of the subject. They did not succeed in suppressing danger, however. In February 1820, Arthur Thistlewood orchestrated the Cato Street Conspiracy, whose intention was to assassinate ministers at a dinner party given by Lord Harrowby at his house in Grosvenor Square. This achieved, the assassins would have seized both the Tower and the Bank of England. The idea was betrayed by a government spy and Thistlewood, together with four others, was executed, while another five were transported.

Such, then, was the background against which Southey gave the world his account of the heroic conduct of British arms in Spain. In choosing his epic, Southey was onto a winner. There had been a huge emotional investment by the British in Spain, symbolised by 40,000 British servicemen killed on Spanish soil. In *The Peninsular War*, Spain is portrayed as the country England once was and, significantly, could revert to being. Nowhere is this more obvious than at Torres Vedras where Wellington's defensive lines forced Massena to withdraw in what became the turning point of the war. The Peninsula was saved. All agreed that the defences of

Torres Vedras were decisive, though not everyone chose to compare that event to the Trojan Wars as did Southey in his book:

> When [Wellington] took his stand there, Lisbon was not the only stake of that awful contest: the fate of Europe was in suspense; and they who, like Homer, could see the balance in the hand of Jupiter, might then have perceived that the fortunes of France were found wanting in the scale. There the spell which bound the nations was broken; the plans of the tyrant were baffled; his utmost exertions when he had no other foe and no other object defied; his armies were beaten; and Europe, taking heart when [it] beheld the deliverance of Portugal, began to make a movement for [its] own[19]

Southey felt that Iberia had done as much for Britain as the other way round. In 1823, when the first volume of *The Peninsular War* appeared, Southey believed that the United Kingdom stood in mortal danger, much as Iberia had in the summer of 1808. But then Southey's readership were implicitly exhorted to take heart from his account of the great Wellington's exploits. As a result of defying Massena at Torres Vedras, 'England once more felt her strength, and remembered the part she had borne, and the rank she had asserted in the days of her Edwards and her Henrys'. The United Kingdom had been delivered in as many important ways as Spain and Portugal. It had fought in strict conformity with the highest principles of justice and sound state policy, while its military reputation had been reasserted after a long decline since the Treaty of Utrecht had brought the curtain down on the glorious victories of the Duke of Marlborough. The book is then brought to something of a moral crescendo with an admonitory passage in which Southey may have had the Liverpool ministry in mind as he exhorted his readership to hold fast to 'resolute perserverance in a just cause' – a nostrum which, as the author had triumphantly demonstrated through three monumental volumes, had been displayed by Wellington. Ever resolute, the Iron Duke had led his troops out of the trenches of Portugal to a triumph in Madrid in July 1812, almost exactly four years since the French had threatened the peace of the world by forcibly investing the Spanish capital. In the very last paragraph, more reminiscent of a disciple of the Clapham Sect than of a dispassionate historian, Southey considers what 'resolute perseverance' could teach a British government faced with: a febrile economy, agrarian unrest, disaffected radicals. For Southey, unreformed Spain remained still in the Garden of Eden while the other nations of Europe had been forcibly cast out by the violence of the French Revolution and the tyranny of Bonapartism. But for Britain, events still lay in balance because of its heroic and successful defiance of the armies of France. If Britain too was to avoid the fate of European monarchies, it could do worse than study Spain: 'These lessons have never been more memorably exemplified than in the Peninsular War, and for her own peculiar lesson, England, it may be hoped, has learned to have ever from thenceforth a just reliance, under

Providence, upon her resources and her strength ... under Providence, I say, for if that support be disregarded, all other will be found to fail'.[20]

For Southey, admonishment and morality balance well-written accounts of the sterling and immortal events of the Peninsular War. The book was much admired, though many of his assumptions rest on claims about Spain, familiar enough to those who had immersed themselves in the writings of the Enlightenment historians, who formed the subject of the first chapter of this book.

The special relationship which Southey, Wordsworth and others thought they saw between Britain and the Iberian countries was put to the test in the years after the final defeat of Napoleon in 1815. Liberals in Britain wrung their hands for Spain when, in 1823, France succeeded – with the connivance of the Holy Alliance – in overturning the Liberal Constitution and strengthening the grip of Ferdinand VII. What had happened was that in 1820 there had been an army rising with the intention of keeping Ferdinand VII faithful to the liberal constitution of 1812 which Spain had promulgated at Cádiz, following the expulsion of the French invaders. From 1820 for three years, liberals of various persuasions – often divided among themselves – tried to sustain a constitutional Spain. However, local anarchy and internecine conflict at the centre between the two strands of liberals – 'moderate liberalism' and the radicalism of the *exaltados* – meant that this interlude, the so-called 'Constitutional Triennium', failed. But while British Whigs followed Holland House in offering benighted Spain sympathy and its exiles something to eat after the liberal experiment ended in 1823, relations between Britain and Spain entered a new and complicated phase. This was because of the difficulty of knowing how to deal with Spain's colonies in South America.

The struggle for mastery in Europe demanded the high seriousness of Miltonic diction by apologists of both sides of the political divide in Britain. A subject which provoked no less moral earnestness, if mercifully a more subdued discourse, was the question of the emancipation of slaves. The slave trade had been abolished from 1 January 1808 largely thanks to the efforts of Charles James Fox, who had initiated matters as Foreign Secretary in Grenville's 'Ministry of All the Talents' of 1806. Without Fox the measure would not have made it onto the statute book, though Fox himself had died while the issue was still in debate. The evils of slavery and the continuing need to campaign against further aspects of the system remained, however, an article of faith at Holland House, but it was no easy matter. Holland had been the legatee of Fox, who had come perilously close to ruining the prospects of his nephew through his addiction to gambling. Matters for Holland had only been saved by a reassuringly fat income from slave plantations in Jamaica. These had accrued as a result of Holland marrying Elizabeth Vassall. Nevertheless, somehow Holland managed to pick his way between self-interest as an impoverished aristocrat, dependent on molasses to sweeten a bank account, and his role as torchbearer of an uncle's humane values. Stepping gingerly along a maze of conflicting interests, Holland was a central figure in the passing of the Emancipation Act of 1833. This granted freedom to the slaves of British dependencies in the West Indies.

The debate in Britain about the tyranny of Bonapartism had concentrated minds on metropolitan Spain. But this new cause which profoundly affected the economic interests of Spain and Portugal meant that the imperial possessions of both Iberian countries came into view: Portugal had a flourishing trade in shipping slaves from West Africa to Brazil, while Seville had been made golden by slaves bound for the Americas. Differences of view as to the economic imperative for Spain of slavery and the moral imperative of its abolition, for many influential public figures in Britain, created tensions. In turn these helped point British policy away from metropolitan Spain and toward its New World dependencies. No one was more important in this shift of emphasis than the British Foreign Secretary, George Canning.

Prince Metternich, the architect of the Congress system evolved at Vienna after the final defeat of Napoleon, described Canning as flashing 'like a malevolent meteor through Europe'.[21] Such was the exasperated tribute from the greatest master of political intrigue since Talleyrand. Arguably George Canning (1770–1827) has been the most adroit Foreign Secretary Britain has ever had, a claim based on the skill with which he outmanoeuvred the governments of Europe. His whole philosophy in representing British interests in Europe was to subvert the rigidities of the Congress system which Metternich and Czar Alexander I sustained as an article of faith. Sustenance was provided by the Holy Alliance of Russia, Prussia and Austria bent upon ensuring not only that the revived monarchies survived, but also that the partners intervene to remove constitutional government. Canning had the foresight to see that such a philosophy could only spell disaster in the medium term, and he had the skill to subvert the chancelleries of Europe.

Iberia was the chess board at which on separate occasions Canning checkmated the aspirations of the absolutists who had glued the reactionary and ineffective Louis XVIII back on the throne of France as they had squeezed Ferdinand VII into that of Spain. Canning's Iberian policy perfectly exemplifies, in the arena of international relations, how an ostensible identification with Spain and Portugal was actually for the purpose of defining and defending 'Britishness'.

Canning succeeded to the Foreign Office in the autumn of 1822, following the suicide of Castlereagh. Unexpected promotion caused him to remark to a political ally that he did not think he would last six months. He held the job for over four years and became something of the lion-tamer of European politics, suppressing the savage instincts of ultras with a mixture of well-judged threats and an instinct for what was going on behind his back. His tenure, however, had begun disastrously: he was humiliated in Spain. Neither sufficiently alert nor robustly forthright enough, he had failed to prevent France from invading Spain in 1823 for the purpose of reinstalling the Bourbon king Ferdinand VII. It was the greatest humiliation in the career of a man thought by Chateaubriand when Foreign Minister of France as having made discoveries in diplomacy which rivalled those of Newton in science. Canning survived.[22] He did so because a majority in the Commons voted heavily against military intervention. He also learned a lesson: he was never caught out again.

Just how profoundly Canning differed from the leaders of the Holy Alliance appeared in high relief after the Congress of Verona (1822). There the Alliance discussed the independence movement in Greece, and the deplorable political developments in Spain prior to the triumph of conservatism heralded by the return of King Ferdinand. Czar Alexander I, whose rapid trajectory from liberalism to paranoid conservatism was sufficiently vertiginous as to justify questions as to his mental balance, declared that 'the continuance of the Spanish system is inconsistent with the happiness and prospects of Spain, and the safety of France or of any other country of Europe'.[23] Diseased himself, the Czar saw politics as an extension of medicine; those with the contagion of liberalism had to be locked away lest they infect the healthy. But Canning was having none of this. He was of the fixed and firm belief that 'Great Britain maintains a policy of her own, suited to her position and constitution. She will be no party to a general interference in the concerns of other States'.[24] Equally, though, Canning was far from being a Byronic defender of the liberties of 'free' peoples. It was all a question of national-self interest, not an expression of a Romantic *zeitgeist*.

The pragmatic exposition of non-interference had to be consistent with the promotion and defence of national interest and, here, out of an interlude of humiliation, came the supreme moment in a career whose tenebrous periods were relieved by a genius for oratory. While Canning espoused the doctrine of respecting the internal affairs of different regimes, to the marked irritation of the European diplomatic corps, this could never mean for Great Britain a neglect of its vital interests. The question was, how had the 1823 French intervention in Spain affected the place of Britain in the world? The Polignac Memorandum (1823) had required Britain to acknowledge that France could not, nor should not, be required to remove itself from Spain in the short term. That was a simple fact of politics, but it was also an imbalance which had to be redressed. Here the key to Canning's thinking was his respect for the traditional order of things and for established spheres of interest. The clue to redressing the French predominance in metropolitan Spain was maritime: the sea having saved Britain from France during the Napoleonic era and would do so again: 'Europe's domain extends to the shores of the Atlantic, England's begins there' was where Canning saw Britain's advantage.[25] It was an apothegm giving the means for Canning to snatch victory from humiliation. For over four years, from 1822 to 1827, Canning – with the significant but isolated support of his superior, the Prime Minister Lord Liverpool – had worked hard to persuade a Tory ministry to recognise the independence of Spain's South American colonies. Canning had early formed the view that the main motive for recognising the Spanish colonies was the French occupation; the second, the designs of the United States to dominate the southern continent; and the third, the completion of a process already far advanced. Canning was always a pragmatist and some of the colonies had been de facto independent since before he had become Foreign Secretary. By December 1824, Canning had submitted a paper known as the 'third memorandum' to the Cabinet on the issue of recognition. In this he had laid out his thinking for colleagues like Wellington who was fixed in his antipathy to the principle that a monarchy should be undermined by a third party giving sustenance to disobedience: ' The great practical question for us seems to be how, in the event of the actual incorporation of the resources of Spain with those of France, such an accession to the power of France can best be counteracted. I have no hesitation in saying that this must be by a separation of the resources of Spanish America from those of Spain'.[26]

Working from within a Tory – not a Whig – governmental regime, Canning showed great courage in pursuing what was effectively a policy of enlightened self-interest. Always controversial, often unpredictable, frequently the object of jealousy, Canning could not have carried off one of the decisive political acts of nineteenth-century Britain without adroit manipulation of public opinion and the support of Liverpool. By the end of 1824 the coup had been prepared and, on Monday 12 December, Canning came to the Commons to defend himself against accusations that he had been feeble in not standing up to the French invasion of Spain. He began by disarming his critics, since he conceded that '[it] would be disingenuous indeed not to admit that the entry of the French Army into Spain was, in a certain sense, a disparagement – and affront to the pride – a blow to the feelings of England'. However, he then appeared to flatter his listeners by posing a series of questions before finally, taking their breath away with the boldness of a policy which he believed would make South America English:

> Was nothing then to be done? ... What, if the possession of Spain might be rendered harmless in rival hands – harmless as regarded us – and valueless to the possessors? Might not compensation for disparagement be obtained, and the policy of our ancestors be vindicated, by means better adapted to the present time? If France occupied Spain, it was necessary in order to avoid the consequences of that occupation – that we should blockade Cadiz? No – I looked another way – I sought materials of compensation in another hemisphere. Contemplating Spain, such as her ancestors had known her, I resolved that if France had Spain, it should not be Spain with

the Indies. I called the New World into existence to redress the balance of the Old.[27]

Canning stepped back from the Mace. The House was spell-bound in the contemplation of his extraordinary boldness: Britain alone among the powers of Europe, and in defiance of the most deeply ingrained prejudices of the Holy Alliance, was about to give formal recognition to the republics of South America. At a stroke a commercial empire had been gained which it had taken the East India Company two hundred years of fighting to accomplish in India. Silence as at the end of a great theatre performance was then broken: Canning was cheered to the rafters. He wrote the next day to Granville of how nothing in thirty five years' experience in the House had been more grateful to the English nation than his declaration that he had called the New World into existence to redress the balance of the old.

Even Wellington was forced to concede the brilliance of the coup. As for his part, George IV was far from pleased, since all this would sanction revolutionary principles and he would be exposed 'to the risk of having a cocoa-nut coloured Minister to receive at his Levee'.[28] For all that, Canning believed the King would accept what had happened and indeed, on the last day of the year, Canning himself announced to Madrid his intention of recognising Mexico, Colombia and what was then known as the colony of Buenos Aires (later to be enlarged to Argentina). But here as so often, intervention in the affairs of imperial Spain had nothing to do with the espousal of generous, liberal policies as might have been advocated by Charles James Fox or William Wilberforce. The Spanish colonies and their fate mattered to Canning only if a way could be found to make them not so much independent as English. Canning was disarmingly frank about what he was up to, and it had nothing to do with the rights of man, with Rousseau, Paine, Godwin or any other philosophers of freedom: 'Spanish America is free; and if we do not mismanage our matters sadly, she is English'. He did not. Britain rapidly came to dominate the economies of South America and this was done at the expense of the Yankees.

Spain and its troubles provoked one of the great oratorical moments in the House of Commons, even by the standards of an age exceptional for the eloquence of its political leaders. Yet the impudence of Canning's claim to have summoned a continent into being was only one way in which Spain and its affairs were dramatised in London. Those who lived in Bloomsbury saw what Thomas Carlyle described so eloquently in his valedictory biography of his friend John Sterling, who had a romantic if disastrous entanglement with Spain.

Sterling was disabled by being too clever. Impetuous and easily distracted, he was a 'young Cambridge democrat', much influenced by Coleridge at whose feet he liked to listen to dicta on life, ethics and religion. Carlyle had little patience for the disintegrated genius which the poet had become by the 1820s, venting contempt for Coleridgean 'moonshine' by describing what Sterling so much enjoyed hearing as 'The moaning singsong of that theosophico-metaphysical monotony'.[29] But then, it seems that Sterling had a temperamental need for heroes and hero-worship, and so, even if Coleridge's musings on the meaning of existence were largely impenetrable, it was clear that General Torrijos, leader of the Spanish exiles in London, was someone who could be looked up to without reservation. By any standards, Torrijos was a romantic figure: in 1823 he had played a major part in resisting 'the Ten Thousand Sons of St Louis' – the reactionary French army which had seen to the reinstatement of Ferdinand VII as king of Spain. As a result Torrijos had had to go into exile in London, and it was there that he came to inspire Sterling and a group of breathless Cambridge romantics. Torrijos began to plot with what Carlyle referred to as the 'Regent Street democrats', a reference to the lodgings Sterling had taken when he had come down from Cambridge. Their scheme was to raise the south of Spain against Ferdinand VII – something they were to attempt in 1831.

In London, Torrijos proved himself to be the most gifted and charismatic of the Spanish refugees; a group whose melancholy, empty days Carlyle witnessed. Indolent, displaced, each figure caught in asymmetrical isolation, community was denied, as Carlyle evocatively suggested that sense of desolation of men for whom the candle was trembling: 'Daily in the cold spring air, under skies so unlike their own, you could see a group of fifty or a hundred stately tragic figures, in proud threadbare cloaks ... Old steel-gray heads, many of them; their brown complexion, dusky look of suppressed fire, in general their tragic condition as of caged Numidian lions.'[30]

Transfer of enthusiasm from Kant, refracted through the chipped but still brilliant prism of Coleridge, to Spanish Jacobinism as understood by General Torrijos led the impetuous Sterling to emotional disaster. Carlyle, an unsentimental dyspeptic, was temperamentally averse to ameliorate pain of any sort and was certainly not disposed to make light of the part Sterling had played in the later death by firing squad, on the beach at Málaga, of Torrijos himself, Sterling's cousin Lieutenant Edward Boyd, and some fifty unlucky *liberales*. The title of the chapter Carlyle devotes to the end of Torrijos is callously brief: 'Catastrophe'.

What had happened was this. Sterling's relative Edward Boyd, an Ulsterman and as such, heir to a respectable tradition of the histrionic in politics, had been a Lieutenant in the Indian Army. In India, Boyd's difficult personality had caused him to resign over some real or imagined slight. He came back, he inherited £5,000 and he looked for adventure. Someone had pointed out that there was 'a worn-out royal gunbrig ... to be had dog-cheap' rotting in an Irish creek. Boyd bought it and immediately proposed 'to go a-privateering' to the Philippine Isles – a Regency

Drake, expecting to make his fortune by stealing from Spanish ships. But before then he went to London where Sterling persuaded him that if he wanted an adventure of 'the Sea-King sort', he could strike a blow for liberty by providing Torrijos with the means of raising revolution in Spain. The General, a 'kind of living Romance', thought he could perceive Spain 'as inflammable as touchwood' through the London fog. Faced as Torrijos was with life on the pavement in Euston Square, this is all too easy to understand. It was a disastrous delusion. A landing was effected near Málaga whereupon the General with his followers were rounded up and fusiladed on the beach one Sunday morning in December 1831. Boyd was the only Briton among the martyrs, though originally there had been a knot of ardent fellow countrymen, anticipating in some ways the youthful British commitment to political idealism in Spain, made a hundred years later by Orwell and Blunt. Boyd thought he was going to be leading a pentecostal band of 'Cambridge Apostles' – that is, a select group of the brightest and most intellectual undergraduates who met to debate political issues of the day. Among those destined for Spain were to have been Sterling himself, Richard Chenevix Trench who became archbishop of Dublin, and the philologist and historian John Mitchell Kemble. Fortunately for the last two, they decided to turn back when they got to Gibraltar.

For bringing Boyd and Torrijos together, Sterling never forgave himself. He had acted the go-between but he had also intended to commit himself to this desperate enterprise, prevented at the last minute by the emotional blackmail of a woman whose hysterics had made him propose and promise to stay at home. The landing was wholly ineffectual, not to say absurd. Extreme bathos and real tragedy ensured that it became a subject not even Carlyle, with all his bold disregard for convention, ever dared raise with Sterling who was, however, to confess to his brother: 'I hear the sound of that musketry; it was as if the bullets were tearing at my own brain'.

Reactions in England to such Byronism were varied. Richard Ford, who together with his eccentric friend George Borrow was the most gifted nineteenth-century British writer on Spain, wholly sympathised with the authorities. Ford was quite clear: Boyd had got what he deserved – 'if anybody of the party deserved shooting, it is a meddling foreigner, who must have known of the existence of the decree under which all rebels, taken *in flagrante delicto*, were liable to summary punishment'.[31] By contrast, *The Times* was splenetic. On Christmas Eve 1831 it reported the death of Torrijos, attributing the summary disregard for the due processes of law, and the rights of a British citizen, to a mixture of the 'unrelenting despotism' of Ferdinand VII and his 'monkish advisers'. Readers were informed that the precipitation of a 'drum-head court martial' had been enforced by the deceits of the Jesuits. Intriguingly, in the issue of February 20 1832, there appeared a reprint of a letter which had originally been sent to the *Dublin Evening Mail*. Surely that letter was a forgery: quite simply it is too good an exit for the young Irish hero – heaven-sent inspiration for Donizetti to bring his curtain down on a lachrymose opera. It was claimed that the letter had been sent from the 'Convento del Carmen' just hours before Boyd was shot. Whether forged or not, the death of this quixotic revolutionary helped to reinforce many prejudices about the turpitude of Spain and the Spaniard:

> My dear Harry,   Convento del Carmen
>
> Before this reaches you, you will have lost a friend who was sincerely attached to you. The preparation for death is going on, and in two short hours 'life's fitful fever' will be terminated. The clanging of chains is ringing in my ears and those harbingers of disaster, being clad in the livery of the grave, are flitting before me, up and down the refectory of the convent where I write from. I am surrounded by them pestering me to recant ... God bless you, my dear Harry – may you be happier and more fortunate than yours, affectionately
>
> Robert Boyd

Torrijos himself lived on within the liberal heart of Spain. In 1842 the citizens of Málaga erected an obelisk to the fifty-three who had been shot on the beach. Curiously enough, it stands in the former Plaza Riego, opposite the birthplace of Picasso – creator of *Guernica*, the most powerful of all icons dedicated to the horrors of war. Boyd along with the others was reburied beneath that obelisk. So much then for the romantic death of one deluded Ulsterman. A year or two later, the emotional bonds between Britain and Spain came to be symbolised not by a gaggle of Cambridge Apostles but by another Irishman, the son of a gentleman farmer from Lisready, Co. Limerick.

Sir George de Lacy Evans (1787–1870) was an astonishing man whose ambition and capacity for self-delusion were on a positively heroic scale. Evans' energy, exceptional even by the exhausting standards of the age, made him the inspiration for a ripping historical yarn by G.A. Henty, the Edwardian imperialist writer of boys' history books.[32] Conspicuously brave as a soldier, Evans had had a dramatic career in the army. But that was predictable, for soldiering was in his genes. Ancestors out of sorts with the Anglo-Irish establishment had been forced to seek military service on the Continent.

With a career clearly stalled after Waterloo, however, Evans had turned to writing and politics. He had become the M.P. for Westminster (1833–41 and 1846–65), and was described by one of his opponents as looking like an 'Italian assassin'. He defeated Byron's friend Sir John Hobhouse on a Radical platform. Evans now stood in a long line of radicals representing a famous constituency, of whom the most notorious had been that scourge of eighteenth-century Ministries, John Wilkes. The major did his best to uphold a great tradition. He was a passionate advocate of that deeply romantic cause, Polish independence, something which was a natural outcome of his dislike of Russia which had extinguished Polish hopes of freedom when they savagely put down the revolt of 1830–1831.On the home front, Evans supported curbing the powers of the police whom he regarded with deep suspicion; he campaigned for the emancipation of the Jews; he visited the Cotton Mills and encouraged trade unions and, although he evidently liked killing, was opposed to flogging in the army.

Evans had ideals, and Spain was a subject about which he had been passionately idealistic since serving in the Peninsular campaign in the 3rd Dragoons. He had fought at Vitoria and on through northern Spain all the way to Toulouse. Evans's gallantry should have been rewarded, but then promotion cost money and Evans was not rich. Such a state of affairs had left him with an abiding sense of the injustice which underpinned the British army in the age of Wellington. He had succeeded, however, in catching the notice of one man who would be important for his future. In 1835 the Spanish ambassador in London was General Alava, who had known Evans when they had been soldiers together in Spain. By May, with Spain once again in crisis, Alava had obtained permission to raise a volunteer army in Britain. This was to be directed against the *Carlistas*; followers of Don Carlos, the brother of the late Ferdinand VII, who to recap, had gone to war because they disputed the right of Queen Isabella II to the throne. This was on the uncertain grounds that Spanish law had specifically ruled out the accession of a woman.

There was a sense in which debate in Britain in 1835 as to the wisdom of once again embroiling itself in Spain had a familiar ring. Back in 1820, General Sir Robert Wilson had tried to raise an earlier British Expeditionary Force to support Riego during the three-year liberal interlude which had followed his rising. But in 1835, and in connection with the Pretender Don Carlos, Whig and Tory divided along the same lines as they had done in 1808 when Holland had represented the views of liberal Spain and Wordsworth the Tories. By 1835, Britain had abandoned Canning's masterly inactivity as the most provident way to manipulate foreign affairs, and had joined France, Spain and Portugal to form the Quadruple Alliance of April 1834. Such a western alliance, Palmerston had argued, would act 'as a counterpoise to the eastern league of arbitrary governments'. Whigs thought of the Carlist wars as a struggle between 'freedom and tyranny, liberty and despotism' while for the Tories they were another deplorable instance of 'revolutionary excitement' challenging the settled order of things. So much for the battle lines of the British political divide. Beyond the confines of Parliament, and as the war developed, there would be a widespread populist interest in the progress of arms. That interest was prurient, reinforcing a conviction among the

British public that the Spaniard was primitive and savage, and that his perceived cruelty and disregard for the rules of war marked him off not only from the British but also, despite the marked and persistent streak of anti-Gallicanism in nineteenth-century Britain, even from the French.

Meanwhile recruitment for the British Legion to fight for the *Cristinos* went ahead very fast: formation had only been sanctioned in June and by 10 July the first detachments of what might have eventually amounted to as many as 12,000 men had landed at north-coast ports. As with so many British Expeditionary Forces since that time, all began with high hopes.[33] Palmerston, chief architect in Britain's renewed involvement with fighting on mainland Spain, depended very heavily on the British ambassador to Spain throughout much of the 1830s. The person in question was Sir George Villiers (1800–1870, 4th earl of Clarendon from 1839), who was a strikingly good-looking man not unlike Wellington, with similar aquiline features and a commanding physical presence. Villiers was to remain on station in Madrid for six years, and his conduct there did much to make his political career. Regarded as something of an expert on foreign affairs, Villiers would twice serve as Foreign Secretary under Disraeli (1865–1856, 1868–1870). Before then, however, on 9 July 1835 Palmerston wrote to suggest that the Spaniards would do best to defer to the superior merits of British military talent and experience: 'Evans's ten thousand will turn the fate of the war. The Spaniards ought to give him the chief command, if he acquits himself well when he gets to the ground'.[34] However, matters turned out to be altogether less straightforward than Palmerston had predicted. For a start, Evans left much to be desired: Villiers thought him 'a man of mighty intentions and small performance'.[35] He could have added for good measure that the *Generalissimo* was also wildly inconsistent and unpredictable. It was remarked that his tolerance of incompetence and corruption was 'amiable and good hearted but highly subversive of discipline and subordination', though he had managed to stir himself sufficiently to have the Legion's two Spanish bakers executed on the rack. They turned out to have been Carlist spies, liberally spicing the bread with oxalic acid. There was also much rowing back in London as to whether Evans was actually ordering a ferocious regime of flogging for ill discipline, something which ill consorted with his credentials as a radical M.P. who had persuaded his constituents that he was adamantly opposed to corporal punishment as degrading and counter-productive.

Perhaps it was just as well that Evans in Spain laboured under the massive misapprehension that he was a great military leader, a delusion which his critics were not slow in unmasking:' The fact is that he cannot help looking upon himself as the Great Captain of the Age, and fancying that he is the Duke of Wellington, that that squinting little boy Don Sebastian is Napoleon and that if he moves from San Sebastian it is to fight the Battle of Waterloo. All of them very great errors.'[36]

Vain, bombastic, and oversensitive, Evans caused great offence in Madrid. He returned the Order of San Fernando because it had been delivered by a person with too low a rank. Nevertheless he had prodigious physical courage. Willingness to lead from the front inspired a rag-bag army which Evans moulded into an effective field force by dint of twelve hours a day spent in the saddle. But there were insurmountable problems. Unfortunately, these started with him. Villiers told Palmerston:' He came out here for English and not Spanish political purposes, and his position with the Government, his operations in the field, and the discipline of his corps have all suffered from the phantom that has eternally pursued him of – What will they say of me in Westminster?'[37]

There had always been an acute problem with the quality of the men under command; Wellington's view that the British soldier was the 'scum of the earth' was certainly confirmed by scrutiny of Evans as a recruiting officer. Those who did best in Spain were the Irish contingent because, so it was claimed, they had long been inured to sleeping on mud floors without blankets. This the Legion had been required to do during its first terrible winter in Spain when, during prolonged periods of snowy weather, it had been billeted in abandoned monasteries open to the skies. As for the equipment, it was reported that Evans's artillery horses had served their time in London cabs.

The Irish did well but not, apparently, the Scottish contingent. A Glaswegian banker thanked one of Evans's officers smugly: 'Well, Colonel Shaw, we are much obliged to you in Glasgow for taking so many black-guards away'. But no less awful was the rabble which Evans had found among the unemployed of his own constituency of Westminster, a crowd who might have been drawn by Cruickshank, then busy illustrating *The Pickwick Papers*. Such were the soldierly qualities of the Westminster crew that Wellington was moved to observe: 'Evans will find a mighty difference between holding forth to a set of constituents in a Westminster pot house and commanding an army in a poor country without a commissariat, and with little or no money'.

Wellington knew about corruption. Accordingly, he cannot have been surprised by the outrage expressed by Villiers as to what was happening in the Quartermaster's department:

> Grindlay informs me that the Spanish Commissary with the Legion is one of the greatest rascals unhung, but not greater than some of the paymasters of the regiments ... One of them, a Mr Burt, brother of two fellows who keep gambling houses near St James's Street, said to a clerk of Grindlay's that it had not answered him as he expected because he had never got hold of swag enough to bolt with.[38]

Wellington was angry; as a Tory he was a convinced supporter of Don Carlos and, on principle, implacably opposed to intervention in foreign countries on behalf of propping up liberalism. But as the most famous soldier of that age, he was also incensed when it became clear that the Legion's public humiliation occurred not on the battlefield, for defeats were usually briskly reversed, but at Vitoria, the site of his own most decisive Peninsula victory. There the British Legion was simply abandoned without proper victualling, despised by the Spaniards and hated by the locals for their disorderly conduct. A winter of immobility in torrential rain rotted discipline as it decimated the ranks. Villiers summoned up a latter-day image of Falstaff and his crew when he reported to London of how:

> Some time since a regiment either quartered in or marching through a friendly village maltreated the inhabitants (I fear killed a good many). Desecrated the church, and robbed the plate, and the ornaments of the images. Evans subsequently sent for the cura and made him give an account of damages which he paid ... I heard (though only from an inhabitant of Vitoria) that they have 800 baggage mules and 500 whores moving about with them which must be pleasant but is not cheap.[39]

The first months in Spain were disastrous for the Legion. But thereafter, discipline improved, *Cristinos* co-operated and victories beckoned. By April 1836, Evans was marching briskly along the road to Santander, persuaded by one of his commanders, 'an old Armadillo [who] likes knocking his head against a wall', to raise the siege of San Sebastian. Against all the odds, the Legion did exactly that; but only because of the timely arrival of the Royal naval ship the *Phoenix* which powdered the city walls with its 15–inch guns. Evans lost eleven officers and 120 rank and file; the defeated *Carlistas* suffered the death of just one officer and 11 men killed. However, it was an important psychological blow and it did much for the morale of the *Cristinos*. By July 1836, Villiers was more positive about what he saw as the contribution the Legion could make to the liberal cause in Spain. He dismissed the contemptuous attitude of a largely hostile British press: 'As for the supposed dislike of the Spaniards towards the Legion of which the English newspapers are full, nothing can be more false. The hopes of all the partisans of the Queen are fixed upon Evans and the Legion. It is felt and acknowledged that they alone have done anything and they alone are likely to do anything'.[40] Evans's reputation was unpredictable like a kite in the wind.

The Carlist wars created a division along the old fault line of British politics: Whigs and Radicals were *Cristinos*, Tories all for Don Carlos. As for Don Carlos himself, the Tories felt he had always cut a better figure than his contemptible elder brother, Ferdinand VII. He had refused to surrender his rights to the throne when in 1808 the family had been trussed like chickens by Napoleon who had bullied first Charles IV and then Ferdinand himself into agreeing that the throne should go to Napoleon's brother Joseph.

Supporters of Don Carlos identified him as a chieftain of a lost race whose relatively small population and confined geography belied the debt Europe owed to a primitive people. It was a reversion to Robert Southey's emotional bond with a savage but still pure Spain. As one anonymous pamphleteer put it: 'The Carlistas were the descendants of free forefathers, who under the hallowed oak of Guernica, first taught to enslaved Europe the lesson of liberty.'[41]

The Carlist Wars broke out when Britain was engaged on a voyage of self-discovery. Don Carlos reinvented himself in 1833; ten years after Walter Scott had reinvented Scotland. Scott had orchestrated a revival of the authentic as he had invented the ethnic, acting as master of ceremonies to the less than heroic figure of George IV who, on a famous visit to Scotland, disported himself at Holyrood in pink tights and a Royal Stewart Tartan. *Carlistas* in Spain and Tories in Britain both subscribed to a Celtic international, a will-o'-the-wisp which could as easily be pursued through the green meadows of the Asturias as among the heather of a Highland glen. Writers in Britain were minded to draw parallels between the heroic Basques and the inhabitants of the peripheral peoples of the British Isles:

> The best sympathies of a bold, warlike peasantry of all Spain are marshalled against the cause of Cristina ... They, like the Highlanders of Scotland, uphold with romantic gallantry the standard of their king, as the Royalists of La Vendée trampled on the tricolor of revolution ... In an evil hour shall we interfere in this contest with which we have nothing to do ... A war of principle, privilege, dynasty, and even religion ... whose sacred cause throws a dignity over the efforts of these half-armed bands of patriotic royalists, as the ample cloak of Spain covers with the drapery of decency the poverty which too often pines beneath its folds. This is the ennobling cause, which will call forth those lofty spirits, which Spain alone brings forth, but for whom she now brings forth too few for her glory.[42]

These are Wordsworthian sentiments, parallel to the instinct of the poet-politician, when thirty years before he had denounced the perfidy of the Convention of Cintra. Then he had looked to Scotland and Wales to find parallels with which a British readership could identify. Writing in 1808, Wordsworth had concluded that these fringe British nations had been an endangered species, but still sufficiently virile and uncorrupted nonetheless, to bear comparison with what he, like this pamphleteer thirty years later, had singled out as unique to Spain. British Tories in 1808 or 1838 were united in their belief that Spain, alone among the nations of modern Europe, could call forth such 'lofty spirits' as could be relied upon to sustain a great cause.

Goya's *Disasters of War* (*Los Desastres de la Guerra*) was unknown in Britain – as indeed it was in Spain, too – since the prints were not published until the 1860s. As far as Britain was concerned, however, that may have been just as well: Tories could continue to admire what they identified as the peculiarly Spanish warrior type, the *guerrilla*. Those in Britain who saw the *Cristinos* as dangerously radical were much taken with General Tomás Zumalacárregui, whose success as a leader of the *Carlistas* was entirely predictable. He was a Basque and 'there has never been wanting a guerrilla leader to a population so disposed and animated'. Basques were held by British Whigs as 'the patriarchs of European liberties' (Figure 3).

Since no one except the hot-head Evans and his desperados had ever been near the Basque provinces, those helots of reaction, soldiers of Don Carlos, encouraged the wildest fantasies. Delusions about the Basque soldiers of the pretender were bred among those in Britain who on an emotional level deeply resented change, as epitomised by what one writer mockingly deplored as the 'glorious days of July' 1832 when Earl Grey had seen to the passage of the Great Reform Bill through Parliament.

Zumalacárregui was seen as one with the heroes of a great tradition of Spanish irregular resistance, whether represented by those who had defied Augustus Caesar or that latter-day Caesar, Napoleon. To his admirers – and there were many among the British – Zumalacárregui seemed to come down in direct line from Sertorius, Viriatus, Pelayo and El Cid. In this connection an important semantic distinction was often employed by British admirers of the timeless Spanish warrior whose incarnation Zumalacárregui was. These heroes were often described not as generals but as 'chieftains', and their tribal status gave them an indisputable authority to lead their peoples into battle. The racial stock of Basque *warriors*, not soldiers, remained untainted since they 'bred among themselves'. Just as Wordsworth had preferred Madrid to Paris as unsophisticated and unindustrialised, so too the robust heroes of Don Carlos' armies, springing unarmed from the oak of Guernica, had never been selected 'from the higher and demoralized classes'. It was predicted that the Carlist leaders were men in whom their troops could place confidence. Ransacking the high romance of medieval chivalry to do justice to the cause of reaction, one British writer recalled the legend of Sir James Douglas, the Scottish aristocrat who had gone off to the Crusades with the heart of Robert the Bruce suspended around his neck like a dried tomato. Douglas had diverted to Spain where Spaniards, being Spaniards, had run off as soon as the Moors had appeared. Douglas, left exposed, had flung the heart of Bruce at the enemy into whose front he had charged to his death. But then it was claimed that those who had been supposed to support the mercenary Douglas had been the soft and corrupt Spanish Andalusians, not Basques. As a people had once been, so they still were. Basques, strong and trustworthy, unlike effeminate southern Spaniards, were ready to support a leader like Zumaracárregui, 'whose red plume they will follow forward, like the heart of Bruce, to death or victory ... They are the unchanged, unconquered Cantabrians ... they still advance singing their ancient national ballads (which have such a spirit-stirring influence on clannish highlanders)'.[43]

3 J.F. Lewis, *Zumalacarregui and the Christina Spy*

The fact that no one, Briton or Spaniard, could have said what a Cantabrian was to save his life was all to the good. Both Tories and Whigs claimed the same ground; both regarded themselves as custodians of liberty. And so it was that Spain, ever since Lord Holland had identified it as the land of promise, had become a battleground fought over in the British Press hardly less ferociously than by Wellington over the fields of Salamanca or Evans through the alleys of San Sebastian. Spain in the nineteenth century, like a drunkard in Gin Lane, lurched intermittently from *pronunciamiento* to fratricide. But then, the Civil War fought out over Spain by the Tory *Times* and the Whig *Morning Chronicle* was one continuous battle which lasted for the first forty years of the nineteenth century.The *Carlistas* in British politics liked to see the Basques as the patriarchs of European liberty. Palmerston thought otherwise. As Foreign Secretary he had the unenviable job of defending the decision, which the Whig ministry had originally made back in the summer of 1835, to allow recruitment to the Legion. He sneered at the picture which the Tories drew of Basque liberties, while those newspapers which he could recruit dilated upon what they dismissed as 'turgid bombast about mountain liberty'.[44]

A Carlist pamphlet published in London in 1837 had the rather despondent title *On the Unchangeable Character of All Wars in Spain*. It was written by Richard Ford, and it served unwittingly to point to certain symmetries about how British intellectuals and politicians divided in their emotional allegiance to Spain whether in the age of Palmerston or that of Stanley Baldwin. Spain in 1836 as in 1936 had as much to do with identifying opponents and discovering political identity as it did with a benighted country where Britons went ostensibly to serve the interests of others. The promoter of political utopias Lord Holland, the minor Regency poet Walter Savage Landor and the novelist Arthur Koestler, each in his own age, wished to make Spain different and each wanted to do it in a hurry. Ford aimed to put the Carlist Wars into the context of what, even then, was a long history of British involvement with conflict in Spain. He put the point well: 'Those who are hurrying on Spain from the extreme of despotism to the chaos of democracy show little knowledge either of human or Spanish nature'.[45] That was a view which Evelyn Waugh, a later splenetic Tory, might have applied to George Orwell, whose book about his experiences fighting in Spain, *Homage to Catalonia*, remains one of the finest English epitaphs to a lost cause. As well, there is a fine collection of Spanish communist posters in the Imperial War Museum, now of more interest to students of design than to zealots of the *International*. But there is an altogether more macabre, regrettably imperishable tribute to the heroes of The British Legion of 1836. The Pathology Department of Edinburgh University holds a vast collection of specimens saved from the surgical theatres of the Carlist Wars. These unlikely trophies of osteology and bottled soft-tissue specimens, accompanied by ten volumes of clinical case notes, were gathered together by Sir Rutherford Alcock

(1809–1897), who would achieve famous things in the Far East as first Consul-General in Japan and founder of Shanghai. But for a year, in 1836, he had been attached as surgeon to the marine brigade in the Carlist Wars. When, on his return from Spain, he taught pathology at the University, he put his specimens to good use.[46] As for Evans, who somehow managed to avoid ending up in a bottle, there is no commemoration. He was never to become 'Evans of San Sebastian'. London boasts no bronze of our pantomime general astride his horse like 'Napier of Magdala' who, mounted erectly, inspects the tulips in Kensington Gardens from his podium at the head of Queen's Gate. The British Legion was the last, the most disorganised and the most eccentric Government-backed military intervention in Spain. Evans's was an inglorious war but it represented a commitment both in *materiel* and emotion which went a long way back – to 1706 and the duel between the armies of the Protestant Lord Peterborough and the Catholic Duke of Berwick across the fields of Catalonia during the War of the Spanish Succession. It is to the question of how religious difference helped focus people's thoughts about Spain we turn in the next chapter.

Notes

1. Edgar Holt, *The Carlist Wars in Spain* (London: Putnam, 1967), p. 17.
2. 'Don Pedro Cavallos on the French usurpation of Spain', *Edinburgh Review or Critical Journal* 13 (Oct.1808–Jan.1809), pp. 215–34.
3. Geoffrey Carnall, *Robert Southey and his Age* (London: Longmans, 1960), p. 97.
4. See *Tesoros de la Real Academia de la Historia* (Palacio Real de Madrid, 2001), cat. No. 216.
5. Leslie Mitchell, *Holland House* (London: Duckworth, 1980), p. 226.
6. Ibid., p. 225.
7. John Hamilton Thom (ed.), *The Life of the Rev. Joseph Blanco: with portions of his correspondence*, 3 vols (London: J. Chapman, 1845), 1, p. 36.
8. W.J.B. Owen and Jane Worthington Smith (eds), 'The Convention of Cintra', pp. 193–415, *The Prose Works of William Wordsworth* (Oxford: Clarendon, 1974), p. 236, line 515.
9. Ibid., p. 292, line 2893.
10. Ibid., p. 328, line 4350.
11. Ibid., p. 337, line 4705.
12. Ibid., p. 332, line 4515.
13. Robert Southey, *History of the Peninsular War*, 3 vols (London: John Murray, 1823–1832), Vol. 1, pp. 604–5.
14. Ibid., Vol. 1, p. 13.
15. Ibid., Vol. 1, p. 6.
16. Ibid., Vol. 1, p. 11.
17. George Borrow, *The Bible in Spain* (London: John Murray, 1879), p. 74.
18. William Edwards, *Notes on British History* (London: Rivington's, 1931), p. 723.
19. Southey, *History of the Peninsular War*, Vol. 3, p. 924.
20. Ibid., p. 927.
21. Harold Temperley, *The Foreign Policy of Canning 1822–1827: England, the Neo-Holy Alliance and the New World* (London: G. Bell and Sons Ltd,1925), p. 456.
22. Ibid., p. 474.

23 Peter Dixon, *Canning: Politician and Statesman* (London: 1976), p. 215.
24 Temperley, 'Attitude towards Constitutions; non-Intervention', in *Foreign Policy of Canning*, pp. 457–61.
25 Ibid., p. 471.
26 Ibid., p. 551.
27 Ibid., pp. 380–1.
28 Dixon, *Canning*, p. 232.
29 Thomas Carlyle, *The Life of John Sterling* (London: Chapman and Hall, 1851), p. 68.
30 Ibid., p. 77.
31 Ian Robertson, *Richard Ford 1796–1858: Hispanophile, Connoisseur and Critic* (Wymondham: Michael Russell, 2004), p. 88.
32 G.A. Henty, *With the British Legion: A Story of the Carlist Wars* (London: Blackie and Son, 1903).
33 Carnall, *Robert Southey*, p. 85.
34 Palmerston to Villiers, Foreign Office, 9 July 1835, in Roger Bullen and Felicity Strong, *Prime Ministers Papers Series: Palmerston: 1: Private Correspondence with Sir George Villiers (afterwards fourth earl of Clarendon) as Minister to Spain 1833–37* (London: Royal Commission on Historical Manuscripts, 1985), p. 264.
35 Ibid., Villiers to Palmerston, Madrid, 12 March 1836, p. 393.
36 Ibid, 4 March 1837, p. 613.
37 Ibid., 30 December 1836, p. 580.
38 Ibid., 23 June 1836, pp. 455–6.
39 Ibid., 13 February 1836, pp. 373–4.
40 Ibid., 16 July 1836, p. 475.
41 Richard Ford, *On the Unchangeable Character of A War in Spain* (London: John Murray, 1837), p. 2.
42 Ibid., p. 63.
43 Ibid., p. 65.
44 Ibid., p. 15.
45 Ibid., pp. 59–60.
46 M.H. Kaufman, B.N. Purdue and A.L. Carswell, 'Old Wounds and Distant Battles: the Alcock Ballinghall Collection of Military Surgery at the University of Edinburgh', *Journal of the Royal College of Surgeons of Edinburgh* 41 (1996), pp. 339–50.

3
Religion

In 1802 Xaviera Wiseman, the Spanish wife of an Irish merchant, took her first-born son Nicholas (1802–1865) and, placing him on the altar of Seville Cathedral, dedicated him to a life in Christ.[1] Half a century later, in 1850, Nicholas, by then a Cardinal and prince of the Roman Church, arrived in England from Rome (Figure 4). It was the moment for which ultramontane Catholics had been praying since the reign of Bloody Mary. Wiseman came to preside over a re-established Roman Catholic hierarchy and so celebrate what some feared would be a victory denied to Philip of Spain.

It is the purpose of this chapter to examine the place of Spain and Spanish Catholicism in that tense, sometimes agonised, dialogue between the Anglican establishment and the Catholic faith which exercised people throughout much of the nineteenth century. What exactly to do about Catholics was something which preoccupied minds as diverse as that of the Regency wit and raconteur Sydney Smith no less than that of William Gladstone, who in the Victorian age made politics out of religious conviction. As Charles Lloyd, Bishop of Oxford, wrote in 1827 to the future Prime Minister Sir Robert Peel, the Catholic question was mixed up with 'everything we eat or drink, say or think'.[2] What a person thought about Catholicism was intimately bound up with how he saw himself as an Englishman, a process of self-definition brought to violent birth by the Gordon Riots of 1780. The riots represented the worst outbreak of sectarianism in British history. Thereafter the drama of Pius IX's pontificate (1846–1878) kept the issue of Catholicism in the forefront of debate. *Pio Nono* marched the Church briskly away from an early espousal of liberalism, pausing only to define the Immaculate Conception in 1854, and – with the issue of the *Syllabus Errorum* and the encyclical *Quanta Cura* of 1864 – condemning rationalism, pantheism, religious liberalism and modern philosophy. All this was good kindling for keeping controversy crackling away, but flame became fireball in 1870 with the promulgation of the doctrine of Papal infallibility. It was a step too far for many English

4 Herbert Watkins, *Cardinal Nicholas Wiseman*

Catholics, who saw it as a deeply regrettable aspect of Papal triumphalism.

The Catholic Cathedral of St George's, Southwark was erected – symbolically and provocatively – on the site of the Gordon Riots, which had taken the form of hysterical anti-Catholic fury whipped up by Lord George Gordon, leaving 500 dead and Gordon himself in Newgate gaol, where he became a Jew shortly before expiring. It would be Wiseman himself, some sixty years later, who was to lay the foundation stone on that field of blood in Southwark. Before then, however, Father Faber had opened the first Oratory in England in a former liquor store, an unlikely beginning for a movement which eventually found respectability in the Knightsbridge baroque of the Brompton Road. The story of the role played by Spain in the great debates on Catholicism in England begins not with the Victorians, however, but in Thomas Rowlandson's age of riot and gin.

The refusal of George III to agree to Catholic Emancipation in 1801 brought down the government of Pitt the Younger. To die-hard Tories, here was evidence if ever it were needed that Catholics were inherently destructive, not to say treasonable. The king was convinced that he could not uphold his coronation oath and agree to emancipation, an impasse which destroyed the Ministry which to many seemed to stand between English liberty and Bonapartism. The issue of emancipation, like that of Ireland, was a running sore: Ireland remains so, but the inflammation caused by the Catholic question was greatly reduced with the passing of the Catholic Emancipation Act in April 1829, during the dying stages of Wellington's disastrous campaign as Prime Minister. For years before then, however, a growing body of literature had served to confirm the worst prejudices of reactionary Englishmen about the true nature of Catholics. No one did more to contribute to this index of prejudice than the extraordinary figure of the Reverend Blanco White (Figure 5). This

5 (?)Joseph Slater, *Joseph Blanco White*

former royal chaplain of the Spanish Bourbons purveyed graphic stories about priest-ridden Spain for Regency England as the former KGB spy Oleg Gordievsky has done about Communist Russia. Both sensationalists in different eras, each has provided compulsive reading.

White described himself in latter days as 'an old nervous invalid'. But he had always been neurotic and self-obsessed, though certainly not without real courage, White holds something of a record in the Victorian era. There can have been no one now so obscure who embarked on quite such an ambitious autobiography, a book which would eventually appear in 1845, and then only after his death. It was over 1,000 pages long, in three volumes, and under the less than encouraging title *A Life by myself*. Not content with that, White also wrote another confessional entitled *An examination of Blanco by White*. With all this, the reader might be forgiven for thinking White had invented schizophrenia. Such painful self-scrutiny was because White conducted an unceasing search for religious conviction – Gladstone in an obituary described how the spirit of his erstwhile friend 'was a battlefield upon which with fluctuating fortune and a singular intensity, the powers of belief and scepticism waged, from first to last, their unceasing war'.[3]

White had once acted as spiritual adviser to the Wiseman family. He was effective – no one would do more to promote the Spanish understanding of Catholicism in England than Nicholas Wiseman, the future Cardinal; but then, so too no one would do more to damn it than this renegade priest, Blanco White. But whatever White may have contributed to the nurturing of Cardinal Wiseman, the most controversial English Catholic of the Victorian age, this was only achieved at great personal suffering. White's experience as a priest in Seville from 1800–1810 left him psychologically scarred. He had never had a vocation, and had only gone down this path because his real weakness was that he was pathologically unable to disappoint those whom he loved. He had been devoted to his parents. Unhappily they had been devoted less to him than they had been to the Church of Rome. They had prayed unceasingly that their eldest son would become a priest. Despite White's own doubts which he had felt from his first day in the seminary, once ordained at Christmas 1800 he made progress. He obtained a coveted position in the royal chapel of S. Fernando at Seville, and that at the early age of twenty seven. But by then he was desperate. Years after he had escaped both the priesthood and Spain, he described how what he regarded as other sheep in wolves clothing experienced a terror like that felt by agents behind enemy lines: 'Spaniards, who have broken the trammels of superstition, possess a wonderful quickness to mark and know one another'.[4] It is doubtful whether White would ever have been released but for the French invasion of Spain in 1808. In the subsequent confusion, White scurried from Seville to Cádiz where he scrambled aboard the British frigate *The Lord Howard*, never to see his homeland again.

White kept moving physically and spiritually: an Anglican clergyman by forty, he ended his life aged sixty six, a Unitarian. But despite inner turmoil and outward disruption, White had 'a sweetness of temper' which made him loved and respected by many. A great admirer was Southey, who – while touring the Iberian peninsula – had famously declared how '[t]he higher classes are, and the whole body of people depraved beyond all my ideas of licentiousness ... Over the departed spirit of Spanish gallantry Mr. Burke might pronounce with propriety a funeral oration. And of what advantage has this journey been to me? Why, I have learnt to thank God that I am an Englishman ...'[5] Despite such contempt for all things Iberian, and Southey's was a stock reaction among the English, Southey did develop a perverse devotion to Spain, whose greatest interpreter he believed he had found in White. Another enthusiast for White was Coleridge, who thought White's poem 'On Night and Death' 'the finest and most grandly conceived sonnet in our language'. History has not agreed. Nevertheless, White was certainly littérateur enough to find a home at Holland House, then the most brilliant salon in London. There he became tutor to the Hollands' son. A skiff such as he, however, cannot have found Lady Holland sympathetic: she was a battleship who bore down upon all who lay in her path. For two years this most fastidious of men endured her furious and overmastering personality. But life had its compensations – library and dining room attracted a medley of Spanish exiles and English Hispanists.

White, encouraged by Lady Holland, became the leading voice in the English-speaking world on Spain, its predicament and its future. This White did through Spanish-language newspapers created and sustained by his enterprise and the network of support provided by the community of Holland House. What White wrote in London, Simón Bolívar read in Bogotá. *El Español* and *El Semanario Patriótico*, both edited by White and both subsidised by Holland, were assiduously distributed by the Foreign Office to provoke fury in the cafés of Cádiz and Buenos Aires. White developed many personae in England as he became adept at concealing things from those who did not need to know. Thus it was as a new recruit to journalism that he wrote to Southey in the autumn of 1812:

> I may now reckon with a sort of pension of £250 a year, which is to be continued during the Minster's pleasure, in order to support the Español which was recommended by the British Ambassador at Cádiz as a work calculated to promote the interests of Spain and Great Britain ... I am paid out of the secret service money, just as those who betray their country and should this be known by my enemies it would be a settled point with them that I could do anything for money.[6]

For White's recipient, Bonapartism seemed a summation of all that threatened the life-sustaining force of tradition. But he was hardly less worried about the internal issue of Catholic Emancipation which exercised Regency England much as Home Rule for Ireland would darken the last years of Queen Victoria. Most Englishmen, if they thought about Spain at all, considered the most characteristic thing about the country was its Catholicism. No one in England did more to oppose natural justice to Catholics than Southey and, for that matter, no one fed his prejudices more adroitly than White who declared to Southey: 'I long to see you; for, of all men in England, I should like to speak to you about myself, and take your advice.'[7] But theirs was a mutual friendship, a mutual dependency. In July of the same year in which White revealed that he was on the secret-service payroll, he was helping Southey with his thinking about Catholics; sending letters in which his experience of working in a Catholic university in Spain gave him, at least in the eyes of his correspondent, the authority to pass judgement on the old religion:

> Motives of delicacy keep me from giving my opinion about the Catholics, but to you I must tell that my internal conviction is, that if those of Great Britain are not dangerous to the Constitution it must be because they are not what Catholics have been, hitherto. The Pope and the Universities may make a thousand disavowals of their former characteristic principles; but I know that a true Catholic will go by the reverse the moment after. I have passed two years of my life in a catholic University, and I know that those who are able to make such concessions as are, and must be demanded in England, have given up Catholicism altogether in their hearts. The rest (remember) adore as yet, Thomas a Becket and Gregory the 7th ... Perhaps I shall undertake to write at my leisure, an article upon Jacobs and Sir John Carr's Travels. The only thing that deters me is the consideration that Spain cannot be described to advantage in the important points of morals, manners, and religion. But I will try.[8]

For all White's invective which certainly coloured Southey's thinking, perversely enough the latter had always admired the expression of this religion as he saw it looming out of the mists of Galicia. But that encounter had been undertaken as an anthropologist might observe head-hunters in New Guinea: 'Even this mummery – this puppet-show popery – is better than that execrable diabolism of Calvin. Here is something to feed the feelings, to satisfy and kindle the Imagination ... Every prayer at a crucifix helps him – and a Mass on purpose – is a fine shove towards Paradise. It is a superstition of hope.'[9]

The distinction between regard for Spanish Catholicism and a fixed antipathy to the same religion in England demonstrates how engagement with Spain has a bearing on some of the great issues of the British nineteenth century. In Spain, Catholicism was a cement which kept the social façade upright. For Britain, popery was a fissure which threatened to split the building asunder. What was good for one was disastrous for the other. For Southey the paramount necessity was to keep Church and State apart. This bifurcation was the basis of his profound antipathy to the Catholic religion as exercised in Britain. Southey was always clear in his own contributions to the print war over Catholic Emancipation that the nature of the Catholic faith necessarily demanded that not only would its adherents disregard the separate integrity of the estates, but they were duty-bound to work for the destruction of the British constitution. They owed a primary allegiance to a separate spiritual jurisdiction which effectively compromised their capacity to render unto Caesar the things that were Caesar's. Furthermore, because they believed their religion to be the 'true' faith, so it was incumbent upon them to work for the destruction of apostasy by the removal of the Anglican Settlement. To allow a Catholic to become a magistrate was only to encourage the destruction of the British Constitution. Catholics in England could never be allowed civil rights. For all Southey's learning, and few Englishmen were as well read in the literature of Spain as he, Southey succeeded in turning the peninsula into a British dependency. This was done at the same time as he was persuading himself that it should be England's high ambition to preserve a country that had not been compromised and destroyed by the Enlightenment and the French Revolution. It was visceral conservatism which allowed him to contemplate the pock-marked face of Spanish politics and somehow find it romantic. In 1800 he wrote of how for Spain: 'I would have had a house of peers, were it only in respect to great names, and those heroic remembrances which are the strength and glory of a nation. The nobles, were, for the most part, deplorably degenerate; but as a bad spirit had degraded, a better one would improve the next generation; and I would demolish nothing but what is injurious.'[10]

So much, then, for the bearing Spanish Catholicism had in Britain during the great crisis of Emancipation. But then, to what extent did an understanding of the idiosyncrasies of Spanish Catholicism have on a popular view of Spain? Perhaps no institution in Europe seemed to the British observer to contain such contradictions. It has been remarked that as a social institution the Church was superior in influence to the nobility. Wellington opined that 'The real power in Spain is in the clergy. They kept the people right against France'.[11] In turn, a French aristocrat observing the scene from the perspective of the 1830s remarked on how 'La constitution du clergé espagnol est tout à fait républicaine', a claim based on awareness of remarkable career trajectories like that of one eighteenth-century primate who had been the son of a charcoal burner, something which would have been quite impossible in the French Church.[12] So too, the lower clergy were often exemplary: before the War of Independence, their 'simple accomplishments were enough to shine out in a world of darkness'.[13] But then White, who coloured the British view of Spain more decisively than any other writer with the possible exception of George Orwell, saw Catholicism as the fundamental cause of the problems which beset the country. It was White's foregrounding of the Regular Orders, by the end of the eighteenth century 'in full organizational and intellectual decadence', which eventually demonised the Spanish Church for a British readership. White undertook something of a personal crusade, for he was concerned to exorcise his own corrosive resentment against a Church which had nearly destroyed him and, as he believed all his life, had certainly killed two much-loved sisters whose death he attributed to the psychic strain of being confined to convents like linnets in a cage. White was a good journalist with a vigorous grasp of the value of the macabre, despite a skin as thin as rice paper. Mary Shelley's *Frankenstein* was published in 1818 and created a sensation. It was followed in 1823 by *Valperga*, a story of fourteenth-century Italy. Between such exercises in horror and romance, there appeared in 1822 White's own *Letters from Spain* by 'Don Leucadio Doblado'. This was the book which formed the settled view of the nineteenth-century Englishman about Spain and its religion. It is a series of letters to a friend abroad, purporting to be written by someone living in Seville. In the letters, all which is exemplary about Spain and its backward condition is described in excoriating detail.

White had two purposes: he attributed universal impoverishment to the destructive influence of the Church in Spain, as he played on the emotions of his readership to build up resistance to the growing agitation for Catholic Emancipation in England. White declared in 1826: 'A Roman Catholic cannot, without guilt, lend his support to a Protestant establishment, but is bound, as he wishes to save his soul, to miss no opportunity of checking the progress of heresy'.[14] Spain was saturated by Catholicism like blood in a sponge – the influence of religion in Spain was 'boundless', White declared, before saying that it divided the whole population into two comprehensive classes, either 'bigots' or 'dissemblers'. But White was more than a political scientist who had absorbed much of the free thinking of Holland, Bentham and Nassau Senior. He believed that what was required in Spain, no less than in Britain, was what Southey had described in a letter to Grahame as 'a sect of moral Oeconomists', a distillation of all that was best from the various contending versions of Christianity.

White was a political and ethical thinker of some penetration, but he was also a sensationalist. He dissected the corpse but then enjoyed rattling the skeleton. The most frightening figure in his Spanish mortuary was the diabolical figure of the Oratorian Father Teodomiro Díaz de la Vega, once Blanco's spiritual director. Vega is a sinister presence in both the *Letters from Spain* and *A Life by myself*, where he is to be found lurking in the conventual house of S. Filippo Neri in Seville. White's vision of this priest and his machinations was his own contribution to the genre of the macabre first created by Mary Shelley and after that vulgarised by Madame Tussaud, who was just then creating itinerant sensations in London before she settled in Baker Street in 1835. In September 1823 the first diorama was designed by Pugin and built in Nash's Park Square off Regent's Park. The graphic and melodramatic aspects of *Letters from*

Spain was a paper contribution to a Regency appetite for sensationalism in wax and canvas.

White describes a group of well-off and devout Spaniards incarcerating themselves within the walls of S. Filippo Neri for spiritual exercises under the direction of Vega. White tells his readers how, on 24 August 1781, Vega 'had heard the last terrified confession' of a woman accused of witchcraft by the Inquisition.[15] The woman had denied everything in the most strenuous terms for a full nine months; despite the best efforts of what appear to have been a whole chapter of canons who worked on her to admit guilt. Finally however she 'confessed'. This she did on her last night, to avoid being burned alive. She was rewarded: she was garrotted in prison and her body taken out and publicly burned. Such an examination of Vega's curriculum vitae was well aimed – the better-read might have recalled that 1781 had seen the publication in France of Rousseau's *Confessions* and in Germany *Die Raüber*; Schiller's stirring drama full of revolutionary feeling and challenge to political tyranny.

White had been six when he saw the bundles of firewood being laid on top of barrels of pitch for the last victim of the Inquisition in Seville to be condemned to death. Perhaps the trauma of that experience had been enough to single out Vega as archetype, allowing general conclusions about how habitually the mind was policed: 'In Spain where every person's conscience is in the keeping of another, in an interminable succession of moral trusts, the individual conscience cannot be under the steady discipline of self-governing principle: all that is practised is obedience to the opinion of others, and even that obedience is inseparably connected with the idea of power'.[16]

White pictures Vega as a dark shadow in a Goya. We are told how meetings with supplicants were conducted: lantern closed on all sides so as to cast a shaft of light on the figure of Christ, 'as large as life, with glass eyes, and the body so coloured as to represent flesh sprinkled here and there with blood.'[17] This scene provokes White into a consideration of *donum lachrymarum* and *hysteria passio* – 'pulses of spiritual transport' which express states of extreme emotion induced by the contemplation of sins and the expiation of the Saviour. But though such hysterics are to be deplored, White makes it clear that his reader would be mistaken if he considered them a sign of weakness. While Vega periodically underwent such transports, nevertheless 'in sternness and boldness, he might be compared to Knox, the Scotch Reformer'.[18] It was as if White thought Vega was as robust as an oak but as sinuous as the ivy which smothers new growth reaching for light.

White insinuates an almost sexual abandonment on the part of Vega. It is difficult to know just what White had felt when he had himself been a priest in Seville and observed his adversary playing on the primitive fears of a credulous congregation. Perhaps the impression was like what the reticent feel today when confronted with Bernini's S. Teresa: for all the astounding virtuosity, some are embarrassed. Vega was a consummate actor and a master at manipulating the feelings of those who willingly surrendered their independence:

> the consecrated wafer was exposed to view ... The sound of music was interrupted only to give way to the almost frantic strains of impassioned tenderness in which Father Vega addressed the Deity, in whose immediate bodily presence he conceived himself to be. I will not repeat any of the remarkable (it would be more correct to say objectionable) expressions used by the spiritual leader [since] ... I consider them not only as irreverent, but as bordering on indelicacy.[19]

The terrifying power which a Spanish priest could wield became something of an article of faith with a British readership. Borrow reverted to a similar kind of sensationalism about their role in the religious life of the country when, while peddling Protestant bibles in Spain, he paused to watch the execution of two brothers. He was much more shocked by the actions of the priests than by the application of the famous iron collar, the favoured method in Spain which rapidly broke the neck of the criminal once its screw was turned:

> God was not thought of; Christ was not thought of; only the priest was thought of, for he seemed at that moment to be the first being in existence, and to have the power of opening and shutting the gates of heaven or of hell just as he should think proper. A striking instance of the successful working of the popish system, whose grand aim has ever been to keep people's minds as far as possible from God, and to centre their hopes and fears in the priesthood.[20]

Letters from Spain was the most influential account of the mores of the country to be published in Britain until the appearance of Ford's *Handbook*, that run-away success of 1845. Part of the appeal of the *Letters* was its metronomic swing from sober analysis to hysterical sensationalism. There was something for everybody. However, the *Letters* is also interesting for what it had to say about Britain. Although there is nothing specifically directed against Catholic Emancipation, the indivisibility of Spanish Catholicism and Spanish corruption which is emphasised inflamed prejudice as it alerted men to the gathering storm. What the *Letters* implied was spelled out in another publication by White, *Evidences Against Catholicism* (1825). Upon reading it, Southey wrote 'as an Englishman and a Protestant', to thank White for all he had said against Catholicism.[21] Its appearance delighted the portly dons of Oxford who promptly awarded White an M.A. for all he had done to keep them comfortable. White left Jacobean Holland House for Jacobean Oriel, the Oxford college soon to become the setting of that supreme crisis of Victorian religious belief, the 'Oxford Movement'. Before that society was torn apart, however, White delighted in becoming a member of the most luminous religious community ever to have been cloistered in one Oxford college. There, he took a special pleasure in playing violin duets with the 'Blessed' John Henry Newman, the future cardinal whose commitment to the faith and holiness of life subsequently obtained for him that appellation 'Blessed' – a title which has him today standing at the threshold of and just one step below sanctity. White and Newman became loving friends, but even as early as 1835 Newman confided to his sister Jemima that White had 'a morbid pleasure in being abused'.[22] White had been a Spanish priest and Spain had always been soaked with the blood of martyrs.

White suffered from a pathological sense of his own inadequacies, yet he impinged upon Spain profoundly. One ancestor had been Murillo's great patron, Don Justino de la Neve; another had founded Los Angeles. But then there was as well something extraordinary about White himself. He was the only Spaniard who had once been a Catholic priest and was now a Protestant clergyman. None was better qualified to reveal the secrets of the country's confessional. White became a decisive influence on those who helped to form a British view of Spain in the generation which succeeded his death in 1841, for several reasons: he had been, successively, central to debates on the political future of Spain after the promulgation of the Constitution of Cádiz in 1812; informant of the colonial revolutionary movements of South America; and finally – through inside knowledge of the mysteries of his former creed – critical to the tumultuous debate on the future of the Catholic faith in Britain.

Lurid descriptions by White of frightened girls being drawn into convents helped to create a popular frisson for the table-top traveller. The lithograph by David Roberts of this very subject, published in the *Picturesque Sketches in Spain* of 1837, took advantage of the repertoire of Hispanic images created first by White whose dismissive, sardonic prose anticipated the quicksilver Ford at his most acerbic. White reviewed two contemporary novels by Valentin Llanos, who was married to the poet John Keat's sister, Fanny. The novels were entitled *Don Esteban* and *Sandoval*. The review seems to anticipate Ford's relish for the outrageous. 'It is this national faculty', White declared, 'of flying off from reality to imagination, of forgetting what they are, and in glorying in what they have been and ought to be, that makes the Spaniards such a peculiar people'.[23] But then White was himself outrageous in his criticism of Llanos. The crude anti-clericalism which White deplored was similar to what he had himself written when he had kicked the ecclesiastical dust of Spain off his feet.

Condemnation of all things Spanish did not, however, go uncontested in the tumultuous decade of the 1820s. As seen in the previous chapter, Wordsworth, Coleridge and Southey all had moved from enthusiasm for the French Revolution to deep conservatism, but the popular social critic and successful writer William Cobbett remained a Radical all his life. Cobbett was not unlike George Borrow: both cussed and touchy, they were never fêted by the Establishment as Carlyle was to be, despite his famously dyspeptic temperament. Cobbett loved unpopular causes. He had a nose for the indefensible. He rested his arguments in favour of Emancipation not on the wholly reasonable grounds of equality before the law but through his belief that Elizabeth I had been a 'virago' and Philip of Spain maligned and misunderstood. Such a view had the attraction of the unexpected but hardly the force of evidence. It represented a wholesale reappraisal of Elizabethan heroics.

Cobbett's eccentric contribution to the on-going 'Spanish Question' in British public life, his *The Protestant Reformation* (1824–1825), had the same format as the polemics of Blanco White. Cobbett's book was again in the form of fictitious letters, issued not from Seville but from under the shadows of Holland House. Cobbett began by suggesting that nothing had been more to the honour of England than the marriage of Philip II and Mary. He compared the generous and gentlemanly conduct of Philip with that of another foreigner who had been betrothed to another Mary, William of Orange. Cobbett knew well enough just how provocative he was being. William was the hero of Anglicanism since it had been he who had secured the 'Glorious Revolution', or 'Inglorious' as Cobbett insists on describing it. Whereas William of Orange had heaped upon his followers 'large parcels of what was left of the Crown estate', Philip of Spain had taken great care that his grandees should not get their noses in the English trough. Cobbett understood well enough that the tap-root of objection to Emancipation was the threat to the constitution which would result from giving Catholics political rights. But then he turned such logic on its head. Elizabeth owed the Protestant Settlement to her Catholic subjects:

> Here we have the great, and, indeed, the only cause, of Elizabeth's success in rooting out the Catholic religion. Her people were, ninety-nine hundredths of them, Catholics. They had shown this clearly at the accession of her sister Mary. Elizabeth was as great a tyrant as ever lived; she was the most cruel of women; her disgusting amours were notorious; yet, she was the most popular sovereign that had ever reigned since the days of Alfred ... they saw nothing but her between them and subjection to foreigners, a thing which they had always most laudably held in the greatest abhorrence.[24]

The Armada had been provoked by Elizabeth's perfidy toward the patient and long-suffering Philip: 'on this occasion, and, indeed, on all others, where love of country was brought to the test, the Catholics proved, that no degree of oppression could make them forget their duty as citizens, or as subjects'.[25] Cobbett's diatribe against *Gloriana* was calculated to create apoplexy among forty shilling freeholders. Whether his bizarre challenge to the canons of historical orthodoxy helped the reformers must be doubted, though it certainly attracted attention. The book sold 60,000 copies in its first year, and Leo XII read it in translation. What is certain is that the debate over the loyalty of Catholics, to which Cobbett made his own popular but eccentric contribution, made people see the importance of history. It became a subject at once pressing, urgent and relevant. Penny pamphlets for and against Catholics fluttered about like gulls in the wind. Notorious episodes in Catholic history were cited as evidence of how what Catholics had once been, they would remain. Thus an open letter addressed to the Right Reverend Beilby Porteous, Lord Bishop of London, reminded everyone what Catholics in France had done during the St Bartholomew's Day Massacre. The message was simple enough: they would do it again. Emotions ran high, and Cobbett struck a note of near hysteria as he turned up the volume. Ludicrously he referred to Elizabeth Tudor as 'gentle Betsy' as if she were some trollop from a Webster play:

> Talk of Catholic Tyrants! Talk of the Catholics having propagated their faith by acts of force and cruelty! I wonder, that an English Protestant, even one whose very bread comes from the spoliation of the Catholics, can be found with so little shame as to talk thus. Our lying Protestant historians tell us, that the ships of the Spanish Armada were ' loaded with RACKS', to be used upon the bodies of the English ... the Spaniards might have saved themselves the trouble of importing RACKS, seeing that gentle Betsy had always plenty of them, which she kept in excellent order, and almost daily use.[26]

Sympathy for Spanish Catholicism appeared from an unlikely quarter again, some fifteen years later. It was in an extended 1840 review of a French book of travels, almost certainly by Harriet Martineau. Neither the credentials of the authoress, nor indeed the preamble of the article, prepared readers for what was to follow. Martineau, a free-thinking, radical feminist from the greatest of the English Unitarian dynasties, was writing in *The Christian Teacher*. That was the organ of Liverpool Unitarianism and this was a fulsome appreciation of Spanish Catholicism. *The Teacher* was the principal publication of a sect which rejected both the Trinity and the divinity of Christ, a process of reduction hardly calculated to appeal to the canons of Seville Cathedral, whose building clearly moved Martineau greatly. Martineau writes in pre-Darwinian terms. She argues that Spanish devotional art was peculiarly adapted to the nation by plunging into the jungle with the great French naturalist and precursor of Lyell and Darwin, the Comte de Buffon (d.1788), and the intrepid naturalist of South America, Charles Waterton (d.1865). She contrasts Buffon's dismissal of the sloth as a *rebut de la nature*, with Waterton's riposte that this creature is beautifully constructed for a green world: 'that is, as far as admirable adaptation to a given purpose is beautiful'. An unlikely parallel between a creature which might have been admired in Martineau's day only by the artist Edward Lear as caricaturist, and the glories of Seville Cathedral, leads to a gentle admonition. Those hostile to Spanish Catholicism must see Spanish society in its own terms, Martineau declares, before gently chiding readers for not considering how outward material substance fitted inner needs:

> And though, no doubt, as once was said, a poor covenanter in peril and privation worshipping his God upon the wild mountain is a spectacle still more sublime, one cannot but respect too that sentiment of a good Catholic – the origin no doubt of this splendour that nothing is too good to be offered unto God – and one cannot but admire the splendour of art, painting, statuary, and architecture devoted to his shrine, and spread out in lavish magnificence for the enjoyment of the mass of the people.[27]

What Martineau was advocating was cultural relativism – her rare capacity to understand Spain in its own terms, rather than falling into that British habit of judging the place according to how far it diverged from British preconceptions and prejudices. The art historian William Stirling, whose writings feature prominently in a later chapter of this volume, was much the same. He prioritised context above all else: for him the worth of a picture lay in its value as an eloquent historical document. He wanted to know about Spain, not to judge it.

If Nicholas Wiseman ever read Martineau's response to Seville, he would have loved it. No one admired Seville Cathedral more. He had been brought up in a highly cultured if overly pious family. His father had been in the liquorice business with Nathan Wetherall, an ex-patriot antiquarian who spent much time trying to preserve the cultural detritus of Andalucía in the face of almost total indifference on the part of the Spanish authorities. The Wisemans had as well acted as agents for Lord and Lady Holland on visits to Andalucía in 1803 and again in 1807–1809.

Martineau had also made a point with which Wiseman concurred. Martineau contrasts what could be achieved in the sacred context of a great cathedral with the secret discouragement which 'creeps upon the soul' in contemplating modern architecture dedicated to secular ends: 'it is vain to expect that man can work with the same noble enthusiasm to adorn the palace of a noble as to dedicate his work in the temple of the Lord'. It was an attitude which exactly accorded with what Wiseman would later express in *The Dublin Review*, a journal of Catholic thought founded in December 1835 when the Irish patriot Daniel O'Connell had invited him to join its launch. Wiseman wrote a 43–page article in the December 1848 edition, entitled 'Spanish and English National Art'.[28] It was two for the price of one. In the first place the article offered a critique of Stirling's *Annals of the Artists of Spain*, which would prove to be the most ambitious account of the history of the Spanish Schools of painting ever to appear in English. In addition, Wiseman was articulating his response to the findings of the Commissioners on the Fine Arts about the decoration of the new Houses of Parliament. Wiseman was not convinced by the programme proposed for the new Parliament buildings, feeling that what was suggested was inappropriate – that it would be soulless. To this extent his criticisms of painted histories for a secular temple accorded well with the views of Martineau.

Wiseman remained devoted to Spain, 'that great and generous country', and indeed it was the uncomplicated, primitive religion of the Spanish illiterate which gave him access to the misery described by his friend Dickens, a directness of sympathy which would gain the cardinal much needed friends in a gathering crisis. Charity in the street – as advocated by Dickens in his novels and practiced by Wiseman in his ministry – had, however, been proceeded by a catastrophic failure of imagination. In October 1850, Wiseman had unwisely issued an infamous pastoral, *From out of the Flaminian Gate*. It was dispatched as he travelled through Germany on his way to oversee the establishment of the Catholic hierarchy in England. The document was a disaster. The nation was in uproar. The pastoral letter demonstrated a breath-taking lack of tact. Its tone and content reflected a life busied hitherto with the publication of the *Horae Syriacae* (1827). Evidently hours bent over manuscripts in the heat of an August afternoon in an empty Vatican Library had not been the requisite background for consistorial diplomacy. Such a contribution to the history of Syriac versions of the Old Testament may have been celebrated in the *Propaganda Fidei* but it could hardly be said to have prepared Wiseman to defend an embattled Church against three hundred years of hostility.

The supreme crisis of the cardinal's life had come. But it was at once succeeded by his finest hour. With great courage, and without previous experience of public controversy, Wiseman responded to the outrage he had caused by the triumphalist tone of his pastoral. He had arrived calling himself Cardinal Archbishop of Westminster. This was a challenge to the status of an abbey where kings were buried and poets remembered. Wiseman was astonished and agitated by what he described as the 'violence of a whirlwind' raging about his head, something which – when the storm had abated – he felt had been 'perhaps unparalleled in our times'.[29] Nevertheless, while in the full blast of the tempest he had found courage to respond magnificently. He immediately issued *The Cardinal's Appeal to the Reason and Good Feeling of the English People on the Subject of the Catholic Hierarchy*. It was a masterly document: a transformation of a desperate and perilous situation. It ran to thirty-one pages with the full text appearing in the five leading London papers. The morning editions printed it for Wednesday 20 November 1850. Yet by the following Monday, the independent pamphlet issued at the same time had sold 30,000 copies. The radical politician and M.P. for Sheffield John Roebuck (d.1879), known as 'Tear'em' Roebuck for the vehemence with which he attacked his opponents, wrote to Lord John Russell on 2 December 1850, launching into Russell for hostility to Catholics, and adding that the subject of the reconstruction of the Catholic hierarchy was an issue about which: 'the public mind of England [was] stirred from one end of the kingdom to the other'.[30] Somehow, Wiseman had steered a vessel off a reef after he had misread the charts and against a tide in full spate. It was an unparalleled transformation in the history of religious controversy in England. Movingly, Wiseman defended his much resented appellation as Archbishop of Westminster not with claims to arrogated prior authority but upon much meeker ground, the need for charity:

> Yet this splendid monument, its treasures of art, and its fitting endowments, form not the part of the Westminster which will concern me. For there is another part which stands in frightful contrast, though in immediate contact, with this magnificence. In ancient times, the existence of an abbey on any spot, with a large staff of clergy and ample revenues, would have sufficed to create around it a little paradise of comfort, cheerfulness, and ease. This, however, is not now the case. Close under the Abbey of Westminster there lie concealed labyrinths of lanes and courts, and alleys and slums, nests of ignorance, vice, depravity, and crime, as well as of squalor, wretchedness, and disease; whose atmosphere is typhus, whose ventilation is cholera; in which swarms a huge and almost countless population, in great measure, nominally at least, Catholic; haunts of filth, which no sewage committee can reach – dark corners, which no lighting-board can brighten. This is the part of Westminster which alone I covet, and which I shall be glad to claim and to visit, as a blessed pasture in which sheep of holy Church are to be tended, in which a bishop's godly work has to be done, of consoling, converting, and preserving.[31]

It was Wiseman's experience of faith in poverty in rural Spain and Italy which made him effective in alleviating miseries, his description of which matches those exposed by Henry Mayhew (1812–1887), one of the co-founders of *Punch*, which had something of the place in Victorian life which *Private Eye* occupies today. Mayhew made himself famous by articles which revealed the sheer extent of the poverty and sweated labour of the capital. They came out under the somewhat alarming title *London Labour and the London Poor; A Cyclopaedia of the Condition and Earnings of Those That Will Work, Those That Cannot Work and Those That Will Not Work*; collected together in four volumes in 1861. But within the compass of the British Isles, it was in Ireland not England that Wiseman was 'at his most responsive and relaxed among a Catholic people of peasant spirituality and unreserved enthusiasm'.[32] Historically, Spain and Ireland had had much to do with each other because of a shared faith, and so Wiseman, born in Seville of Irish extraction, had been delighted when after forty years he had revisited the country of his birth in 1844, gratified by so many in Seville who could still remember his family.

Wiseman may have saved the future of the Catholic hierarchy in England by his masterly appeal to universal charity, but he remained a figure of deep suspicion to the British establishment; a suspicion hardly allayed by his temperamental preferences and habitual appearance. Wiseman's sternest critic was Father Faber, one of his own flock, who sustained a passionate dislike of him. Often prone to excess, Faber had the regrettable habit, when excited, of referring to the Virgin Mary as 'Mamma'. But he was not disposed to overlook what he regarded as excess in others. Once, particularly exasperated by the splendour of the cardinal, he remarked 'when in full tog he looked like some Japanese God'.[33] While to a stern ascetic Wiseman might have seemed to anticipate a figure out of the Mikado, to others the cultivation of an appropriate gravitas was beyond this 'mountain of flesh'. Given the physical appearance of the cardinal, some doubtless thought it unfortunate that he had been Bishop of Melipotamus *in partibus infidelium*.

For Wiseman, the Church was best celebrated with Te Deums and the full magnificence of Catholic ceremony: a triumph of brocade and brass, trumpets and mosaic which in its refulgent splendour seemed to picture a *Presentation in The Temple* by Rubens. Upon his return to Seville, Wiseman was struck by the paradox of a Church continuously persecuted by successive liberal governments, or so he believed, with an ecclesiastical establishment, splendid in misery:

> The cathedral here is magnificent beyond all my expectations, and what is wonderful is that, thanks to the firmness of its clergy, its gorgeous treasures have escaped unhurt from the rapacity of the French and the cupidity of successive revolutionary governments. The profusion of gold and jewels almost surpasses belief; and as for silver, it seems of no more account than brass amongst us. The same is to be said of the vestments, etc., which are surpassingly rich, *sed de hoc alias*.[34]

The other great figure of the Victorian Catholic revival was the Blessed John Newman. Newman's published letters are only surpassed in quantity by those of the inexhaustible Gladstone. But it is hard to find in all this mass a similar enthusiasm for outward appearance. To the contemplative Newman, the re-establishment of the Catholic hierarchy in 1850 was a reconfiguration on the long strand of British history – a sand bar changing shape over the centuries, washed by waves of barbaric invasion, or the gentle lapping of the word of God. Newman had a sense of the poetic wholly alien to the busy Wiseman. Faith for Wiseman was buttressed less by contemplation, so essential to Newman, than in the outward ceremony which he had admired at its most refulgent in Spain. These differences seem to be suggested in the best of a number of cartoons published in *Punch* during late 1850 when the furore over the re-establishment of the hierarchy was at its height. A portly Wiseman with dough-like face, and looking more like Mrs Beeton than a spiritual confessor, proffers a 'writ' to a furious looking John Bull. Newman, with the profile of a macaw, is hiding behind the skirts of the archbishop as he bends down to scrutinize John Bull's dog. Behind, an Irish serving wench, half concealed behind the open door, is brought on to symbolise all that was most despised about Catholicism in the British Isles. Incredulous but clearly amused by what she is witnessing, she stares agape at the proceedings (Figure 6).

Looking down from his pulpit at the assembled Catholic hierarchy, Newman had declared in a famous sermon of 1852 how the presence of all of them once again in England was 'a second spring': 'I listen, and I hear the sound of voices, grave and musical, renewing the old chant, with which Augustine greeted Ethelbert in the free air upon the Kentish strand'.[35] Wiseman had a keen sense of history too. Intellectual roots spread widely but they were friable: he had an informed interest in an astonishing range of issues, but breadth was achieved at the cost of depth. When compiling *Essays on Various Subjects*, three fat volumes of 1853, he had declared complacently: 'I have not formed an opinion or a feeling that I have ceased to entertain'.[36] 'St Nicholas of Seville', as *Punch* liked to call him, had something to say on almost anything – a point not lost on the poet Browning who produced a likeness of the cardinal in the poem 'Bishop Blougram's Apology' (1855):

> Writing ... my articles
> On music, poetry, the fictile vase
> Found at Albano, chess, Anacreon's Greek.[37]

Wiseman remained usually an object of suspicion, sometimes of grudging admiration, in part at least because of a settled belief in the virtues of Spain. These he tended to see as an earthly trinity, an indivisible connection between society, religion and culture. He felt certain that English Catholics owed an enormous debt to Spain because it: 'gave us shelter in our day of distress, and provided us with the means of educating, for centuries, that clergy which, in spite of the rack, the gallows, and the quartering knife, kept true religion alive in England'.[38] These were virtues which Wiseman took every opportunity to promote through his highly successful career as essayist and reviewer for *The Dublin Review*, that publication which nurtured the hopes of Catholics as *The Edinburgh Review* kept the altar of the Enlightenment smoking and as *The Quarterly* stoked Tory prejudice.

Wiseman had a passion for the visual arts. He was proud that 'it was in the church of the Holy Cross, which Murillo so loved, and in which he wished to be buried, that [I] ... received the inestimable blessing of baptismal regeneration'.[39] Wiseman's love of art had been nurtured while he was a seminarian in Rome. There, friendships had been established with Canova who had helped carry the litter bearing Pius VII back in triumph to Rome after the Napoleonic exile. As well, Wiseman had become close to the Nazarenes, the circle of German painters like Overbeck, Cornelius and Platner who anticipated by forty years the quest of the pre-Raphaelites for innocence, grace and purity. Immersion when

Religion

6 Served with a Writ, Punch, 1850

young in such a brilliant artistic circle in Rome made it predictable that in Wiseman's *Essays on Various Subjects* much attention is given to art and its social impact. *Papers on History, Antiquities and Art: Spain*, also by Wiseman, is a review of three books, all a 'manifestation of a holy horror of Popery in connection with Spain'. Wiseman suggested that the greatness of the 'Golden Age' was not that the sun never set upon the Spanish empire, still less because of Stirling's understanding of painting or Ticknor's of Iberian literature. It was due to the number and distinction of Spanish saints:

> At a time when the rest of Europe was convulsed with religious throes, that gave birth to the hydra-headed creeds of modern times, while Britain and Germany were producing, and fostering, such living calamities as Knox and Cranmer, Luther and Munster, Spain was richer in great and holy characters than almost any part of the world ... Suffice it to say, that in the hall of the bishop of Valencia's palace, which yet remains, there were once assembled together in the time of its bishop, St Thomas of Villanueva, no fewer than seven persons, who were afterwards canonized by the Church.[40]

Wiseman regarded himself as an authority on art; a subject upon which 'his knowledge was minute', and which he used to address the Marylebone Literary Society in June 1857 on the subject of 'The best mode of Collecting and Arranging a National Gallery of Pictures'. Wearing his biretta, Wiseman wished to encourage a style of church architecture which would affirm the right sort of spirituality for that peculiar hybrid, English Catholicism. This was not easy. At much the same time as Wiseman was thinking of 'correct' building, Newman was busy casting about for the right style in which to build a cathedral for Birmingham. Consequently he had written to the Birmingham Oratorian, Richard Stanton:

> I wish you could learn for me which are the best engravings of churches in Spain e.g. Robert's? – and whether it would be possible to get a second hand copy cheap – Considering that everything is going the way of Gothic ... it is very important we should do something really good. The Spanish and Sicilian style seem to me one, which *must* strike; whereas the Roman, or most ancient Basilica, is somewhat like an omnibus.[41]

Newman was more fortunate than Wiseman. Wiseman had to work with Augustus Welby Pugin and he was impossible. Pugin was in minor orders but he took all opportunities to preach a gospel of hard work. While Wiseman strolled arm in arm with O'Connell through the gardens of the seminary at Oscott, Pugin, always driven and often indignant, accosted an Oxford convert whom he chanced upon angling in a nearby stream: 'Fishing, my dear sir!' he said, in pain and disgust, ... 'life is not meant for that sort of thing. At six o'clock this morning I was at the top of St Chad's steeple'.[42] Pugin was more opinionated even than Ruskin: his writings contain as many ideas about propriety for a church as the book of Deuteronomy has rules for the Ark of the Covenant. Yet Wiseman kept his sense of humour with a man who had none. He sublimated his irritation by busying himself with books like Stirling's *Annals*, in which connections were made between Spanish faith and Spanish art. Wiseman was a capacious and inquisitive reviewer whose writing helped him to think how art could encourage faith. Attention was drawn by him to passages in the *Annals* where Stirling wrote of Spanish Catholicism and how art in the service of the Church was the purest of all streams. 'Spanish art is, more eminently than any other, the daughter of Religion', as Stirling declared before intriguing Wiseman by adding: 'it is still in Spain – constant, when seeming most false – religious, when seeming careless of all creeds – that the pious Catholic looks hopefully to see the Faith of Rome rise, refreshed, regenerate and irresistible'.[43] It was acknowledgement of a naive faith, here confessed by a Scotsman whose generous calm in the face of religious difference was the consequence of parents who were wise enough to agree to differ over religion, peaceably divided between their respective loyalties to Presbyterianism and Episcopalianism. What Stirling declared Wiseman seconded, for it accorded with Wiseman's own experience of a happy return to Spain in 1844. The connection he had then observed between the strength of faith and the absence of materialism was to be confirmed in Ireland in 1858.

Wiseman went to Ireland to consecrate a church at Ballinsaloe, but his visit became a second entry into Jerusalem. Everywhere he was met with devout who strewed his path as they knelt for his blessing. He returned renewed in his hopes for creating a people's spirituality in England, something he observed was lacking in the Anglican Church. Accordingly Wiseman often went out of his way to defend Continental folk worship. As has been remarked, 'he was aware that contemporary English culture assumed all Catholicism overseas to be superstitious and empty'.[44] With characteristic bravery, Wiseman defied what he saw as Establishment contempt for primitive religion. His Spanish roots and his appreciation of the intimacy between the art and faith of that country helped to promote a vision for his Church in England which traditionally had always been so different from its sisters in Europe. English Catholicism had been an unholy alliance between old Catholics, ultramontanists and an Irish labouring class – three boats tethered to the same capstan but forever drifting apart. Wiseman was a far from athletic boatman, and he found it a difficult business jumping from one to the other. One of the sternest critics of ultramontanism was the extraordinary Lord Acton. Acton was decidedly unusual for an academic: the first Catholic to be made a peer since the Glorious Revolution, his grandfather had been Prime Minister of Naples and his uncle a cardinal. No one of such social distinction was better read, but no one of comparable reputation produced so little. Acton had a famous library of 60,000 volumes and he had a famous book. The first he sold in a quixotic humour, the second, a *History of Liberty*, remained only in the mind after thirty years of cogitation. Nevertheless Acton was revered by Gladstone who appointed him to the Regius Chair of History at Cambridge in 1895. Although, judging by his publication record, it is to be doubted whether today Acton would obtain even a senior lectureship, his influence on Victorian historical studies has attracted an industry of exegesis normally reserved for the homilies of an early Christian martyr. Acton was chained to his *History of Liberty* as the alchemist to his stone, but he was a magician with a short article. He became one of the formative opinion-makers of late Victorian England through that quintessential expression of Victorian opinion, the *Review*. Reading ten pages by Acton is to masticate a Christmas pudding – so rich are the ingredients, so learned and dense the allusions.

Acton used a powerful position to criticise much of what he thought regrettable about *Pio Nono*. Although Spain was one of the few European countries where Acton did not feel at home – he had four languages perfectly – he brought a wonderful mind to consider the place of the Inquisition in Europe. What he had to say on the Holy Office was stimulated by a biography of the famous Spanish humanist Cardinal Ximénez. Acton, reviewing that biography in *The Rambler* (a journal which he had taken the precaution of buying to make himself infallible), contrasted how the Inquisition operated in Rome and in Spain. Roman practice had been to point out the danger from heretical books and so 'caution men against it'. In Spain by contrast, the dread of error had been so great that it 'lead to a fear of all mental activity'. The tragedy for Spain was that in the lifetime of Ximénez, letters had revived and 'it seemed for a moment that Spain was to rival Italy on a far wider field ... But all this splendid promise faded away; and when in Italy, France and England, learning began to be more sound and literature more rich, in Spain they were already nearly extinct.'[45]

Thereafter it had been downhill all the way. The Inquisition was a slow strangulation, and Acton was settled in his view that if there had ever been a 'Golden Age' it had been poignantly short. It was precisely during the course of the sixteenth century that Spain had ceased to breathe, since the crushing of the 'whole intellectual movement' was to be ascribed to the reigns of Philip II and Philip III. It was the injury done to the intellect, whether dedicated to theology or science, which represented the enormity of the damage which the Inquisition had inflicted. Here Acton makes a revealing connection. As a liberal he passionately believed that the Church must not be afraid of new ideas however challenging they might be. But in writing what was ostensibly a dispassionate analysis of a notorious institution, Acton was recruiting history to fight a controversy in which he was in mortal danger of excommunication, a state of affairs which left Gladstone to remark laconically: 'His work may be put on the Index, but that is all. They will never excommunicate an English peer'. The Prime Minister was right, the Vatican did not. This close combat was between English Catholics who were divided between those who believed their faith must make them reject the progressive and those who considered a different path to salvation. For the latter, and Acton carried their standard, the Church could only survive by being seen to do battle in the dust and heat of pure intellectual debate. As Acton contemplated the unhappy history of the faith in Spain, so he was helped to define his own uneasy relationship with what he regarded as the threat posed by ultramontanism.

Wiseman disliked and distrusted Acton, while for his part Acton closed down his *Home and Foreign Review* in 1864 before the cardinal did it for him. But someone for whom Wiseman might have had a natural sympathy, wearing his biretta as an authority on the arts, was George Edmund Street (1824–1881). Strikingly handsome, energetically learned and supremely gifted, Street was one of the architectural pugilists of the great Victorian debate as to style, meaning and purpose in architecture. He was the favoured architect of Gladstone, who was not merely an eminent Victorian but the pre-eminent Victorian. Gladstone was possessed of an unparalleled intellectual range, ceaseless energy and burning curiosity, keeping himself informed about the course of the medieval revival of architecture through his devotion to High Church Anglicanism, while he held the highest political offices. Street dedicated to Gladstone his great book of 1865 on Spanish architecture, *Some account of Gothic Architecture in Spain*. It did his career no harm. After much debate a committee was established to oversee a competition to design the Royal Courts of Justice in the Strand. Gladstone appointed himself to the panel – wholly justifiably since no other member of the committee knew as much about architecture as he. Stirling too was selected for this jury to sit in judgement upon the law. Both understood that Street could represent more architectural schools of thought than other competitors, and this was almost as valuable as Street's own huge gifts as a designer. Street could reflect the prejudices of serious High Church architects like Bodley and Butterfield, while also expressing the values of the Anglo-French 'art architects' Willliam Burges and E.W. Godwin. Street had not only written a first and authoritative account of Spanish gothic architecture, he had also made a serious and respected excursus into the field of the history of building materials with his *Brick and Marble in The Middle Ages: notes of a tour in the North of Italy* (1855). The Royal Courts selection panel consisted of eight men whose voting resulted in three and three deadlocked for candidates other than Street and a minority of two, Gladstone and Stirling, who manipulated things thereafter in such a way as to give the competition to Street. It was to be the summation of a career. Street had trailed in fifth in the competition for Palmerston's Foreign Office but what he then went on to produce for the English judiciary was a fulcrum sustaining in perfect balance the joint graces of 'verticality' and 'repose'. Here was a skyline from the *Très Riches Heures* hanging luminously above massed, classically proportioned spaces sufficient to dignify the wig of the most pompous of Lord Chancellors. The Royal Courts at once established itself as one of the great buildings of nineteenth-century Europe. It attracted unusually vigorous responses: the 'militant' Street was described as a 'fighting ecclesiastic' who produced in the Strand a building of 'fearless muscularity' and 'ruthless violence'.[46] Street's *chef-d'oeuvre* represented the consummation of the Gothic Revival. But finally he found peace. All the impassioned debates about architecture and worship ceased as Street was buried under the central aisle of Westminster Abbey. There he lies under a medieval revivalist brass: kneeling in prayer with hands clasped in front of him as a Latin scroll issues out of his mouth with the words: 'O Lord I have loved the habitation of thy house'.

That was the problem. In life Street had loved the houses of the Lord too zealously – with such passion, indeed, that some regarded him as hardly more balanced than the fervid Pugin. Yearly excursions abroad provided Street with ammunition with which to take pot-shots at rivals from within the ramparts of his own certainty. Street's *Gothic Architecture*, a masterpiece of Victorian architectural history, had appeared in 1865, three years before the Law Courts competition and in the year in which Wiseman died. Much in it would surely have appealed to Wiseman. He would have been struck by some of Street's animadversions about social fabric and sound fabric – the relationship between a properly ordered society and its buildings. *Gothic Architecture* remains a great but neglected contribution to an understanding of Spanish culture. What Ford had ridden past, Street lingered in. 'Andalusia' hardly appears; its buildings were hybrids of the Christian and the Moslem. By contrast, the cathedrals of Galicia, Castile and Catalonia are fully explored because they lay astride the dusty path of pilgrimage. But for all the disinterested analysis and scrupulous draughtsmanship Street brings to his subject, the book was a tract for the times. It addressed the architectural student as it challenged those who marched under the banner of the Ecclesiological Movement. Spain 'undefiled' was emotionally important to the Victorians: painting, politics and piety, but also pointed architecture – all retaining admonitory value as *exemplae* of a culture which had been swept away in other parts of western Europe. Street was clear about one thing: Spanish architecture could provide lessons which should be applied to all those bitterly contested shibboleths which made the profession of architecture in Victorian England not something to be entered upon by the faint-hearted. The battle of the styles, the Ecclesiological Movement, gothic versus classicism, new materials versus craftsmanship, restoration and conservation – all were controversies which, Street believed, could benefit from lessons to be learned from what had been the largely neglected ecclesiastical buildings of Spain: the churches of Castile, Galicia and the northern provinces.

However, Street was not the first to notice in print some of the finest of these. He had been anticipated by the most eccentric of all Victorians in Spain, George Borrow, the heroic evangelist for Protestantism in Iberia whose combination of strident eccentricity, great literary gifts and the dauntless courage of Bunyan's Pilgrim both attracted and irritated the quizzical Ford, who seems to have cultivated Borrow much as Scott had once promoted the Ettrick Shepherd.

Perversely but characteristically, Borrow had declared in his most celebrated book, *The Bible in Spain* (1842), that the Alcázar in Seville 'is in every respect more magnificent than the one of the same name within the Alhambra of Granada'. That idiosyncratic view should not detract from the impression that Borrow seems to have had a genuine interest in the buildings of Spain and an inquisitive eye.

Borrow found León – largely ignored by the British – 'an old gloomy town', but he greatly admired its cathedral which he saw as a counterpart to its 'beautiful sister' at Palencia whose advantage over León was that, when Borrow visited, it was still 'illumined by some beautiful paintings of Murillo'.[47] Milton guiltily, but famously, had been ravished by some exquisite singing in a church in Rome, and Borrow too, like many apparently adamantine Protestants, found himself all too susceptible to the Catholic art of theatre. He greatly enjoyed a journey in high summer over land from Coruña to Santiago. Once in the great basilica, he found his resolution weakening:

> The cathedral, though a work of various periods and styles of architecture, is a majestic, venerable pile, in every respect calculated to excite awe and admiration; indeed, it is almost impossible to walk its long dusky aisles, and hear the solemn music and the noble chanting, and inhale the incense of the mighty censers, which are at times swung so high by machinery as to smite the vaulted roof, whilst gigantic tapers glitter here and there amongst the gloom, from the shrines of many a saint, before which the worshippers are kneeling, breathing forth their prayers and petitions for help, love, and mercy, and entertain a doubt that we are treading the floor of a house where God delighteth to dwell.[48]

Street, more earnestly if less poetically, stuck to the contested issues of restoration rather than to the contemplation of how the spirit could be seduced with an artful combination of the five senses. 'The tide of "Restoration" has hardly reached Spain', Street was relieved to tell his readership at one point in *Gothic Architecture*. He declared that in Spain there are no Salisbury Chapter-houses or Worcester cathedrals 'to puzzle over as to whether anything about them is old, or whether all may be dismissed or discussed as if it were perfectly new'.[49] Spanish architecture afforded a field of study whose value could not be overrated – certainly it should not be neglected. Street gathered seed in Spain but it is difficult to know how well it took root in England. The difficulty is highlighted by looking at the tense relationship between Street and his most gifted pupil William Morris, founder of *The Society for the Protection of Ancient Buildings*.

While still an undergraduate at Exeter College, Oxford, Morris had decided to become an architect. He wrote to tell his mother that as far as the profession went, Street was the best. In January 1856, he took out articles with the Street firm, then established in Beaumont Street.[50] But a year later he was gone. Morris had decided architecture was not his vocation – but was that actually the whole story? Perhaps the novitiate had realised that with Street, it was better to attend to the preaching than to the practice. Perhaps it strained credulity too far to hear Street declare 'that it was absolutely impossible to be too conservative in everything that one does', while Morris knew perfectly well that at Oswestry church, Street had summarily covered over 168 grave slabs. That was described as 'an act of sacrilege'. The 'Society for the Protection of Ancient Buildings', or 'SPAB' as it is now known, was founded in 1877 to counteract the highly destructive 'restoration' of medieval buildings being practised by many Victorian architects, Street among them. But what had happened at Oswestry had not been an isolated act. Street perpetrated some of the most egregious restorations of minsters and cathedrals himself. He was as happy to take out the arms of King George because they made a sanctuary look like a hotel as he was to replace medieval tiles, glazed and crumbled like honeycomb, with Minton replacements: acid in colour and Bakelite in texture. When Morris was passing through the pretty village of Burford in the Cotswolds in the summer of 1876, he stopped to look at what his erstwhile employer had done. He rushed from the graveyard to establish his hugely influential preservation society.

However, it would be unfair to suggest that the abiding achievement of Street was the vicarious establishment of Britain's first national conservation campaigning group: Street was a great and timeless designer whose best buildings possess a 'purposeful solemnity'.[51] Street had a passionate belief in handwork – so too did Morris, founding father of the Arts and Crafts Movement. Street felt strongly that an architect should be a craftsman – twenty years later Morris would be writing the minutes of the SPAB in a hand stained blue with dye.

For Street, the unique glory of Spanish ecclesiastical architecture was its furnishings. Much of Street's learned exegesis on the origins of the great Spanish cathedrals centred upon the extent to which French influence had travelled the long road to Compostela. But for Street, the interior of a Spanish church was quite unlike anything in Europe – it possessed Street's own 'purposeful solemnity'. The great triumph of Spain was the retable (*retablo*).[52] As Street conveyed something of the refulgent splendour of Toledo or Miraflores, his readership was treated to thoughts as to what in the Middle Ages had been right in Spain and wrong in England. Taking a leaf out of Ruskins' *Stones of Venice*, Street's own stones of Spain suggested that the church interior was more authentic as an expression of devotion because the craftsmen themselves were devout and their profession respected:

> In every one of these works Spanish workmen excelled, because they devoted themselves to them ... and consider how people interested themselves in the matter; how they were excited in the contest between Borgoña and Berruguete, and no doubt in the others also, and we see at once how different was the position which these men occupied from that which, so far as we know, their contemporaries in England held.[53]

Catholicism covered Spanish society as leaves a tree: Southey had approved the primitive expression of religious belief, Wiseman had sighed for a naive faith, Street felt that until English churches were in everyday use there was little chance of obtaining an authentic standard of ecclesiastical architecture. Although the shadow of Ruskin falls across the occasional page, Street calls people to repentance rather than to cleansing the temple, as Ruskin liked to do. Street quarrels with the acerbic Ford as he is indignant with the complacent Stirling.[54] Treatment by Stirling of painters before Velázquez is dismissed as peremptory. For Street, the spirit of what he calls 'the earlier men' was so described as to make it seem as if medieval Spanish painters were an Oxford eight practising for the boat race. Such cleanliness contrasted with the morbid temperaments of Golden Age painters whose productions were in truth never golden, but copper blackened by the poison of religious bigotry:

> [T]he works of Borgona at Avila, the paintings round the cloister and choir-screen at Leon, the painted Retablos at Barcelona, Toledo, and elsewhere, seemed to me to be often very full of beauty both of drawing and colour. Their number is very great, and most of them are still in the very places for which they were originally painted. Their character appears to me to be utterly different from that to which we are accustomed as marking Spanish painting ... the work of a school of painters who, adopting religious art as their special vocation, and shutting themselves out almost entirely from any representation of any other kind of subject, contrived unfortunately to take the gloomy side of religion, and to paint as though an officer of the Holy Office was ever at their elbow. How contrary this spirit to that of the earlier men, who, so far as I have seen, painted just as naturally religious men, cheerful, hearty, and unaffected by the souring influence of the Inquisition, might be expected to paint![55]

Street could have called his book a social history of architecture – besides morphology, there is much on the genesis of buildings, the charity of abbots and the status of architects. But he also rummages in the mason's yard: stones and bricks, crystal and wood, sculpture and stained glass, all are turned over and examined. Stones high on a tower in Castile are dismantled for an ideal church in England. Contritely, Street accuses himself of ignoring the value of rough stone in promoting light and shade for texture – a sensual delight, undreamt of by those who have never seen anything but 'our own smooth, smart and spiritless modern brick walls, built with bad bricks and no mortar'.[56] The difference between touching walls in Lérida and those in London seems to have been for Street a contrast as between the rind of a Seville orange and the skin of a Worcester apple.

For the Victorians, what made for appropriate figurative sculpture was a subject as brittle as icing sugar. A ferocious and famous row later developed with Morris about Southwell Minster when Street set about restoring it.[57] The problem may have had to do with Street's dislike of anything which defied the basic law of good ornament – that is, truth to materials. For example, the glory of Southwell – a neglected minster in a remote corner of Nottinghamshire – was in the leaves of its capitals, thought to be miraculously naturalistic, but they offended Street. What he liked was the figurative sculpture of Spain. Relatively restrained, its urge to simplicity and abstraction found him nodding approvingly: 'thoroughly architectural in character' was how he described it. If Street was opinionated with sculpture he was overexcited about stained glass, something upon which he had strong opinions as indeed on everything else. Having stridden into S. Isidore in León, he was able to pontificate about the lamentable state of the art in England. In León the contemplation of the windows showed that beauty in glass had to do with colouring, not drawing. It was disastrous to try to 'reproduce some sentimentality of a German painter'. Drawing as defined in painting had of course an important place in the promotion of worship, but 'we should not try to get these in the form of windows'. Rather the parish should instead employ artists like Burne-Jones as he had painted at St Paul's Brighton, or Dante Gabriel Rossetti with his work at Llandaff.[58]

The experience of Spain made Street change views radically about architects in the Middle Ages. Who they were and their status was a whimsical subject which provoked Victorians into firm but uncharitable argument on the basis of almost no evidence. Street had gone to Spain believing that the Walsinghams and the Wykehams were the architects, and not just the men who held a bag of gold on the margin of a manuscript. Then, the Peninsula changed his mind. He came to believe that Spain was well ahead of England in having a professional caste, that the 'distinct position of the architect [was] understood and accepted a good deal earlier in Spain than in England'.[59] Foreign travel was something of a mixed blessing for Street. A close study of Lombard marble and Spanish terracotta enhanced a natural love of texture and colour, but then a wide geographical acquaintance narrowed views. Street was right because he had seen so much.

The central issue for the religious of Victorian Britain was what to do about Rome, and yet this chapter has been about Spain, because the Church of Rome was often observed through the prism of Spain in the contest within Britain for emancipation and the establishment of a new hierarchy. Here, the unusual figure of Lord Acton has appeared as an active controversialist in the agonised battle over religion in Victorian England. Acton was unusual in many ways, however, not least because he was an English aristocrat of exceptional intellectual breadth who was both a Catholic and a historian. The next chapter is concerned to explain how a cluster of Protestant historians, British and American, sought to understand how relations between Church and State had developed in Spain.

Notes

1 Edward Norman, *The English Catholic Church in the Nineteenth Century* (Oxford: Clarendon, 1984), p. 120.
2 G.I.T. Machin, *The Catholic Question in English Politics* (Oxford: Clarendon, 1964), p. 1.
3 Martin Murphy, *Blanco White: Self-Banished Spaniard* (New Haven and London: Yale University Press, 1989), p. 203.
4 Don Leucadio Doblado, *Letters from Spain* (London: Henry Colburn, 1822), Letter III, p. 60.
5 Southey to C.W. Williams Wyn, 26 January 1796, in M. Fitzgerald (ed.), *Letters of Robert Southey: A Selection* (London: Henry Frowde; Oxford: Oxford University Press, 1912), p. 9.
6 White to Southey, London, 31 October 1812, Bod. Lib., Ms. Eng. Letters d.74, fol. 93.
7 White to Southey, 67 Edgware Road, London, 5 May 1812, Bod. Lib., Ms. Eng. Letters d.74, fol. 86.
8 White to Southey, 67 Edgware Road, 10 July 1812, Bod. Lib. Ms. Eng. Letters, d.74, fol. 90.
9 Southey to Charles Danvers, 13 September 1800, quoted in A Cabral (ed.), *Robert Southey, Journals of a residence in Portugal 1800–1801 and a Visit to France in 1838* (Oxford: Clarendon, 1960) p. 109.
10 Southey to Walter Savage Landor, 19 December 1821, C.C. Southey (ed.), *The Life and Correspondence of Robert Southey*, 6 vols (London: Longman, Brown, Green and Longmans, 1850), 5, pp. 106–7.
11 Carr, *Spain*, p. 45.
12 Marquis de Custine, *L'Espagne sous Ferdinand VII*, Paris, 1838, ii, p. 58.
13 Carr, *Spain*, p. 46.
14 Norman, *English Catholic Church*, p. 17.
15 Murphy, *Blanco White*, p. 5.
16 Thom, *Life of Blanco*, p. 33.
17 Ibid., p. 38.
18 Ibid., p. 37.
19 Ibid., p. 49.
20 Borrow, *Bible in Spain*, p. 72.
21 Murphy, *Blanco White*, p. 133.
22 Ibid., p. 176.

23 Ibid., p. 124.
24 William Cobbett, *A History of the Protestant Reformation* (London, 1824), Letter X, paragraph 305.
25 Ibid., Letter XI, para. 322.
26 Ibid., Letter XI, para. 346.
27 Anon., *The Christian Teacher*, vol. 2 (1840), pp. 431–9.
28 His Eminence Cardinal Wiseman, *Essays on Various Subjects in Three Volumes*, 3 vols (London: C. Dolman, 1853), 3, pp. 393–438.
29 Norman, *English Catholic Church*, p. 126.
30 Wilfrid Ward, *The Life and Times of Cardinal Wiseman*, 2 vols (London and New York: Longmans, Green and Co., 1897), 2, p. 8.
31 Ibid., 1, p. 568.
32 Norman, *English Catholic Church*, p. 119.
33 Ibid., p. 118.
34 Ward, *Life and Times of Wiseman*, 1, p. 422.
35 Ibid., p. 200.
36 Norman, *English Catholic Church* p. 116.
37 Ward, *Life and Times of Wiseman*, 2, p. 157.
38 Wiseman, *Essays*, 3, p. 7.
39 Ibid., 3, p. 74.
40 Ibid., 3, p. 112.
41 Cardinal John Henry Newman to Father Richard Stanton, 'Oratory Bm. June 6/51', Ian Ker and Thomas Gornall (eds), *The Letters and Diaries of John Henry Newman* 27 vols (Oxford: Clarendon, 1975–),14, pp. 293–4.
42 Ward, *Life and Times of Wiseman*, 1, p. 357.
43 Wiseman, 'Spanish and English National Art', *The Dublin Review* 25, (Dec 1848), p. 483.
44 Norman, *English Catholic Church*, p. 143.
45 D. Woodruff (ed.), *Essays on Church and State* (London: Hollis and Carter, 1952), pp. 392–3.
46 N. Pevsner, *Some Architectural Writers of the Nineteenth Century* (Oxford: Clarendon, 1972), pp. 303–4.
47 Borrow, *Bible in Spain*, p. 129.
48 Ibid., p. 157.
49 G.E. Street, *Some Account of Gothic Architecture in Spain* (London: John Murray, 1865), p. 433.
50 Morris to Emma Shelton Morris, 'Ex: Coll: Oxon', 11 November, 1855, Norman Kelvin (ed.), *The Collected Letters of William Morris*, 3 vols (Princeton NJ: Princeton University Press, 1984), 1, p. 24.
51 Fiona MacCarthy, *William Morris: A Life for Our Times* (London: Faber 1994), p. 107.
52 Street, *Gothic Architecture in Spain*, p. 433.
53 Ibid.
54 Ibid., p. 68, note 1 for Street's disagreement with Ford over the sculpture on the *retablo* of S. Maria l'Antigua, Valladolid.
55 Ibid., p. 443.
56 Ibid., pp. 226–7.
57 MacCarthy, *William Morris*, p. 378.
58 Street, *Gothic Archicture in Spain*, pp. 120–1.
59 Ibid., p. 464.

4
Historians

Richard Ford had a marked poetic vein which allowed him to respond movingly to the geographies of the Peninsula, but Borrow saw the history of Spain running through its stones like quartz through granite. In *The Bible in Spain* the temperaments of famous men arise as naturally from that implacable country as the colour of its soil:

> There is an air of stern and savage grandeur in everything around which strongly captivates the imagination. This savage coast is the first glimpse of Spain which the voyager from the north catches, or he who has ploughed his way across the wide Atlantic; and well does it seem to realize all his visions of this strange land. 'Yes', he exclaims, 'this is indeed Spain – stern, flinty Spain – land emblematic of those spirits to which she has given birth. From what land but that before me could have proceeded those portentous beings who astounded the Old World and filled the new with horror and blood – Alba and Philip, Cortez and Pizarro – stern colossal spectres looming through the gloom of bygone years, like yonder granite mountains through the haze, upon the eye of the mariner? Yes, yonder is indeed Spain – flinty, indomitable Spain – land emblematic of its sons[1]

The purpose of this chapter is to consider how famous historians wrote about some of those legendary figures Borrow was thinking about when he contemplated an altogether harsher environment than the lotus land of Andalucía, so beloved of the British. There will be particular emphasis on the two dominant figures of sixteenth-century Spain: Charles V and Philip II. By 1850 Robertson's work had lost something of its lustre but although many disputed how Robertson interpreted his subject, none denied his mastery as a stylist. Robertson had been the first historian to write a historical biography in English to become an international best-seller. However, by the mid-Victorian period Gibbon's *Decline and Fall* was regarded as not only great history, but greater literature. Robertson, by then far behind, was becoming fast forgotten, until the American historian W.H. Prescott issued an edition of *Charles V* in 1856. Today there is a new interest in Robertson; a revitalisation of a reputation symbolised by the recently published edition of his complete works and a collected letters in progress.

Historians on both sides of the Atlantic came to a consensus about the nature of Charles V, which can be accounted for by common values and an educational system in America modelled on that of the ancient British universities. Those who wrote 'modern' history in the high Victorian period had been educated as classical scholars, and so the 'Caesarism' of the Emperor – a word which first appeared in the English language in 1857, just a year after the appearance of Prescott's edition of Robertson's *Charles V* – was perhaps the most important aspect of their presentations. The three historians whose interpretations of Charles V form the substance of this chapter were well versed in Tacitus and Suetonius. The range of territory over which Charles had held sway, and the heroism of his leadership, made Charles V for historians nearly as distant and distinct as the emperor Augustus, though Charles had been dead less than two hundred years. Whereas for Robertson and Smith the laws of economics, the movement of peoples and social custom were held to be important in the dynamics of history, the Victorians thought of the reign of Charles V in terms of personalities. For them the peculiar temperament of Charles V contrasting with that of Francis I, was decisive in the shaping of early modern Europe. And yet despite such a close focus on individuality in the case of Charles himself, our writers failed to be overborne by the contradictions of a personality which runs through his image like a tear across a canvas. Over thousands of pages, Charles remains a hero to all, though none concealed what was regarded as the sinister, or elided the depraved, in a mind always held to have been commanding in an age unparalleled for the greatness of its leaders: 'It was the peculiar glory of that period to produce the most illustrious monarchs who have at any one time appeared in Europe. Leo, Charles, Francis, Henry and Solyman were each of them possessed of talents that might have rendered any age wherein they happened to flourish conspicuous'.[2]

The men who are treated in this chapter were born within a 22-year period – Prescott in 1796, Motley in 1814, Stirling and Froude in 1818. Although Prescott was older, all grew to maturity during the silver age of the hero, an epoch symbolised by David's image of Napoleon crossing the Alps, and within the lifetime of Napoleon. Could early years spent hearing about how Bonaparte had struggled for the domination of Europe have drawn them to the last pan-European figure before Napoleon? Grasping for tyranny as Napoleon had done at the dawn of Romanticism could hardly have been more inspiring, and it was because Charles V partook both of Charlemagne and of Napoleon that these historians found the heroic to contrast with the chivalric: Charles V to pit against his great rival Francis I, with whom he was locked in desperate combat for the mastery of Europe.

The point of departure is William Stirling, later Sir William Stirling Maxwell Bt, whose *Cloister Life of Charles V* of 1852 anticipated Prescott on Charles V, and Froude on the Tudors, by some four years (Figure 7). Stirling chose the title of his study with care: *The Cloister Life* is focused on the final nineteen months of the life of Charles V when he retreated to the monastery of Yuste in Estremadura; that is to say, from February 1557 until his death on 21 September 1558. By contrast, Prescott's work, in two volumes rather than one, takes the form of an extended commentary on Robertson's *Charles V*. Stirling, Prescott and Froude were on terms of

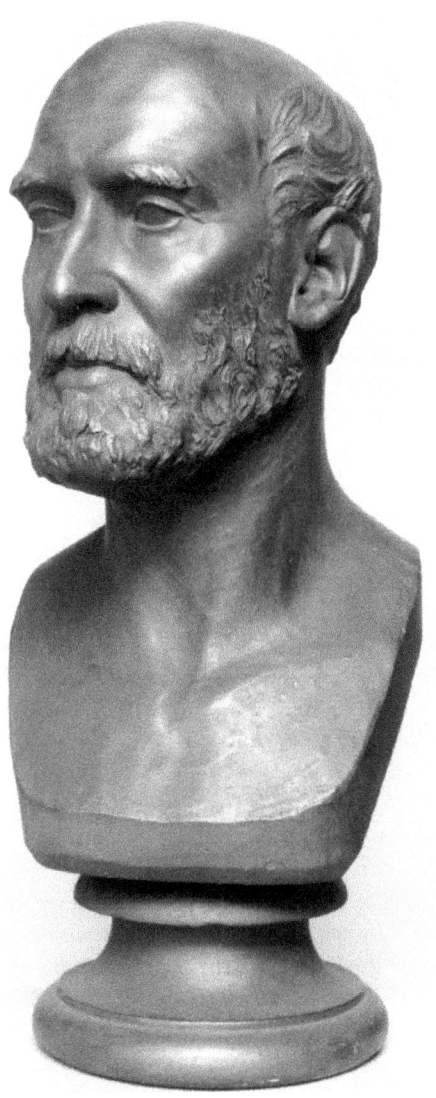

7 Francis Williamson, *Sir William Stirling Maxwell, 9th Bt*

friendly rivalry during the 1850s when they were all publishing. Yet there are intriguing presentational contrasts which make their pioneering contributions to Golden-Age history markedly different. In some ways it is easiest to distinguish their idiosyncrasies by thinking of Stirling as playwright, Froude as novelist and Prescott as chronicler.

But in what sense can Stirling's popular and successful *Cloister Life* be regarded as a play? As with a Jacobean drama, and early modern theatre had been Stirling's first love, the entourage with which Charles V was surrounded at Yuste is presented as a kind of *dramatis personae*. Attendants whose personalities are characterised in sharply contrasted ways glide around the 'ardent, reserved and commanding mind' of the main character, only to disappear off-stage in a drama of retreat, resignation and death. Early in the book the hypocrisy of the Emperor's confessor is suggested as he 'knew how to make ladders, to place and favour, of the ropes which girt their ascetic loins'.[3] Issues of religion and conscience, however, are relieved by a marked streak of burlesque as Stirling enjoys regaling his readership with details of Charles's personal habits. Thus the steward Quixada, sympathy for whom is aroused by the difficulties he encounters in victualling the household, is driven to distraction by frustrations in preventing his master from indulging an appetite for forbidden fruits: athletically he 'interposed [himself] between his master and an eel pie as, in other days, he would have thrown himself between the imperial person and the point of a Moorish lance'.[4] Charles is portrayed as being nearly as zealous and bigoted as his attendant Hieronymites, but he is also revealed as a martyr to gout and, should that not sufficiently lower the tone, to piles as well. The inventory of what Charles possessed at Yuste, an appendix to the book, has inserted after a piece of the true cross, 'two bracelets, and two rings of gold, and one of bone, all good for the hemorrhoids (almorranas)'.[5] Here, subversively, it is suggested that for the Catholic mind of sixteenth-century Spain, bones were a good all round investment: efficacious for sickness of body and soul.

How Charles suffered the agonies of the damned for indulging his appetites forms a kind of Falstaffian relief to the stratagems of hovering Churchmen, bent on overcoming a strength of mind which had been seen at its most heroic when the Emperor made his famous abdication speech in the Hall of the Golden Fleece at Brussels on 25 October 1555, before his final departure for Spain from Flushing on 17 September 1556. Stirling believed that such an interior but disastrous conquest – won by friars amid the holm oaks of deserted Spanish sierras – was to be of far greater significance to the future of Spain than the clash of steel which Charles had won at Mühlberg and Titian had immortalised: 'But once within the walls of Yuste, he assumed all the passions, prejudices and superstitions of a friar ... Religion was the enchanted ground whereon his strong will was paralyzed and his keen intellect fell grovelling in the dust.'[6] The poisonous spider of Catholic bigotry had stung its prey. This passage points to a metronomic quality of the *Cloister Life*: between vast and airy realms of the spirit and a close focus on the corruption of the Emperor's body, worthy in its putrescent detail of the sacks of a martyr's torn flesh carved by Morales to exhort the faithful. Adopting the eyewitness roles of the attendant physicians Cornelio and Mole, Stirling's style changes from straining for effects which are consciously archaic, even Augustan in syntax, pompous and rolling periods of text reserved for matters of State and Faith, to a colourless and factual account of minute particulars such as when the physician informs his readership of how '[h]is throat was constantly choked with phlegm, which, being too feeble to expectorate, he endeavoured to remove with his finger'.[7]

Stirling writes with theatrical flourish, but there is much too about the structure of the *Cloister Life* which is theatre. There is unity of action since the 'play' unfolds in the church, the palace rooms and the gardens at Yuste. Stirling always liked to pace the boards upon which he set his play. For the *Cloister Life*, he shows himself to have been sensitive to the *genius loci* by skilful evocation of a topography which he had closely inspected, but which Prescott never did. Indeed, Stirling was sufficiently committed to the site to have been offered the monastery when it came up for sale.[8] Stirling writes of the despondency of Charles's followers as they waited until Yuste was ready to receive them. Here tensions are raised only to be dispersed in a stage direction as the page is turned on a distant prospect of buildings described like a landscape painting: 'Dimly seen over the wintry woodlands, and through a November mist, Yuste had appeared to the household at Xarandilla a place of penance; but their dismal forebodings were by no means realized in their new quarters on the fresh hill-side, bright with the sunshine of a budding spring'.[9]

Stirling was intent upon scotching a number of myths which clung to the reputation of the emperor like lichen to his cloister walls. He concedes the distinction of William Robertson as a pre-eminent stylist while condemning him for his superficial treatment of Charles at Yuste. Admirers of Robertson found his style graphic, not to say painterly, and Stirling was no exception. He describes Robertson's account of the evening of the Emperor's life as 'masterly as a sketch' but copied from the canvas of an earlier 'unscrupulous' historian. But then there is harsh condemnation for Robertson's credulity in believing that Charles V actually went so far as to descend into his own coffin during a famous dress rehearsal for his funeral in the chapel at Yuste. In the face of the melodramatic, Stirling feels it impossible to 'offer any defence' since everything about the account is absurd except for the style in which the story is told.[10]

There is, however, a more substantive myth which Stirling succeeds in exposing, though not one to which Robertson ever subscribed. The slaying of this particular dragon is what made the book a serious and lasting contribution to history. This abiding misapprehension had to do with the romantic notion that Charles V at Yuste was an Egyptian father. Although Stirling never darkened the doors of a Spanish archive, ambitious exploitation of the primary archival researches of others gave him a broader factual base than had been available before. Accordingly, he was able to demonstrate not only that the emperor entertained some of the most important political figures of the day, but that he made decisive and sometimes disastrous interventions in the affairs of Spain and the Empire from a sparsely furnished upper room looking over a monastery garden. Of these unhappy initiatives, the most destructive, according to Stirling, was the encouragement Charles gave Philip in a codicil to his will to hunt down religious dissent without regard to degree of error or distinction of station. It was a rigour toward Protestantism which Stirling turns to good effect by adding parenthetically that Charles committed such thoughts to paper as he 'watched with fatherly kindness over the fortunes of grooms and scullions'.[11] Here Stirling seems to anticipate those historians who express their bafflement at the contradictions within the psycho-pathology of the tyrant by telling us what in other contexts would be sympathetic if trivial detail such as the fact that Hitler was a vegetarian and liked dogs.

Stirling was a notable art collector, and this may explain why he exaggerates the assiduity of Charles V as patron of the arts, an aspect of taste and temperament largely ignored by other biographers. Here Stirling is guilty of casting a myth out of Robertson only to replace it with one of his own. There seems to be no evidence that Gaspar de Vega, the architect of the new buildings at Yuste, worked from a sketch 'drawn by the emperor's own hand', but this was not all that Stirling erroneously claimed: an oratory, further additions to Charles V's own quarters, and a new wing to accommodate a son who never visited – all, Stirling says with no evidence, were considered by the emperor in the form of his own sketches.[12] There is a vivid account as well of Charles summoning up remembrance of his long-dead wife, Isabella of Portugal, while sitting in the shade of his terrace, contemplating a posthumous portrait by Titian.[13] The passage cried out for the brush, and indeed it inspired Alfred Elmore, a popular melodramatist of the paint box. Elmore produced one of the great Victorian historical inventions, worthy to hang alongside that lachrymose contribution to Stuart martyrology, W.F. Yeames's *And When Did You Last See Your Father?*. Elmore's picture was entitled *The Emperor Charles V at the Convent of Yuste*, a painting which will be the subject of further scrutiny in the final chapter of this book, devoted to the painted image of Spain.

In what is an epilogue about the impact Charles V made upon early modern Europe, Stirling pays handsome tribute to the emperor as a patron of the arts on a Continental scale: 'The name of Charles is connected, not only with the wars and politics, but with the peaceful arts of his time: it is linked with the graver of the Vico, the chisel of Leoni, the pencil of Titian, and the lyre of Ariosto; and as a lover and patron of art, his fame stood as high at Venice and Nuremberg as at Antwerp and Toledo.'[14]

There are several occasions when a reading of the *Cloister Life* suggests the extent to which Stirling's quest for the greatest of Spain's monarchs reveals as much about the values of a Victorian plutocrat as it does about the Golden Age. Some time is spent by Stirling musing on the significance of the year 1558, which he considered decisive for Spain. It was the moment when it was discovered that Protestantism had infiltrated the country, and when Spain made the decision to root it out with fire – thus, according to Stirling, denying itself the chance to escape the tyranny of the old religious ways. Here Stirling wants his reader to believe that, by turning its face against progress, Spain was left behind by the North. Thereafter the Protestant countries, the Netherlands and Britain especially, not only became more progressive, but had a moral authority which Spain had relinquished. The moral and ethical superiority of the North was by no means derived wholly from the fact that the reformed religion represented truth distilled from Catholic error. Any society, regardless of its religious sympathies, by embracing progress was – by that act alone – enhancing its moral capital. Stirling sat in his study at Keir near Glasgow, looking over fields as plump as cushions with their promise of a good harvest of rents, and with a wad of dividends on his desktop. His was never the life of the poor scholar, and personal experience shaped how he saw the lost world of sixteenth-century Europe. His instinctive sympathy with progress, even then making Glasgow the engine room of the world, was expressed thus:

> In that year was decided the question whether [Spain] was to share in the intellectual movement of the north, or lag behind in the old paths of mediaeval faith; whether she was to be guided by the printing-press, or to hold fast by the missal. It was in that year that she felt the first distinct shock of the great moral earth quake, out of which had already come Luther and Protestantism, out of which was to come the Thirty years' war, the English commonwealth, French revolutions and modern republics.[15]

Although Stirling was both the promoter and the beneficiary of 'northern' progress, antecedents predisposed him to be sympathetic to Spanish Catholicism, ostensibly so alien from immediate experience. But then, his parents had taught him to respect religious difference, and it had never made sense for Stirling to defend a particular encampment. Thus the paradox of a Protestant Scotsman becoming a most distinguished Victorian apologist of the 'Spanishness' of Spanish culture is perhaps not so strange. Nevertheless there were limits – even for Stirling – and the Spanish Inquisition was one. Stirling took the opportunity of remarking on the defunct to attack the threatening: the Catholic Church as it had evolved in his own lifetime. A life-long fascination with book production and the history of the printing press made him impatient with the idiocy of a licensing system which had once prevailed in Spain. But then somehow there is a sense too in which Stirling can understand better the cruelty of the Inquisition than the mindless authoritarianism of a Catholic Church presided over in his own day by Pius IX. Pius had abandoned an early espousal of liberalism for insistent, intransigent orthodoxy, causing grave doubts in the British establishment of which Stirling was a railing though never a pillar. The Catholic hierarchy had been re-established in Britain after the Reformation only a year before the appearance of *The Cloister Life*, while Holland, originally created out of Catholic bigotry, obtained a Roman priesthood again just the following year. All this may explain the polemical strain with which Stirling mixes history and current controversy when he turns his contempt upon the efforts of the Spanish hierarchy to gag freedom of opinion:

> Thus it came to pass that Mariana and Soli, Cervantes and Calderon, had to wait upon the pleasure and tremble at the caprice of licenser after licenser; that the beauty, the integrity, and even the existence of some of the finest works of the human mind were jeoparded in the dirty hands of a stupid friar. There were ages in which the church, as the sanctuary of art, and knowledge, and letters, deserved the gratitude of the world; but for the last three centuries she has striven to cancel the debt, in the noble offspring of genius which she has strangled in the birth, and in the vast fields of intellect which her dark shadow has blighted.[16]

Stirling shared with many Victorian writers a marked streak of anti-Gallicanism. If you were for Spain, you were against France. Such bi-partisanship appears to have originated with the alliance between Britain and Spain during the Peninsular War. What is altogether more certain is that the most acidic French-hating Hispanist was Richard Ford. Ford worshipped the Duke of Wellington – an adulation he combined with rigid faith in the principles of high Toryism expressed through a brilliantly sardonic mind. Ford loathed France and made no secret of saying so whenever he could. Now Stirling dedicated the *Cloister Life* to Ford as his intellectual mentor, and so Stirling too makes several gratuitous asides which add up to the implication that as the French have been, so they always will be: the moral turpitude of Francis I, it is insinuated, need hardly surprise a British reader who was well versed in the history of the Bourbons. Early in the book it is declared that although the ancient dynasty of France was usually noted for courage, courtesy and good humour, 'the first king of that name added, in full measure, that laxity of principle and instability of purpose which seem to belong to his blood'.[17] Later, when considering the perfidy of the duke of Vendôme, Stirling cannot resist a further swipe at the French monarchy, since Vendôme 'like a true Bourbon, was intriguing both with France and Spain, and capable of any treachery to either for the slightest gain to himself'.[18]

Stirling was a typical upper-class Victorian. He had no problem whatever in proclaiming his prejudices to anyone who would listen. He did not like Frenchmen and he did not like Jews: though such dislikes seem never to have stood in the way of exchanging invitations with the Duc d' Aumâle, son of the recently deposed king of France, Louis-Philippe.[19] Stirling also maintained a correspondence with Disraeli, receiving an engaging note after he had presented Disraeli with one of his lavishly decorated visual histories of early modern Europe: ' Although I was born in a library, wch was, not infrequently, increased and adorned by some of the most eminent who have indulged in the luxury of private printing, I can recall no work wch can, for a moment, compare with the magnificent volume, wch you have done me the highly-appreciated honor of conferring on me.'[20]

Stirling imagines the contrast between Charles V and Francis I in an intensely visual way. Francis appears glittering in armour as he 'adorns the pageants of war', a figure whose heroic limbs glisten like the pistons of a Futurist poster. By contrast Charles appears as puckered as a leather purse. It is a significant contrast which reveals much about the values of the society to which Stirling belonged. The differences drawn out between Charles V and Francis I are those between the amateur and the professional. Amateurism was something which the Establishment in Britain had made a religion of. Heroic failure, such as the life and reign of Charles of Ghent demonstrated so affectingly, had always appealed to the British ever since the British seventeenth-century historians Clarendon and Burnet had sanctified the tragic figure of Charles I of England. Those earlier British historians had thought that the manner of death became Charles I as nothing he had done in life.

Stirling was writing at a time when the central contradiction of the British public school system was becoming a hallowed article of faith: young men were to be sent to Peshawar or Peking armed with the unhelpful belief that to hold the line sustained by manly straightforwardness was more noble than to succeed in caddish and underhand ways. Accordingly, the character of Charles V was bound to be understood better by a British readership than was the more romantic and winning personality of Francis I. Influenced perhaps by the cult of the martyr which had sanctified Charles I of England, Stirling described another still more heroic failure in much the same Christ-like terms. It is declared that Charles V relieved his brow of its thorny crowns as soon as he had placed 'his son Philip on the rival throne of the heretic Tudors'.

William Hickling Prescott, a near-blind American, enjoyed astonishing success as the pre-eminent historian of imperial Spain in the nineteenth century. The plinth of his reputation remained his *Ferdinand and Isabella*, published in November 1837; within four years it had run to a third edition in England, such was its success on both sides of the Atlantic. It was his first and it was his best book. By November 1855, when the first two of the three volumes of an uncompleted life of Philip II appeared, Prescott was exhausted. Then he could only use his one good eye for an hour a day. He confessed to Strling, friend and rival, how beguiling he found the appeal of abandoning his study in Boston for the green lanes of Peperell, the family estate forty miles away, where Prescott enjoyed the local round of two or three 'polished families'. But then Prescott's output had been miraculous. He was tied to his noctograph – writing instrument for a blind man – as a diver to his rope, while for twenty years bails of manuscripts had been crossing the Atlantic as ballast in steam ships and clippers. His method of mastering mountains of paper was auricular, and this called forth extraordinary powers: a capacity to memorise perfectly upwards of sixty printed pages.

One of the last projects Prescott completed had been his edition of Robertson's *Charles V*. A reissue was justified by Prescott's belief that the archival material which had been excavated from the Spanish royal archives at the obscure town of Simancas, and of which Robertson had been unaware, had completely changed perceptions about the final years of the Emperor's life. Although Robertson had nodded in deference to the importance of obtaining information on the ground, not merely out of leather-bound folios, the romance of archival work was something which the early nineteenth century was the first to discover. The Scottish painter Sir David Wilkie had felt a vision of his friend Washington Irving, pouring over manuscripts in the archives of Seville, worthy enough to make into an affecting canvas.

As it was, the romance of Simancas, a small town on the road from Valladolid to Salamanca, was palpable. Although the Napoleonic Marshal Kellerman had used manuscripts for kindling when there in the Peninsular War, a vast amount still remained; hardly surprising, since the archive had been established in the moated slate-roofed castle as far back as 1545. Simancas held most of the stirring manuscript material associated with the Austrian Habsburgs, and that alone went some way to countering the vast frustration induced in anyone actually trying to use the place. Prescott, and before him Stirling and the French historian Mignet, had scrutinised primary sources made available to them by the industry of Gayangos, the pre-eminent Spanish historian in the nineteenth century. Armed with the Gayangos material, these historians came to the settled view that Charles had been much more active in his retirement than Robertson had allowed. For his part, Prescott deplored the disastrous effects of the final retreat to Yuste. It had been out of the compass of the emperor's four modest rooms attached to this comparatively modest religious community, and not from the spiritual power station of the Escorial, like Yuste a Hieronymite monastery, that a great shadow had spread over the land. Prescott shared the belief held by Stirling that the 'corroding influence' on Charles of

Yuste had had a disastrous effect on Spain. But there is an important difference. Prescott was much more forthright than Stirling in his condemnation of the bigotry of the Emperor. He saw the corrosive arsenic of religious bigotry not merely getting into the mainstream of spiritual life in Spain but, no less disastrously, seeping deeper into Spain's water table. In time the poison had surfaced, only to destroy essential aspects of nationhood. Convinced of the fundamental 'intolerance of [Charles's] disposition', while being himself fretted by the gathering storm of the American civil war, Prescott had delivered an impassioned indictment of a man whom he had worshipped for so long: 'No one of his line did so much to fasten the yoke of superstition on the necks of the Spaniards. He may be truly said to have stamped his character not only on his own generation but on that that followed it. His example and his teachings directed the policy of the pitiless Philip the Second, and through him, of the imbecile Philip the Third.'[21]

Prescott believed that the suppression of religious dissent, and by extension, freedom of thought, contaminated the sub-soil of Spain. It was a view summarised not in the life of Charles V but in that of Philip II, and in a chapter on 'Protestantism in Spain'. The argument had begun by a declaration that because science represented progress and an open mind, the ecclesiastical establishment had put an interdict on its study. But apparently the worm had been moving in the bud before it even opened. Although the phrase the 'Golden Age' had been one first coined by Spaniards in the early eighteenth century, despite such a settled epithet, for Prescott sixteenth-century Spain had been an era not of gold but of tin. Since the condition of science is progress and progress was anathema in the Peninsula, everything in Spain 'not only looked to the past, but rested on the past'. The effect of this retroversion was everywhere, and so by a kind of knight's move in logical thought, the blame for the anaemia of the Spanish economy was laid by Prescott on religion:

> The hand of the Inquisition drew the line which said 'No further!' This was the limit of human intelligence in Spain ... Hence those frantic experiments, so often repeated, in the financial administration of the kingdom, which made Spain the byword of the nations, and which ended in the ruin of trade, the prostration of credit, and finally the bankruptcy of the state.[22]

British and American writers felt deeply ambivalent toward Philip II; a dark prince who caused many who wrote about him to fall into difficulties. Prescott died with his own study in fanaticism unfinished before he had been able to turn to the Armada which for Americans would have been the most affecting episode in the long reign of Philip. For Prescott, as for others from long-established New England families, the Armada had been a struggle to ensure that the candle of conscience shone out of the shadows of religious bigotry. Prescott was a Unionist Northerner identified with the anti-slavery campaign. As such it might be supposed he would have risen to the challenge of doing justice to the sea battle which stemmed the tide of bigotry and removed the threat of mental enslavement. Those events, however, became most famously described for Victorians not by Prescott but by James Anthony Froude, who will be discussed in the last part of this chapter.

Nevertheless, Prescott's biography of Philip II contains an account of the battle of Lepanto good enough to be included in any anthology of American prose. But with the exception of this great passage, *Philip II* lacks the extended allegro of the first and best of the five great themes dealt with by him: the life and times of Ferdinand and Isabella, a book which appeared in two volumes in 1837. Prescott's quest for Spain had been refracted through the lenses of a microscope with variable intensities of magnification. The most powerful of these was focused on Philip II because Prescott believed that in contrast to his father whose 'tastes were all Flemish', Philip 'was in everything a Spaniard'.[23] However, while Prescott always retained his vision of Philip as the most Spanish of the Austrian Habsburgs, it was stated early that a study of him was a study of Europe. A corollary of this belief was that to understand Philip, it was necessary to look as much outside as inside Spain. These claims were made in a history the gestation of which took the form of a painful accumulation of material gathered over several years with significant periods when writing was laid aside. This may explain potential difficulties in reconciling what was said first with what came later. The real difficulty arose when Prescott tried to handle what a non-Spaniard and a non-Catholic found a peculiarly challenging aspect of early modern Spain: the Inquisition. Historically the Prescotts had exchanged the corruption of the old world for the supposed freedoms of a new, and Prescott himself was proud of the fact that his grandfather had been a commander at Bunker Hill when the British had been badly defeated during the American War of Independence. Accordingly, a monstrous machine of repression such as Prescott believed the Inquisition to be was peculiarly repugnant to this righteous New Englander who attributed to the Inquisition a powerful influence on the fortunes and future of Spain. For Prescott, huge consequences arose from the establishment of this engine of tyranny in Europe early in the thirteenth century, a disaster perpetrated during the reign of Prescott's heroine Isabella by the impetus given to the proceedings of the Inquisition by Torquemada from 1487 onward. The complicity of Isabella in the rigours perpetrated under the direction of the Spanish Dominicans required considerable sophistry to jump a heroine from jail.

As Prescott tried to convey his feelings toward the end of his unfinished study, he presented his readership with a contradictory view of the place of Spain in Europe to what he had argued at the beginning of his biography of Philip II. He had begun his first volume by claiming that the history of Philip II was the history of Europe. But by the middle of the second book he offered an argument somewhat at odds with this. Prescott wrote that a consequence of the Inquisition was that 'Difference of faith made a wider gulf of separation than difference of race, language, or even interest. Spain no longer formed one of the great brotherhood of Christian nations'.[24]

If Prescott had been English, it is doubtful whether he would have thought these evils could be attributed to the presence in Spain of the Inquisition. For Prescott's contemporary James Anthony Froude, morality in the face of historical experience became a relative matter, mediated and best understood through exigencies of time and place. To the extent that Froude tried harder than Prescott to understand Spain by the standards of the sixteenth century, he was the more sophisticated historian. For Prescott in America, unencumbered by the disasters perpetrated in the name of religion in Europe, yet living in a society which connived at the enslavement of an inferior people, the Inquisition demanded not merely the expression, but the preaching, of moral outrage. Prescott's condemnation of the Inquisition was aimed not at the sort of bodily enslavement which confronted him in the Southern states of America. Rather, it was a question of mental thraldom, sustained in sixteenth-century Spain by all means at the disposal of Church and State.

For Adam Smith, by contrast, there had been no necessary cause and effect between the mechanism inhibiting freedom of thought and the inhibition of free trade. Smith had argued some seventy-five years earlier, that gold and silver fruits on the New World tree of plenty should have been seeded, invested in new fields of mercantile enterprise instead of being allowed to wither on its branches. However, Prescott went still further than just blaming the Inquisition for the atrophy of the Spanish economy. He claimed that it had choked up free-thinking altogether:

> But in Spain, every thing not only looked to the past, but rested on the past ... The effect was visible in every department of science, – not in the speculative alone, but in the physical and the practical; in the declamatory rant of its theology and ethics, in the childish and chimerical schemes of its political economists. In every walk were to be seen the symptoms of premature decrepitude, as the nation clung to the antiquated systems which the march of civilisation in other countries had long since effaced.[25]

Prescott considered Philip as military commander a pale shadow of Charles V. He wrote of how Philip was essentially a strategist, not a man of war, his chosen ground the council not the camp. He summarised the difference epigrammatically: 'Charles calculated the chances of success; Philip, those of failure.'[26] The comparison between Charles V and Philip II was commonplace; though Prescott insisted upon it in order to play up the contrast between one he described as being 'in everything a Spaniard' and Charles V who found Spain profoundly antithetical. But as to whether Spain was European or as 'the most individual country in

Europe' essentially a law unto itself, Prescott created difficulties for himself. His quest for the true nature of Philip's 'dark and inscrutable character' led him into confusion. During the course of an examination of Philip's policy in the Netherlands, he encouraged his reader to believe that Philip was 'one prepared to leave events to take their own course rather than try to direct them'; but then, when an explanation was attempted as to why Spanish policy failed in the Spanish Netherlands, he claimed that Philip did not understand the character of the Netherlander 'as dogged and determined as his own'.

Prescott was heavily influenced by Washington Irving, whose huge success as the first American to command a European readership had as much to do with his versatility as to the elegance of his pen. Irving was both popular historian and belletrist. Although Prescott's work contributed something of real value to the growth of scholarship in America in proportion to the extent to which his methodology differed from that of Irving, he bought heavily into the romance of Moorish Spain which had been so suggestively evoked in Irving's publications of the 1820s. Writing of the fall of Granada in 1492, Prescott claimed that the siege had 'rivalled that of Troy in its duration and surpassed it in the romantic character of its incidents'.[27] However, where a Spanish Homer was to be found Prescott declined to say.

Something which betrays Prescott's specifically 'American' angle on Spain is what he wrote about the fate of the Moriscoes – a racial, not merely individual, victim of the Inquisition. The decision of the 'imbecile Philip III' to expel the Moriscoes 'must be regarded as one of the principal causes of the subsequent decline of the monarchy'.[28] Prescott then added something of interest for us in light of the debate about immigration in Britain today:

> But it was the mistake of the government that it opened to them no future. Having destroyed their independence as a nation, it should have offered them the rights of citizenship, and raised them to a position of equality with the rest of the community. Such was the policy of ancient Rome towards the nations which she had conquered; and such has been that of our own country towards the countless immigrants who have thronged to our shores from so many distant lands.[29]

Because he was an American, what Prescott had to say about persecution and bigotry in Spain was pitched at a higher key than was the case with those who were seeking to understand Spain from their studies in London and Edinburgh, or in the libraries of Oxford and Cambridge. Prescott represented a new class of American historian, someone whose books constituted a real advance in methodology. Disability meant that he had to sustain a nest of workers who burrowed into the anthill of the Spanish archives carrying crumbs and morsels out into the sun. Yet Prescott himself was by no means passive. Indeed he was open and receptive to much that was new in historical research. Thus there is a progression from what Prescott saw as the proper kind of evidence to be used in *Ferdinand and Isabella* and what had become admissible in *Philip II* of 1855. In the preface to the former, Prescott argued that the literature of Spain could tell its readership about matters of the period besides battles and councils, though no other aspects of cultural studies were allowed at this relatively early stage of his intellectual progress as historian: 'I have devoted a liberal portion of the work to the literary progress of the nation, conceiving this quite as essential a part of its history as civil and military details'.[30] He was as good as his word. Material was included not merely on literature, but upon enlightened cardinals and humanist universities.

What then came to make a difference was the epistolary friendship with Stirling, begun in 1850. Although Prescott was more than twenty years older, he learned more from Stirling than vice-versa. The increasing importance given by Prescott to engravings after portraits and anecdotes about the relationship of patrons to artists was because of the work done in the 1840s by Stirling on Spanish art. Although Prescott did not think to acknowledge his intellectual debt to Stirling, he did offer an apologia for including the street-sweepings of history. This is to be found in the Introduction to *Philip II* of 1855: 'I have endeavoured to present a picture of the intellectual culture and the manners of the people. I have not even refused such aid as could be obtained from the display of pageants and court ceremonies, which, although exhibiting little more than the costume of the time, may serve to bring the outward form of a picturesque age more vividly before the eye of the reader.'[31]

Although there were many finer historical minds than Stirling's, he certainly anticipated Prescott in finding value in what historians hitherto had not noticed. Stirling had been the first to appreciate ephemera as historical evidence and to use it as such: state entries, street traders, costumes, book plates, armorial bearings, fables, frontispieces and emblems, all were considered and some included in his books. This was leaf mould which nurtured root-and-branch issues of politics and religion. Stirling's awareness of the importance of material culture had developed when he had been quite small. As an adolescent he had watched – if not helped – his mother compile scrapbooks, subversive variations on the famous *History of England* published by James Granger in 1769 which had included blank leaves for the insertion of portraits usually cut from other books. Still to be seen at Pollok House near Glasgow, where the remnant of a once great collection is housed, outwardly these appear as portentous as the *Oxford English Dictionary*. Once opened, however, volumes blossom into a riot of such whimsy as to make a Surrealist collage seem like an ordinance survey map: portraits, views of country seats, advertisements, newspaper articles, caricatures, all are jumbled together to undermine the pretensions of the Regency age.

It may be suspected that without the inspiration of Stirling, Prescott would not have written so affectingly about the cause of the death of Charles V in terms reminiscent of how small boys in England used to be helped to remember their kings: they would recall that Henry I had died of a 'surfeit of lampreys', while King Billy had tripped on a molehill. By contrast, Charles V died from looking at Titian:

> He then passed to the contemplation of another picture, – Titian's 'Agony in the Garden', and from this to that immortal production of his pencil, the 'Gloria' as it is called, which is said to have hung over the high altar at Yuste, and which after the emperor's death, followed his remains to the Escorial. He gazed so long and with such rapt attention on the picture as to cause apprehension in his physician, who, in the emperor's debilitated state, feared the effects of such excitement on his nerves. There was good reason for apprehension; for Charles at length, rousing from his reverie, turned to the doctor and complained that he was ill. His pulse showed him to be in a high fever. As the symptoms became more unfavourable, his physician bled him, but without any good effect ... no earthly remedies could avail. It soon became evident that the end was approaching.[32]

Dress, once a neglected aspect of culture, had by this time become important for Prescott as he contrasted the richly-tinted habits of the Spaniards with the solid magnificence of the English and Flemings when describing the marriage ceremony of Philip II and Mary Tudor at Winchester Cathedral in 1554.[33] It was an insidious comparison, for the reader prefers the clothes of the robust northerner to the shallow picturesqueness of the Latins. Prescott asked his reader to believe that Philip II's dress denoted his character, and brilliantly caught the *Zeitgeist* when, with a nice paradox, he described existence at the Escorial as having been 'a life of splendid humiliation'.[34]

But there is a larger paradox at the heart of Prescott's method. He was much more heavily dependent than others on amanuenses. He was a Boston Brahmin whose status in Massachusetts owed as much to social position as any success accruing from his books. If he had not been virtually blind, and thus unable to undertake primary work for himself, research trips to Europe would have been conditioned as much by the East Coast social calendar as by the demands of an unfinished chapter. But Prescott had workers lodged in libraries from Simancas to Vienna, all gathering primary material for his books, and many absorbing the methodological changes then transforming history into an academic discipline. Prescott too was aware of this: in *Philip II* tribute is paid to Ranke's books and to his *Ottoman and Spanish Empires* specifically. But Prescott became hubristic – believing not merely that he was engaged on a 'quest' for Spain, but that he had actually achieved a surer grasp of historical truth than those who had witnessed a living king 'who surrounded himself with a veil of mystery which the most cunning politician could not penetrate'.[35]

There were greater historians in Victorian Britain than Froude, but none offered a better epitome of the public and controversial nature of the discipline (Figure 8). Born in 1818, Froude went up to Oxford in 1836.[36] Together with his gifted brother Hurrell, James was drawn to the exceptional personality of John Henry Newman, then a Fellow of Oriel and now revered in Rome. But the community of like-minded souls, the so-

8 Sir George Reid, *James Anthony Froude*

called 'Oxford Apostles' centred upon the colleges of Oriel and Exeter, was short-lived. The death of Hurrell Froude in 1836, and the parting of friends because of religious differences, helped to direct James toward his great and abiding work, the magisterial: *History of England from the Fall of Cardinal Wolsey to the Defeat of the Spanish Armada.* Conceived in 1854 and laid to rest only in 1870, it appeared at intervals in twelve volumes between 1856 and 1870. Six out of the twelve were devoted to the reign of Elizabeth I. That was a startling imbalance which surely reflected the priorities of an age pleased to see the map of the world turning red – the colour of the British Empire. Imperial greatness was perceived to have sprung from the heroic defiance by Elizabethan seaman of the Spanish colossus. Elizabeth I is immortal. Froude had intended to continue his history up to the end of the Tudor dynasty in 1603, though in the event it finished with the glorious victory of the Armada. There was no point in doing more. Froude had celebrated the glories of a Protestant and a free people. The job was done.

Choices historians make as to what to study is sometimes autobiographical: a subject chosen by which to come to terms with personal conflict. Such was the case with Froude when he embarked on his great epic of the Reformation in England. Froude's examination of the final shipwreck on the Reformation of that 'ruler of almost limitless potential', Henry VIII, and the prevarication of Elizabeth I in the face of religious difficulties, had a bearing on the confusion Froude felt over matters of faith which was a permanent legacy of his broken friendship with Newman. As one perceptive critic of Froude's place in nineteenth-century Oxford put it, 'As Tacitus is supposed to have condemned the government of Domitian through the history of Tiberius, so Froude disputed and opposed the ideas of the Oxford Movement through the history of the Reformation'.[xxxvii] And so it was that in the face of personal uncertainty and painful events conspiring together to ruin a promising academic career in Oxford, Froude made a significant choice in becoming a historian. He settled upon what true-hearted Victorians agreed was the most glorious and ebullient moment in the history of the English nation: the reign of Elizabeth I. Spread by Froude over various books, each one more popular than the last, was the exciting story of a vulnerable woman, an isolated nation and a hostile Europe – all requiring Spain as ante-masque to a final vision of triumph and reconciliation. Of all this, Froude himself once said, when specifically referring to the Armada, 'I shall use my materials badly if I cannot make it as interesting as a novel'.[38] He succeeded beyond his boldest estimation, so well indeed that Lytton Strachey described him as 'one of the salient figures of mid-Victorian England'.

And yet, although Froude's histories gave him a more prominent platform than he could ever have aspired to from a set of college rooms, he came to despise his heroine, bountiful muse and the source of both his wealth and his public acclaim as she had proved to be. In the eyes of Froude, William Cecil supplanted Elizabeth I as the presiding genius of the late Tudor age. But such a change of heart only came in 1870. When Froude had begun his great enterprise in 1854, then he had certainly expressed strong attraction to a woman he liked to call 'our glorious *semper eadem*'. Such an epithet was revealing since the Latin tag – meaning 'Always the Same', Elizabeth's favourite motto – provided a salvational figure much needed by Froude after the tumults of the Oxford Movement. Elizabeth was attractive as he set out to trace her path through the maze of religious conflict because he was seeking insight into his own conflict of religion; by then a decade old but still something which he needed to confront. Failure by Froude to reconcile spiritual anguish had meant that he had abandoned the complacent comforts of an Oxford high table for London and the uncertainties of life as a monthly contributor to *The Westminster Review*. It comes as no surprise, therefore, that when he turned to the writing of history he should have slipped behind the arras of the Tudor Age. After all, the agonies which Froude and his friends had endured in Oxford in the late 1840s about religion had only been surpassed by the tumultuous religious events of the 1540s.

What interest, then, did Spain hold for Froude? He was the closest anyone got in Britain to being a disciple of Ranke, and for one whose work was dedicated to expressing the vitality of England in the age of the Elizabethan seaman, a contrast with consumptive Spain was attractive. Froude's discipleship, together with the character of his subject, conspired to make him the first British historian to work in the Spanish royal archives at Simancas. Often accused of slipshod inaccuracy and always the object of jealous colleagues, Froude rumbled onward as criticism bounced off a shell constructed from his twelve-volume history. Periodically, however, an arrow found its way in and Froude would be stung into attempted refutation of the more intemperate views of fellow historians jealous of his huge popular success. Then Froude would ambush his critics in the recesses of Simancas, inspired by recollection of many hours marooned in that old castle, so described as to evoke Faversham Hall:

> I had to cut my way through a jungle, for no one had opened the road for me. I have been turned into rooms piled to the window sill with bundles of dust-covered despatches, and told to make the best of it. Often I have found the sand glittering on the ink where it had been sprinkled when a page was turned. There the letter had lain, never looked at again since it was read and put away.[39]

Hyperbole was second nature to Froude. He strained to emphasise the privations he had endured as a defence against a growing consensus about his place in Victorian historical studies. This was summarised by one obituary writer who described him as having been hobbled by '[t]he demon of inaccuracy, of mistake, of reckless statement, [which] stayed by him all his life in all that he wrote. His persistent half-avowed disregard of fact was an ingrained, constitutional and unmistakable characteristic of the man.'[40] But such damnation, it should be remembered, was delivered at the end of the nineteenth century when there was still a naive faith that all which was needed was to find the documents, and the facts would tell the story. The rehabilitation of the historical novel which today has gained a new and unlooked-for respectability, may now call for a reappraisal of the achievement of Froude. Perhaps after all, it may come to be believed that Froude was never in Hell but only Purgatory, from which now he can perhaps be delivered. Come what may, it is worth remarking that a distinguished modern assessment of Froude has concluded that '[h]is research descended to a depth never previously envisaged, and there is a sense in which all subsequent work on the Tudors rests on his shoulders'.[41]

To Froude, melodrama was the weft and web of a broad canvas, whether it was employed in self-defence or, more disinterestedly, to sympathise with some of the many victims of a brutal age. Froude was a hugely gifted storyteller whose books were to be found in family parlours where conceptions as to the greatness of England had been formed on the bedrock of the Victorian review. The more Froude wrote, the less he thought of Elizabeth I; though curiously enough, he managed to find some unlikely sympathy for her elder sister Mary. Perhaps the sad queen's winter personality and exhausting devotions appealed to one whose vigorous personality blew like a gale through the airless chambers of Victorian historical research. Froude was what Lytton Strachey called ' a man of letters who was also a man of the world, an accomplished gentleman, whose rich nature overflowed with abundant energy, a sportsman, a yachtsman, a brilliant and magnificent talker'.[42] Public success had succeeded in masking earlier agonies, and Froude of the London club not the college chapel, outwardly now the ebullient English gentleman, perhaps felt honour-bound to rescue a withered and deluded virgin from a husband described in terms more recognisable in a bronze satyr than in a portrait by Antonio Mor. The setting is the Bishop's Palace at Winchester. Froude, with the stroke of a master, exposed the emotions of a vulnerable queen by pretending to let fall the curtain on something altogether too painful to behold. It is the literary equivalent of De La Roche's *Execution of Lady Jane Grey*:

> The queen was at the bishop's palace, but a few hundred yards distant. Philip, doubtless could have endured the postponement of an interview till morning; but Mary could not wait, and the same night he was conducted into the presence of his haggard bride, who now, after a life of misery, believed herself at the open gate of Paradise. Let the curtain fall over the meeting, let it close also over the wedding solemnities which followed with due splendour two days later. There are scenes in life which we regard with pity too deep for words. The unhappy queen, unloved, unlovable, yet with her parched heart thirsting

for affection, was flinging herself upon a breast to which an iceberg was warm; upon a man to whom love was an unmeaning word, except as the most brutal of passions. For a few months she created for herself an atmosphere of unreality. She saw in Philip the ideal of her imagination, and in Philip's feelings the reflex of her own; but the dream passed away – her love for her husband remained; but remained only to be a torture to her. With a broken spirit and bewildered understanding, she turned to Heaven for comfort, and instead of heaven, she saw only the false roof of her creed painted to imitate and shut out the sky.[43]

So much for Kings and Queens. The place of that 'false roof,' as Froude described Spanish Catholicism and indeed the Spanish priest, was something which featured prominently in Chapter 3 of this book. Predictably enough, it was as well a theme which attracted travel writers and historians. Borrow, for example, on a visit to Valladolid much enjoyed a tour of the English College conducted by the affable Rector. It made a deep impression, one which came to be recorded in *The Bible in Spain*, a book which anticipated Froude's engagement with Spain by some ten years:

> Of all the curiosities of this college, the most remarkable is the picture-gallery, which contains neither more nor less than the portraits of a variety of scholars of this house who eventually suffered martyrdom in England, in the exercise of their vocation in the angry times of Edward VI and fierce Elizabeth. Yes, in this very house were many of those pale smiling half-foreign priests educated, who, like stealthy grimalkins, traversed green England in all directions; crept into old halls beneath umbrageous rookeries, fanning the dying embers of Popery, with no other hope nor perhaps wish than to perish disembowelled by the bloody hands of the executioner, amongst the yells of a rabble as bigoted as themselves; priests like Bedingfield and Garnet, and many others who have left a name in English story. Doubtless many a history, only the more wonderful for being true, could be wrought out of the archives of the English Popish seminary at Valladolid.[44]

Borrow was forcibly struck by heroic connections between Spain and English Recusancy. But his readers were no less struck by the power with which he described what Victorians saw as the fanatic country. Ford thought Borrow half crazed, but he was deeply fascinated by and drawn to a man he recognised as *sui generis* among his literary acquaintance. Never one to pay tribute easily, Ford nevertheless paid fulsome tribute to his friend's understanding of the Peninsula. Shortly after the appearance of *The Bible in Spain*, he wrote to the editor of the *Edinburgh Review* in the warmest terms about the man and his book:

> You remember Borrows Gipsies in Spain [*The Zincali*, 1841] for which Merivale tells me he did you that paper: This *strange* Missionary has now and much by my advice, printed *The Bible in Spain*. It will be published on Saturday so Murray writes to me: since the days of *Gil Blas*, nothing in my

mind has been written so passing rare and Spanish: I envy you the reading the book: The matter is prima materia for a *grand article*, and should be done by some one who knows the country and the people therein most graphically drawn. It offers an opening which the Ed: R: peculiarly ought to seize of pointing out as never has been done, some of the philosophy of Spanish fanaticism, and the slavish effect of Popery *which I abhor*. I have written a *protestant and liberal and antigallic paper. I detest the French* ... Lockhart *now* sees Borrow as I do; and is in raptures.[45]

As for Froude and his attitude to the tribe of priests, toward the end of the second volume devoted to the reign of Elizabeth, he examined Philip II himself through the blood-stained glass of the Inquisition. The personality of Philip, and his enthusiasm for purifying the dominions of Spain from the heretic, he so described as to allow generalised claims not only about the inherent nature of the Spaniard as a racial type, but also about the idiosyncratic nature of Spanish Catholicism, *obiter dicta* which in their gratuitousness and audacity are worthy of Ford at his most uninhibited. Froude began by stating that each priest and monk – and we are informed that there were no dissenters – was without mercy in pursuit of the heretic because the God of a Spaniard was himself without mercy. Froude thought of Spanish Catholicism much as he might have regarded 100% proof alcohol – once it was drunk, immediate intoxication of the drinker led to blindness. The baneful effect of Catholicism in Spain he then contrasted with the conditions in that area of Italy under the immediate control of the papacy where art and science flourished within the framework of Machiavellian statesmanship, 'but there was not religion enough to make men care whether their creed was true or false'.[46] So much for Froude's old friend, John Henry Newman.

Froude, like Stirling and Prescott, established early in his preamble to war in the Netherlands a logical corollary between the atmosphere of the Low Countries as the most thriving part of Europe and a sympathetic reception there to the tenets of the Reformation. He then moved on to consider the disastrous intervention of Philip II whose policies were not borne down by the impersonal forces of economics, religion or geography but by the application of a baneful personality – a character presented by Froude as a farrago of contradictions. Perhaps the Victorian reader registered how what was said of Philip's character in one chapter was contradicted in another. If all this went unnoticed, that may have been due to the vigour with which Froude turned his kaleidoscope of highly coloured biographical details which in their mesmeric qualities suggested symmetries which were not actually there. For example, there are difficulties with what was said of Philip in Winchester in July 1554 and what Froude asked us to believe as Philip moved against heretics in June 1567, when the Duke of Alva arrived in the Low Countries to initiate his notorious Council of Blood:

> The most important of the national characteristics were combined in the person of Philip II. The energy, the high-mettled spirit, the humour, the romance, the dash and power of the Spanish character had no place in him. He was slow, hesitating, and in common matters uncertain. If not deficient in personal courage, he was without military taste or military ambition. But he had few vices. During his marriage with Mary Tudor, he indulged it is said, in some forbidden pleasures; but he had no natural desire for such things, and if he did not forsake his faults in this way, he was forsaken by them. He was moderate in his habits, careful, business-like, and usually kind and conciliatory.[47]

Froude characterised the Duke of Alva as an epitome: 'In him the Spain of the sixteenth century found its truest and most complete representative'. The delineation of Alva began 'in colours black as if he had been dipped in the pitch of Cocytus'.[48] Then pain from the old wounds – inflicted by the Oxford Movement and the trauma of abandoning an early vocation as a priest – uncovered in Froude a sublimated undercurrent of cynicism about the absolute truths of religious beliefs. He declared that religious history was partial in its verdicts: the efficacy of religion was contingent upon and compromised by historical circumstances, not to mention the inadequate understanding of humanity. All this Froude reinforced toward the end of a masterly paragraph in which he blocked in the character of Alva, describing the Duke's latter-day crusade when he arrived in Flanders; but then Froude could not resist scandalising the rural deans among his readership. When Alva arrived in Brussels in August 1567 with his 10,000 bent upon the massacre of the innocents, trooping along behind were 2,000 prostitutes, somewhat to their chagrin, themselves under the famous Alva 'military discipline'. Alva was the most representative figure of the Golden Age for Froude, whether sanctity, slaughter or sex was on the agenda: 'careless of pleasure, careless of his life, temperate in his personal habits, without passion, without imagination, with nerves of steel, and with a supreme conviction that the duty of subjects was to obey those who were set over them – such was the famous, or infamous, Duke of Alva'.[49]

It is no coincidence that in Froude's book the scene switched in the twinkling of an eye from the iron commander of Philip II's storm troopers to the pathetic figure of Mary, Queen of Scots. She was shut up in Loch Leven Castle and it was the same month in which Alva set out for the Netherlands to begin his campaign of mass torture and pillage. A Brueghel of lancers in the snow was spirited away to be replaced by a Rossetti of a swan-necked maiden and her swooning attendants. It all helped to make his books best-sellers.

So much for Froude's view of the impact of Spain on the Low Countries. Others held strong opinions too, not least J.L. Motley, the pre-eminent American historian of the Netherlands who identified not with Castile, as was the case with his fellow American Prescott, but with Flanders. Here there was a certain symmetry with the eighteenth century. If fellow Bostonians Prescott and Motley bifurcated Spanish Europe into Spain and Flanders for the Victorians, so the contemporary eighteenth-century Scotsmen William Robertson and Robert Watson had done much the same for their earlier generation. One Principal of Edinburgh University and the other of St Andrews, Robertson had taken the Spain of Charles V while Watson of St Andrews had written two well-received volumes on Flanders. Watson's *History of the Reign of Phillip II* published in two volumes in 1777 was actually nothing of the kind.[50] The reader was immersed in the watery sluices of Gelderland as Watson described the heroic struggle of the Dutch for religious freedom, Spain being almost absent. The book was an apologia for Protestantism written at a time when Scotch Presbyterians, in an ironical twist which one suspects was lost on Watson, were having to face the uncomfortable fact that religious toleration was going to become an urgent and controversial aspect of British public life. That Watson was able to get away with a title which wholly fails to describe the contents of his book is an indication of the extent to which history writing in the Hanoverian period was committed history.

As for Motley writing some eighty years later, he chose to throw Philip II into relief, less by contrasting him with his father than by comparing him with William of Orange, the hero of his *The Rise of the Dutch Republic* (1856). Here a single paragraph separated two sketches which hung as closely together as a pair of portraits. The scene was the hall in Brussels in which Charles V abdicated. A tall handsome youth of twenty-four stepped forward. Motley has told us that whereas Philip had a vast mouth and monstrously protruding lower jaw, William was the fortunate possessor of a cast of features which were dark, well chiselled and symmetrical. His eyes were full, brown, well opened and expressive of profound reflection. By contrast, Philip, though surrounded with counsellors, could have benefited from counselling: 'He looked habitually on the ground when he conversed, was chary of speech, embarrassed, and even suffering in manner.' But as for William, he was quite different. He added a burden of open and direct thought beyond his years to a young and handsome physique, the contrast between lithesome appearance and gravity of perception, the essence of that romantic hero who was to call forth the Dutch nation.

Motley reserved his most powerful invective for Alva, more roundly condemned than anyone else. Alva was unique in having no virtues of any sort and, though narrow in range, his vices were colossal. It was admitted that Alva did not partake of the usual Spanish vices of lust and intemperance, but then this was more than made up for by 'enormous' avarice, stealth, ferocity and 'patient vindictiveness and universal bloodthirstiness' of a type which, in a phrase redolent of the Psalms, was not found even in the beasts of the forest.[51] Having drawn up his index of vice, Motley felt the need to defend himself in case his readership thought he protested too much. At the end he provided an extended footnote where asides were offered on the nature of historical evidence and the process of revisionism before the condemnation of Alva is restated in the light of documentation. Motley cited the importance of the archival material at Simancas as well as the project to publish the most significant part of the eighty volumes of the papers of Cardinal Granvelle which had lain long neglected in St Vincent's Besançon, the home town of Granvelle himself. In 1834 Guizot, then Minister of Public Instruction under Soult as Prime Minister, and distinguished historian in his own right, had ordered that these should be published.[52] This had begun with the appearance of a first volume in 1841. Armed in part with these fresh materials, Motley finished off the man who epitomised all that was most terrible about the Spanish character:

> the character of the Duke of Alva, so far as the Netherlands are concerned, seems almost like a caricature. As a creature of fiction, it would seem grotesque: yet even that hardy, historical scepticism, which delights in reversing the judgement of centuries, and in re-establishing reputations long since degraded to the dust, must find it difficult to alter this man's position ... The publication of the Duke's letters in the correspondence of Simancas and in the Besancon papers, together with ... [the] 'Sententiem van Alva' these in themselves would be a sufficient justification of all the charges ever brought by the most bitter contemporary of Holland and Flanders.[53]

John Lothrop Motley often enjoyed a Havana with Froude. A perfect sitter for Charivari, a writer of sparkling and brilliant letters, Motley had a sharp eye for the weakness of a man which he successfully concealed under a cloak of suave manners, as befitted one of America's most sophisticated mid-century diplomats. Motley was sympathetic, with a generous intelligence and a 'wonderful resemblance' to Byron, all of which doubtless contributed to the decision by the Civil War hero President Grant to send Motley as American Minister to London in 1869, and why indeed, once arrived, Motley was so much in demand with political hostesses. Unfortunately he soon fell victim to in-fighting back in Washington and he was recalled only a year later. Long before a posting to London, however, Motley had travelled extensively in Europe, for he was always a public man who sustained a wide circle of friends. In Paris he had met Guizot and heard Thiers in the Chamber of Deputies. In Frankfort in 1855 he had called on his old friend Bismarck who 'could not have shown more warmth and affectionate delight in seeing me'.[54] It was well-nigh miraculous that Motley composed anything, but he did. Letter-writing seems to have been his release from historical composition and, at the end of May 1858, he sent one of numerous letters to his wife in America. In this Motley suggested the extent to which history and contemporary affairs were intermixed:

Late in the evening I went with Arthur Russell to the Cosmopolitan ... this ... is a club which meets late in the evenings twice a week ... in a large room which is the studio of the painter Phillips, in Charles Street, leading from Berkeley Square. The object seems to be to collect noted people and smoke very bad cigars. This evening I found Mackintosh there, and among other men were Higgins, a gigantic individual who writes in The Times under the name of 'Jacob Omnium', Layard the Ninevite, Stirling, the author of the 'Cloister Life of Charles V', Monckton Milnes, besides other personages connected with literature and politics.[55]

Motley fell into conversation with Stirling, to whom he instinctively warmed as an amiable, scholar-like Member of Parliament and man of fortune. Talk soon settled on mutual interests as Motley learned of Stirling's current writing on Don John of Austria then in gestation. As for Prescott's biography of Philip II, both agreed that 'his Philip was altogether too mild and flattered a portraiture of that odious personage'.[56] Motley was more positive about Froude. He told the Crown Princess of Prussia, herself an enthusiast of the great storyteller, that he was himself a friend of Froude and of how he 'entertained the highest opinion of him as a historian',[57] adding, however, that he had not been converted to Froude's faith in Henry VIII.

But then, what of Motley's faith in Philip II? It can hardly be expected that Motley was to find unlikely heroes in those he conceived of having strained every nerve to destroy the nascent republic of the United Provinces. Motley was fascinated by appearances. He paid minute attention to the faces of both Charles and Philip, alighting on the forehead and then hanging on the lower lip of the Emperor like a fly upon meat. As the eye passes over the fleshly contours of father and son, it is if all that was dark and disastrous about Spain could be predicted by physical deformities so painfully inventoried. Were these most intimate examinations influenced by the mid-Victorian vogue for phrenology then fashionable but long since discredited? In Motley's time those who professed this quack science were asking a credulous public to believe that the psycho-pathology of murder, and by extension, the crime of religious persecution, could be predicted by the size of a man's cranium. Motley described the physical appearance of Charles V when a young Emperor in positively Herculean terms:

'he had been able ... to vanquish the bull with his own hand in the favourite national amusement of Spain'.[58] But then Motley went further by suggesting that what all writers saw as the physical deformities of Philip were genetic defects passed on by a father who had been hardly less deformed. Others had glossed over the unfortunate appearance of Charles V as they manipulated physical traits to the disadvantage of Philip so as to set Charles V in higher relief. But Motley was different. He spared neither. The description of the father summoned up visions of a monstrous arachnid, while to Philip was ascribed all the potential malignancy of a stinging insect. Charles had a heavy and hanging lower lip with a protruding jaw so prominent as to prevent him from bringing the few fragments of his teeth together – Motley told that Charles was unable to speak a whole sentence in an intelligible voice. Philip had thin legs, a narrow chest and the shrinking, timid air of 'an habitual invalid'. Motley insinuated the racial superiority of 'proper men in Flanders and Germany' by reference to Philip's dismay at first meeting specimens of his northern subjects, a frightening experience which induced Philip to try to gain their favour by making unsuccessful forays at the tournament: 'Such was the personal appearance of the man who was about to receive into his single hand the destinies of half the world; whose single will was, for the future, to shape the fortunes of every individual then present, of many millions more in Europe, America, and at the ends of the earth, and of countless millions yet unborn.'[59]

Like an unscrupulous barrister, Motley could make what is accidental seem important. Here, the reader is expected to accede to the idea that because Philip was physically unprepossessing, he was unfit to rule the world. Motley stood apart from his contemporaries in attributing such potency to Philip II. Philip II too was a Hercules, though not the slayer of the Cretan bull like his father, but that other Hercules who carried the world upon his shoulders.

Motley, like Froude, was a master at subverting Catholicism, as he ran straight into a description of the saturnine nature of Philip after stressing the king's neurotic addiction to the confessional. Here Motley made his own contribution to that thickly perfumed aura of royal licentiousness which hung as heavily around the kings of Spain as the liquefied shadow of a Velázquez portrait. In the case of Philip II, the juxtaposition between contrition and concupiscence was well calculated to provoke righteous indignation in a Protestant readership which believed that Catholicism was an international system of hypocrisy, and the confessional a morbid exercise in self-indulgence. Motley was a sufficiently professional historian to cite evidence for his claims. But he was also a fine arranger and by no means averse to 'spin'. In the case of Philip's fondness for the stews of Brussels, a primary source was duly transcribed in the original Italian at the foot of the page. Here then was 'authenticity' for an indictment of Philip's morals and the rotten hypocrisy of the system of religious belief upon which Philip himself relied. But it is the manipulative way in which Motley allowed his reader but a pulse of thought between the confession of sin and its fresh commitment which betrayed the essential hostility felt for the whole system of Spanish Catholicism as it had been sustained by Philip II, its most fervid supporter. There can be no disputing that Philip was lustful just like his father, but it was the artful way in which Motley placed the pallet behind the *prie-dieu* which damns the man and his beliefs. There is something mildly comical as Motley would have the reader believe that Philip got off his knees, climbed out of the window behind his confessor and straight into a carriage waiting to take him to his favourite brothel:

> He consulted his confessor most minutely as to all the actions of life, inquiring anxiously whether this proceeding or that were likely to burthen his conscience. He was grossly licentious. It was his chief amusement to issue forth at night, disguised, that he might indulge in vulgar and miscellaneous incontinence in the common haunts of vice.[60]

There was seen to be a crucial difference between Phillip II and his father. Charles could be vindictive, cruel and bigoted, but some of his Victorian biographers detected a scepticism, even a cynicism, toward the relationship of Church and State which allowed a father to be spared while his son was condemned. Both Stirling and Motley thought they saw in Charles V a streak of doubt which, though suppressed, represented something of a redemption when contrasted with the adamantine certainty of his monstrous son. Thus, although Stirling evidently felt that the final months at Yuste represented a moral disintegration, at one point in *The Cloister Life* Stirling suggested that Charles knew that Protestantism represented the truth, though he could not bear to look:

> He knew the danger, especially for the unlearned, of parleying with heretics who had their quivers full of reasons so apt and so well ordered. Suppose one of their specious arguments had been planted in his soul, how did he know that he could ever have got it rooted out? Thus did a great man misread the spirit of his time; thus did he cling, to the last, to the sophisms of blind guides who taught that gross ignorance was saving faith, and that the heights of spiritual perfection were to be attained only by those who walked with stopped ears and hoodwinked eyes.[61]

In much the same spirit, Motley concluded that the emperor thought more of realpolitik than of the rosary. This, he argued, was the priority of Charles when locked in combat with the formidable Maurice of Saxony for the control of the Empire: 'Charles hated Lutherans but he required soldiers, and he thus helped by his own policy to disseminate what, had he been the fanatic which he perhaps came in retirement, he would have sacrificed his life to crush ... No man, however, could have been more observant of religious rites ... He was too good a politician not to know the value of broad phylacteries and long prayers.'[62]

These ideas were published in the period 1850–1860. The Great Exhibition of 1851 appeared to set the seal on Britain's superiority as the turbine of the world. That exhibition, the votive offering to Victorian material well-being, perhaps gave those who looked to Spain a certain degree of impatience as they contemplated the destruction of all that promise which Prescott was the first to suggest Isabella the Catholic had offered. Here were men from societies who had grown rich through economic diversification looking at Spain which had grown poor through investing in a moribund religion as it had turned its face against the great challenge of building a new world from the wealth of the Americas.

None of our writers was blind to the cruelties and intransigence of Charles V. Philip was demonised, but his father remained something of a hero. Although much of the point of Robertson's magisterial account of the Mediterranean world was how the present connected to the past, there was confusion at the heart of that wonderful account. Robertson excused the defects of Charles V because he was the last representative of a lost world of medieval chivalry. For historians of the Victorian age, Charles V was the son of Philip the Fair but not the father of Philip of Spain, or as those writers really liked to see him, Philip of the Escorial, that fortress for God which was to the nature of the Spanish kingdoms as Milton's description of the realm of Beelezbub in *Paradise Lost*. The contrast between the judgement passed upon Charles and that directed against Philip is another instance of the Protestant discourse about Spain in the nineteenth century. Ironically, given Prescott's commitment to New England Puritanism and his culturally conditioned aversion to Old World deference, the blind man never lived to complete his history of Philip II with an account of the decisive triumph of Protestant seamanship. Accordingly there was never a breathless description of the great fight off Gravelines and of how 'when the west wind came with terrible fury' the *Santa María de Visón* and other galleons were wrecked in Donegal Bay; something which had it been described by Prescott would surely have matched his unforgettable description of Christian and Turk meeting to change the world on a morning of serenely inappropriate beauty in the faraway gulf of Lepanto. But although for an English-speaking readership complacent affirmation of the superiority of Protestant liberties was denied, in some sense such a pleasure was redundant. Charles V is made the hero and Philip the villain of Victorian histories – not, in truth, because the emperor was more tolerant, but because Philip threatened England. Tacitly these historians acknowledged Philip II to have been the most Spanish of monarchs, but he was cast as the villain of Spanish history because he was the monarch who had actively threatened the integrity of the British Isles. A consequence of the first scholarly accounts of Philip II's life which have been the subject of much of this chapter was to reinforce a new specifically Victorian and Edwardian imperialism.

In 1908 a history book for 'boys and girls' appeared, entitled *Our Empire Story*. The cover shows Elizabeth I and Sir Francis Drake, standing at half length and close quarters, heads in strict profile, as the scourge of the Spaniards bends to kiss the hand of 'Gloriana'. Between the two figures, as if it were some tapestry, is a map of South Africa. It is painted 'Imperial red'; the colour of the British empire. South Africa figures prominently because the British had just, with considerable difficulty, defeated the Boers. The foreword starts with the cliché so often applied to Spain: that Edwardian Britain possessed an 'Empire upon which the sun never sets'. At a time when the British empire was beginning to disintegrate, greatness was perceived to have begun with the Armada when Spain had started its own slow decline as an imperial power. But, then, just how differently Imperial Spain might have been handled by those who did not subscribe to Anglo-Saxon cultural values would surely be revealed by a careful scrutiny of French nineteenth-century historians of the Peninsula. That, however, is another book.

Notes

1 Borrow, *Bible in Spain*, p. 177.
2 John Foster Kirk (ed.), *The Complete Works of William Hickling Prescott*, 12 vols (London: Gibbings and Co., 1896), 7, *The History of Charles the Fifth*, 2 vols, 1, p. 369. Hereafter all references to Prescott's published histories are to Kirk's collected edition.
3 William Stirling, *The Cloister Life of the Emperor Charles V* (London: J.W. Parker, 1852), p. 40.
4 Ibid., p. 39.
5 Ibid., p. 268.
6 Ibid., p. 221.
7 Ibid., p. 202.
8 Gayangos to Stirling, 27 May [1856] n.p., MLG T-SK 29/64/3, 'If you should feel inclined to buy the Monasterio de Yuste, it is now for sale. The owner Borja Farrius, wishes to part with it.'
9 Stirling, *Cloister Life*, p. 91.
10 Ibid., p. xiv.
11 Ibid., p. 201.
12 Ibid., p. 34.
13 Ibid., p. 196.
14 Ibid., pp. 211–13.
15 Ibid., p. 159.
16 Ibid., p. 171.
17 Ibid., p. 21.
18 Ibid., p. 107.
19 Henri d'Orléans, Duc d'Aumâle to Stirling, Twickenham, 13 June 1856, MLG T-SK 29/7/242.
20 Disraeli to Stirling, Grosvenor Gate, 7 April 1870, MLG T-SK 29/51/118.
21 Prescott, *The History of Charles V*, 2, p. 636.
22 Prescott, *History of the Reign of Philip II*, 3 vols, 1, p. 380.
23 Ibid., 1, pp. 6 and 56.
24 Ibid., 1, p. 379.
25 Ibid., 1., pp. 380–1.
26 Ibid.,1, pp. 204–5.
27 Ibid., 3, p. 6.
28 Ibid., 3, p. 252.
29 Ibid., 3, p. 251.
30 Prescott, *The History of the Reign of Ferdinand and Isabella The Catholic*, 2 vols, 1, p. ix.
31 Prescott, *Philip II*, 1, p. xii.
32 Ibid., 1, p. 283. Compare how closely this is modelled on the passage in Stirling's *Cloister Life*, p. 196.

33 Ibid., 1, p. 106.
34 Ibid., 3, p. 363.
35 Ibid., 3, p. 355.
36 For Froude as historian see John Kenyon, *The History Men* (London: Weidenfeld & Nicolson, 1983), pp. 115–25.
37 Algernon Cecil, *Six Oxford Thinkers* (London: s.n., 1909), p. 158.
38 Kenyon, *History Men*, p. 121.
39 Ibid., p. 120.
40 Ibid., p. 119.
41 Ibid., p. 123.
42 Ibid., p. 124.
43 James Anthony Froude, *History of England*, 12 vols (London: 1856–1870), (Everyman edn, London: J.M. Dent and Sons Ltd, 1909), *The Reign of Mary Tudor*, p. 143.
44 Borrow, *Bible in Spain*, p. 125.
45 Richard Ford to Macvey Napier, Hevitre, Exeter, 7 December 1842, BL Add. Ms. 34623, fo. 274.
46 Froude, *History: The Reign of Elizabeth*, 5 vols, 2, p. 433.
47 Ibid., 2, p. 436.
48 Ibid., 2, p. 440.
49 Ibid.
50 Robert Watson, *The History of the Reign of Philip the Second, King of Spain*, 2 vols (London: printed for W. Strahan and T. Cadell; and Edinburgh: J. Balfour and W. Creech, 1777).
51 J.L. Motley, *The Rise of the Dutch Republic: A history*, 3 vols (London: J.Chapman,1856), 2, p. 107.
52 For a full account of the revaluation of the Granvelle Papers, see Prescott, *Philip II*, 1, pp. 466–8.
53 Motley, *Rise of the Dutch Republic*, 2, pp. 504–5.
54 Motley to his wife, Frankfort, 27 July 1855, in G.W. Curtis (ed.), *The Correspondence of John Lothrop Motley*, 2 vols (London: John Murray, 1889), 1, p. 174.
55 Same to same, London, 28 May 1858, in ibid., 1, p. 227.
56 Ibid., 1, p. 228.
57 Ibid., 2, p. 105.
58 Motley, *Rise of Dutch Republic*, 1, pp. 116–17.
59 Ibid., 1, p. 104.
60 Ibid., 1, p. 145.
61 Stirling, *Cloister Life*, p. 176.
62 Motley, *Rise of Dutch Republic*, 1, pp. 116–17.

5
The Spanish School

This chapter is concerned less with questions of who bought which pictures and where they came from than with looking at the most interesting art historians who emancipated the 'Spanish School' from it subservient role as an offshoot of Italian art. Until Ford and Stirling published on Spain in the 1840s, the art of the country was seen as a subspecies of the genus of Italian art, its best practitioners defined as good only insofar as they approximated to the great canon of Italian design.[1] Early nineteenth-century catalogues of historic collections contained references to Spanish art certainly, but these were habitually subsumed within a section or chapter entitled 'Italian'. All that began to change from the 1830s, however, and Spanish painting was finally liberated in 1848 with the appearance in that year of William Stirling's three-volume account of Iberian art entitled *Annals of the Artists of Spain*. Much of what follows is concerned with the birth, development and growth into independent adulthood of that 'Spanish School'.

Nevertheless for all the prescience of Stirling, in a critical sense he was behind the times because his style was archaic. Subliminally he saw himself as belonging to the age of Reynolds, not to that of the Great Exhibition.

Long before Stirling started to write on Spain, British commentators had always found it hard to come to terms with the art of a country so profoundly Catholic. Just how difficult this could be is vividly suggested by Sir William Eden. He visited Spain in the summer of 1788, accompanied by his family. By the end of May the party had arrived in Valladolid, ancient capital of Castile and hardly changed since the days of Charles V. Eden found it trying because of the crowds, though it was not the curiosity of the townspeople which upset him so much as the presence of a Church which clung to the city like seaweed to a rock:

> This is an extraordinary place, and gives me melancholy ideas. There [are] above eighty churches in it; and monasteries and nunneries in every street:

and the state of bigotry is in the extreme and as great as it was in England in the time of Queen Mary. The whole people of all ranks and ages appear to have no object or occupation but religious ceremonies:- processions and singing through the streets:- images in almost every corner and people kneeling to them:- The chamber in which I am now writing is almost covered with Pictures wretchedly executed of Martyrdoms; and with images of the Crucifixion of different sizes:- and at the window we here [hear] the people singing in the Convents near to us – – In the Churches there are lists hung up of *Heretics* burnt here by the Inquisition, which in former days exercised great power here and to a very bloody extent: It was impossible to pass thro[ugh] the great square this evening where the executions were without shuddering. We tried to walk out with some of the children: but it is utterly impossible; the people collected around us in a few minutes so as to make it difficult to move and we were forced to return.[2]

A recent historian of Victorian Venice dismissed Spain as a country nobody visited.[3] This is certainly an exaggeration. Lord John Russell, eventually twice Prime Minister, visited Spain three times when young, the Hollands – who 'kept a knife and fork for him at Holland House' – taking him with them in 1807. He returned once in 1810 and then for a third, extended visit in 1812/13. Disraeli, trying to play Lord Byron, wallowed in Andalucía in 1830; Edward VII when Prince of Wales visited Seville; and there was always the intermittent appearance of colourful or wealthy English. The Baroness Rothschild descended upon Cádiz in 1876 and swept off with a Murillo for which she had paid £1200, just when Murillo's critical *fortuna* in England, sustained for two centuries, was at last entering what was to be its long eclipse. Then there was Sir Henry Thompson 'the well known surgeon and cremationist', reported in the autumn of 1876 as being at Granada 'with his daughter who are [both] painting away'.

But for British diplomats during that interlude of optimism one hundred years before this period, despondency beat upon the British embassy as oppressively as the July sun. Although Lord Grantham (ambassador 1771–1779) was affable, talented and popular, particularly enjoying the company of fellow diplomats with a taste for music, there were times when life in Madrid for those who did not have inner resources to fall back on was almost as melancholy as it had been for Sir Charles Cornwallis, who had gone to Madrid after peace had been concluded with Spain at the beginning of the reign of James I. In 1604, Cornwallis sometimes went a whole month without meeting any Englishmen – a state of affairs which had hardly been ameliorated when Grantham first arrived. The problem for Grantham was that Madrid had no 'society' for a young aristocrat bowling along on his Grand Tour. A British visitor could only find a roost in the *sitios* of the diplomatic corps; private palaces were shut up like the tomb. The cloistered nature of the grand houses of Madrid was something Gautier would notice even in 1840 after a period of considerable urban expansion. Some sixty years before, Grantham would sometimes pine for company only to find thereafter that what he got he did not care for. This he explained to an old family friend: 'I have passed some agre[e]able Days lately, with some Travellers of a good sort which is not always the case when an Englishman comes into Spain. He is often some queer body, who has nowhere else to go to, or who travels because he has no home, whom I know nothing of and yet by our way of life am saddled with him all day.'[4]

Here Grantham was confiding to the mother of a young visitor who was to prove utterly different. This was Thomas Pelham, 2nd Earl of Chichester (1756–1826), who in 1801 would serve briefly as Home Secretary in the Addington ministry. At an earlier stage, he had had a hand in moments of high drama, opening proceedings in the impeachment of Warren Hastings in 1787, and in 1791 entrusted with letters from the British government to Barnave and Lafayette, appealing for the life of the French king and queen. Before then and to polish studies at Peterhouse, Cambridge, Pelham had gained an experience of Spain, as unique for the length of time spent in the Peninsula as it proved to be for the distinction of his *ciceroni*. The Pelhams and Grantham's family, the Robinsons, had long been friends. Grantham had interested Pelham in coming out by explaining how he and his brother 'Fritz' or Frederick, were about to read *Don Quixote* together:

> I cannot furnish you with the least article of amusement from hence, you may be assured that your life at Cambridge is checkered with more variety than ours. We are much at home in the Evening, and shall very soon begin to read *Don Quixote* together, Fritz has already read it, but proposed this scheme to me, which I approve of highly. I am convinced I had to understand or at least to taste that Book, one must have seen this country. *Gilblas* which is exceedingly clever is by no means so Spanish.[5]

By December Pelham had arrived; met at the Escorial by Grantham riding out from Madrid. Pelham could hardly have been in better hands; Grantham was quite exceptional for his receptivity to Spanish art among the British in the eighteenth century. Grantham had long been friends with Anton Raphael Mengs and he had developed an unusual passion for Velázquez whose works he was then cataloguing. This Grantham did in the most ambitious possible way. He engaged the services of what he described as the mad German artist, Wenceslaus Pohl (or Pahl), to copy the royal portraits in Madrid. He then planned to use Goya's services as an etcher to illustrate what was to have been a *catalogue raisonné*.[6] Nothing seems to have come of all this and, though it appears that Grantham got quite far, what were presumably his notes have not materialised. However, because of his enthusiasm for Velázquez, Grantham has the distinction of being the first Englishman to have noticed Goya.

Pelham was warmly welcomed into the ambassadorial entourage, becoming extremely close both to Grantham and his unmarried brother Fritz. Pelham went to Aranjuez where he was fortunate to find the king away shooting woodcock and so could see superb pictures in the royal bedchamber, while when in Madrid he was tutored by Grantham in the rules of architecture: 'I have begun S^r W[illiam] Chambers's Book on Architecture with Lord Grantham and hope to make sufficient progress for giving plans of buildings when I return to England as by that time I suppose my Father will be at a loss for improvements; unless as Master of the Wardrobe he new furnishes the King's Palaces'.[7]

By February 1776 Pelham was able to take advantage of a critical contact Grantham had been able to arrange. Antonio Ponz, the great Spanish art historian, became his language tutor. Together in Madrid they visited the pictures in Sacchetti's *Palacio Real*, substantially completed by Charles III in 1764. By high summer, Pelham was ready to undertake a tour of the south, en route for Italy. For this, the travel writer Henry Swinburne was recruited: 'I have enquired of Sr Thomas Gascoigne and Mr Swinburn about Spain. They have left me their plan of their Tour with an account of all the places and things worth seeing, from which we calculate that I shall be near two months going through it'.[8] But then Pelham did not leave Madrid until after a visit to the *Buen Retiro* with Mengs, who dominated art at the court of Charles III as Velázquez had done that of Philip IV. Saying farewell to Grantham, whose kindness and support had been untiring, Pelham set off for Italy, promising Ponz to keep up his Spanish. From Málaga Ponz advised about who and what to see in Andalucía.[9] Of this Pelham told his mother:

> I began *Don Quixote* in Spanish from which I expect great Pleasure, the Inns we stop at being the same as those in which he met with so many Adventures: ... in our way hither we saw the Puerte Lapeche where *Don Quixote* was knighted, but had not time to stay and Receive that Honour tho' Mr Waddilove on his Horse and I on my mule were from our Appearance, inceptors in knight errantry. I have just now been interrupted by a party of Gipseys who attend the Inns and posadas of the South of Spain and entertain Travellers with Fandangos and Sequidillas etc.[10]

Waddilove, in Madrid as chaplain to the embassy, was the same Robert Waddilove whom we first met helping Robertson with his *Charles V*. But when free from acting as a research assistant to the Scottish historian, Waddilove was a keen amateur of painting who liked to scour the markets of Madrid in search of a bargain. In La Mancha, however, the cleric was guarding the morals of a young Cambridge graduate who had recruited him for just such a purpose. Pelham had prissily told his mother that it had been a necessary precaution, 'on account of the indifferent Company we shall meet in the Sea ports particularly ladies and Gibraltar where there is much drinking, which I think Mr Waddilove's profession and age will greatly assist me in avoiding'.[11]

Pelham made no distinction between the cultures of Spain and Italy, where he was commissioned by Grantham to help him pursue a particular passion. This was to amass as full a collection of Velázquez copies as possible. These were in lieu of originals which were not for sale. Grantham now trusted the judgement of Pelham – as well he might, since his erstwhile guest could not have had better tutors than Ponz, Mengs and Swinburne:

> My copies from Velasquez have succeeded so well, that I am quite eager about his works, and am making a catalogue of them to which I mean to add a short account of his life, and some observations on his style. I do not promise that it shall be printed as I have neither wit, nor press, nor Strawberry Hill. You are to assist me in my researches, and I will in due time send you a note of directions. In ye first place, you must find out if there [are] any at Turin. The collection in ye Palace is fine.[12]

Grantham pursued Pelham with requests for Velázquez while his protégé established himself at Rome, dining with Mengs twice weekly at the Spanish embassy and dealing with James Byres who in turn dealt in pictures for the Grand Tourist. Pelham also took a long hard look at Gavin Hamilton, whose indolence did not impress him. He told his father what he thought of the Scottish Neo-classical master: 'Mr Hamilton dined with me yesterday, and as you may think made many Enquiries after you. He has just finished a Portrait of [the] Duke of Hamilton with Mr More who travelled with him in Italy, He has been very Indolent for some years, but seems to be willing to return to paint with more Ardour than he had before.'[13]

Meanwhile, Grantham was shooting off long letters about the state of the arts and the temperature of the court as it moved from one residence to another. No notice is made of the young Goya, but what was wrongly taken for years to have been one of his more scandalous subjects, the duquesa de Alba – the supposed sitter for the *Naked Maya* – does appear to have raised an eyebrow: 'The little Duch^{ss} of Alva I fear gives her friends much trouble, and is likely to be very wild'.[14] When not distracted by coquettes, Grantham took a quieter interest in the growing confidence of Pelham as critic, patron and connoisseur. Perhaps he flattered his protégé when he told Pelham that the Spanish ambassador's civilities would be very useful and how in time he himself would be 'proud to pick up from you, the good instructions and observations which you will hear from Mengs, with his usual sagacity'.[15]

The creative friendship between Grantham and Pelham has a certain poignancy in the longer perspective. For Pelham there seems to have been little distinction between the treasures of the Escorial and the temples of Rome. One followed the other. So too, but for the accidents of history, the British tourist might have oscillated between Bourbon Madrid and Bourbon Naples. But then Napoleon's armies marched into Spain, and decades of chaos ensued. Grantham was certainly not the only British ambassador of the eighteenth century to develop a profound respect for Spanish culture: Sir Benjamin Keene was also a great enthusiast. But Grantham alone thought to present a picture to the Escorial. As for Pelham, no one after the French invasion would again be able to receive the kind of induction to Spain which he had enjoyed. Pelham had had an unusually long stay in the country when it was under the beneficent rule of the enlightened Charles III, during which time life looked promising in ways which had not been the case since the days of Ferdinand and Isabella. Instead, violence and bloodshed meant that neither for the grand tourist nor the later railway traveller was Spain to mean what it might have done.[16]

Nevertheless, Spain remained a subject of sustained interest. The presence in London of Carlyle's exiles was decisive to a growing awareness of the place of early modern Spain for European literature.[17] Spanish Liberals gravitated to Holland House, the most prominent of the great Whig salons of the Regency period. There, Golden Age literature was much discussed while the libraries of some of those who enjoyed Lord Holland's hospitality were concurrently sold at auction to stave off penury. By the time exiles returned to Spain, following the death of the reactionary Ferdinand VII in 1833, there existed important holdings of Spanish literature divided between collections in London and Edinburgh.[18] Educated people were ready for Spain. Besides the new interest in literature and the arts, historic sympathy had been felt since British expeditionary forces had first landed in the Peninsula in 1808. But most people stayed firmly at home and only travelled to Spain in front of their library fire, in response to the endemic political instability and inept government which were characteristics of the country throughout most of the nineteenth century. For the tourist, then, it was something of a miracle that by 1860 Spain had railways, though it was a system hardly calculated to induce access, since in defiance of the rest of Europe the country had adopted a broad gauge which effectively precluded through trains from France and Italy. Had there not been all these difficulties, however, there would surely have been a well-worn track from Madrid to Granada. The middle classes would have been shepherded on to the railways by Thomas Cook and armed with Richard Ford's *Handbook for Travellers in Spain*, the most interesting and distinguished Victorian guidebook to any European country. Despite all impediments there remained a special affinity between the two countries and in the field of painting, a curiosity as to the nature of a school whose right to a life independent of Italy was first recognised by the Victorians.

British collectors of the eighteenth century favoured Murillo, and it is not hard to see why. The artist was the most receptive of Golden Age painters, susceptible not only to Italians, for whom the English had a warm appreciation, but influenced by Flemish and Dutch art. Murillo was as near to an Italian as it was possible to find in Spain, and his pictures could often look more Italian than Spanish. A seductive technique and warm palette, at the service of an emotionalism bordering on the sentimental, suggested a combination of all that was best in Titian, Correggio and the North Italian schools. Murillo's powers of gentle persuasion – what his first English biographer described as his 'delicacy and moderation' – paralleled a transformation within the mainstream of European Catholic education from the rigours of St Ignatius' *Spiritual Exercises* (1548) to the accommodations of Fénelon's *Explication des maximes* (1697). Murillo's meekness allowed Anglicans to overlook an obvious if regrettable devotion to Catholicism. Just how 'reasonable' Murillo was thought to be by Anglicans is suggested by the response of the periodical *The Athenaeum* to the celebrated painting of *St Thomas of Villanueva Giving Alms*. The reader might have been forgiven for assuming that the art critic who was here responding so favourably to a work extolling the virtues of charity had in fact been describing Murillo's famous *Flower Girl* now at Dulwich. Curiously, the writer felt the *St Thomas* exuded a 'gipsy air of enjoyment from an eternal summer life and thoughtlessness about the morrow'.[19]

Murillo's sub-genre of 'fancy pictures', his images of street children, had an especial appeal because of their eclecticism. Current orthodoxy recognises that, toward the end of his career, Murillo was interested in Rembrandt and his followers, some of whose works were in Seville by the 1660s. Murillo's late awareness of Netherlandish art was a response to Dutch patrons in Seville. Dutch and Flemish art appealed strongly to eighteenth-century British taste, and it was easy to respond to Murillo who assimilated these schools.

The first English biographer of Murillo makes an improbable art historian, while his book offers an account markedly different from current attempts to understand the artist. Edward Davies, 'Late Captain in the First Regiment of Life Guards', published his biography of Murillo in 1819, having got to know the oeuvre – or what was left of it – in Spain during the Peninsular War. For Davies, if a man could appreciate Van Dyck it was easy enough to extend that sympathy to Murillo, since Van Dyck was one of the best-represented painters in England at a time when not only was Murillo more popular than any other Spanish painter, but he was also more sought-after in Britain than most Italians. Davies argues for a congruity between Murillo and Van Dyck – Murillo's *Death of Santa Clara* appeared as if 'touched by the hand of Van Dyck'. He was fascinated by apparent sympathy between the two. He digressed as to how the females of the *Santa Clara* 'possess all the grace, delicacy, elegance, and attraction' of a copy of a Van Dyck by the fashionable Regency portraitist, Sir William Beechey.[20] Some of Murillo's most important works are also approved by Davies because they look like Van Dycks: the figure of St

Elizabeth of Hungary from the Hospital of the Caridad in Seville, for example, 'appears as if painted by Van Dyck',[21] and the *Don Justino Neve* is praised 'for the pains with which he executed it ... for it might be taken for Vandyck, whose tints and colour he imitates perfectly'.[22] A Murillo Virgin could fit snugly enough between blowsy ladies of the bedchamber by Van Dyck on the walls of a Georgian gallery. Davies was proud to become the 'apologist of so great a man' as he described Murillo, going on to claim that a notion of his powers 'can be formed by those only who have seen his paintings in Andalusia'.[23] He was less concerned with coming to terms with the Spanishness of Murillo's art than with those occasions when Murillo could be mistaken for another – for Van Dyck, an artist admired by the Regency connoisseur as much for what he had done to immortalise a period of English history as for any alchemy he may have worked with his brush.

Part of the appeal of Murillo was what made his work look un-Spanish, but other aspects served to reinforce his attractions. Murillo was unusual for a Spaniard in using drawings extensively. Such preparation appealed to the British connoisseur, pre-eminent as he then was in Europe as collector of old-master drawings. In the 'fancy pictures' there is evidence of Titianesque loose brushwork stiffened by skilful use of drawing in anatomy and foreshortening. By combining painterly technique with command of line, Murillo seemed to offer something for everyone. It comes as no surprise therefore to find that Murillo, the last of the great painters of the Golden Age, should have been the first to find space on the walls of the English interior.[24] Yet Murillo's attractiveness is not something that can be explained simply by what a collector might make of his technique. His appeal was never narrowly confined. For eighteenth-century British eyes there was something in Murillo which anticipated sentiments later found in Wordsworth's *Lyrical Ballads* of 1798. Poet and painter exploited fundamental contradictions which demanded willing suspense of disbelief. They offered pre-lapsarian innocence which glossed over a reality of disease, squalor and misery – a quality one reviewer described as Murillo's 'sunburnt squalidity'. The boy with teeth as white as china in Murillo's *Invitation to a Game of Argolla*, is the equivalent of the 'little cottage Girl' with curly hair and fair eyes, interrogated by Wordsworth in '*We are Seven*'. Wordsworth stresses the same combination of rude health, ragged dress and simple fare taken under the skies as is used to mawkish affect by Murillo. Wordsworth's poem provides a striking parallel to Murillo's most celebrated image of innocence, his *Spring as a Flower Girl*, which was acquired in 1795 for what would later become the Dulwich College Picture Gallery. Three years later Wordsworth published *We are Seven*, which establishes the congruity:

I met a little cottage Girl:
She was eight years old, she said;
Her hair was thick with many a curl
That clustered round her head.

She had a rustic woodland air,
And she was wildly clad:
Her eyes were fair, and very fair
Her beauty made me glad

[Then did the little Maid reply]

My stockings there I often knit,
My kerchief there I hem;
And there upon the ground I sit,

And sing a song to them.
And often after sun-set, Sir,
When it is light and fair,
I take my little porringer,
And eat my supper there.'[25]

With Zurbarán, the story was different. Zurbarán was a challenging artist for British taste. It is something of a surprise to discover that the earliest and one of the most important group of Zurbaráns to find its way outside the Spanish empire, *Jacob and his Twelve Sons* (thirteen separate paintings) came to Britain as early as the 1720s. The group was the only significant holding of Zurbaráns for generations. They were brought around 1726 by Sir William Chapman, a director of the South Sea Company, and consisted of a series of 'portraits' representing the patriarch and his children from whom the twelve tribes of Israel descended. Each figure is shown life-size; some with an awkward stilted appearance faintly reminiscent of puppets. Heroic physiques are decorated with spectacularly coloured draperies roped with fine jewels, curious hybrid images which create an uneasy fusion between Meissen *commedia dell'arte* figures and the prophets of Michelangelo. The emphasis which Zurbarán gives to the colour and idiosyncratic costume, amounting to a kind of ethnicity, points to a strong element of the bizarre. It is intriguing that this striking series by a leading artist of the Golden Age came to rest in the palace of an English bishop.

Jacob and the Twelve Tribes were acquired in 1756 by Richard Trevor, Bishop of Durham, from the estate of the Jewish merchant Benjamin Mendez. Trevor hung them in his palace at Bishop Auckland. Today the Zurbaráns are considered among the most important Spanish pictures in Britain. But Trevor almost certainly viewed them differently. He had played a notable role in removing some of the disabilities which had impeded British Jewry, and this may have been why the Zurbaráns came to be in an episcopal palace in Protestant Britain.[26] He had bought them after the death of Mendez, a Jew who had naturally identified with them. The presence of these remarkable pictures in County Durham was, therefore, almost certainly not an expression of enlightened taste, for no one else in Britain had paid any attention to Zurbarán.

It may seem improbable that Trevor could possibly have regarded his pictures as 'portraits', but such a view was bound up with a literalist interpretation of the Bible. It was part of the mindset of a pre Darwinian bishop. James Ussher, the Restoration archbishop of Armagh, had calculated that the earth was created at 6.00 p.m. on 23 October 4004 BC, something which was taken seriously by rational theologians for generations afterward.[27] Such credulity was little different from that manifest by the great Italian humanist Paolo Giovio whose villa near Lake Como was full of 'portraits' of *uomini illustri* like Julius Caesar and Plutarch.[28]

If the first holding of Zurbaráns owed as much to racial toleration as to antiquarian pedantry, the artist came to be annexed by the Romantics. The acquisition by the National Gallery in 1853 of one of Zurbarán's most inquisitorial pictures was an exciting but controversial move which provoked a spirited correspondence in *The Times*, pro and con. Richard Ford had always been somewhat equivocal about Zurbarán, but after his death his views were resurrected and changed. Sir Austen Henry Layard, the Middle-East explorer and ambassador to Madrid (1870–1877), was commissioned by John Murray to rewrite Ford for a revised edition of the *Handbook*. Layard made Ford much more critical about Zurbarán, but then Layard had none of Ford's refinement and subtlety. In Layard's revised 1882 (6th) edition of the *Handbook*, Zurbarán is declared to be 'characteristic of Spanish bigotry and the Inquisition'. Layard, now using Ford as a ventriloquist's dummy, has Ford concede the merits of the most ambitious of Zurbarán's paintings, the celebrated *Apotheosis of St Thomas Aquinas* (Seville), but thereafter damning him with faint praise. Ford is made to declare that Zurbarán was too sombre in his colouring, while 'a few figures of female saints prove that he was not insensible to grace of form and beauty of colour'; nevertheless, he was 'usually mannered, and without dignity'.[29]

By contrast to the massive presence of Spanish art in Paris, there was very little understanding of Spanish painting in mid-century London. It was not until the late 1840s that The British Museum acquired its first etchings by Goya. The story was much the same at the National Gallery. There were remarkably few Spanish paintings at Trafalgar Square until the 1860s and 1870s, and no Goya until 1896 when several were acquired simultaneously. Failure to buy even representative pictures of the Golden Age – let alone works of later periods – comes as something of a surprise, since Sir Charles Eastlake, the first director of the National Gallery, was a close friend of Stirling whose *Annals* was the first synoptic account of Spanish art.[30] The *Annals* had received critical approval by the time

Eastlake became Director of the National Gallery in 1855. Yet Eastlake remained indifferent, his most progressive contribution to the Gallery being his inspired purchases of notable early Italian panel pictures. Eastlake may have neglected Spanish art, but Stirling certainly did not. Stirling makes clear at the very start of what turns out to be the *Annal's* 1,400 pages that portraiture is the pre-eminent genre of painting; just as it was the particular province of the best painters in Spain. For Stirling, portraiture was

> the most useful and valuable department of painting, which lightens the labour and points the tale of the historian and the biographer, embalms beyond the arts of Egypt, and gives to beauty centuries instead of years of triumph – the Spaniard obtained a proud eminence. All the greatest painters of Spain have produced admirable portraits.[31]

This was predictable in one whose major works of political history were biographies – case studies of those whose likenesses Stirling fondly thought had been recorded. What was rather more unusual, however, was the real appreciation Stirling showed for Spanish sculpture, then entirely unknown in Britain. Although that enthusiasm was singular, Stirling's appreciation stemmed from the importance placed throughout the *Annals* on milieu. Stirling passionately believed in context, and no branch of the arts in Spain survived so well as its idiosyncratic polychrome sculpture. Drawn to art which had had a physical provenance, not just a previous owner, he was attracted to cycles depicting the life of a saint because the panels might have come from some monastery famous in Spanish history. Spanish art came alive for Stirling in context. Stirling felt uneasy visiting a gallery, just as nowadays so many find a zoo oppressive. For him art needed the right environment in which things could 'live and move and have its being', to use Stirling's own echo of a sacred text. The effect of site was movingly conveyed when Stirling described work of the important Spanish art theorist and painter Carducho:

> Like many other trophies of Spanish art, these fine works of Carducho have lost much of their significance by removal from the spot for which they were painted. Hung on the crowded walls of an ill-ordered museum, his Carthusian histories can never again speak to the heart and the fancy as they once spoke, in the lonely cloister of Paular, where the silence was broken only by the breeze, as it moaned through the overhanging pine forest, by the tinkling bell or the choral chant of the chapel, or by the stealing tread of some mute and white-stoled monk, the brother and the heir of the holy men of old, whose good deeds and sufferings and triumphs were there commemorated on canvas. There, to many generations of recluses, vowed to perpetual silence and solitude, these pictures had been companions; to them the painted saints and martyrs had become friends; and the benign virgins were the sole objects within these melancholy walls to remind them of the existence of woman. In the *Chartreuse*, therefore, absurdities were veiled, or criticism awed, by the

venerable genius of the place; while in the Museum, the monstrous legend and extravagant picture, stripped of every illusion, are coolly judged of on their own merits as works of skill and imagination.[32]

Stirling's admiration for the painted sculpture of Spain represented a bold departure from the Regency world of Apollo and the anthemion. By the 1840s, taste in Britain had extended far beyond Greece and Rome to include Islamic, Chinese art even. However, the profoundly Catholic renderings of Christ on the *via dolorosa*, such as can still induce a shudder when looking at a Pedro Roldán, were the things Stirling felt most Spanish, most in need of discovery. Writing of the museum in Valladolid, Stirling makes a bold claim indeed when pointing out that Berruguete, Juan de Juni and Hernández, were sculptors whose 'statues of painted wood rival in life and spirit the marbles of Greece – [here they] must be studied; they are the tutelars of the place.'[33] Stirling's taste for sculpture was broad and generous, his appreciation no less profound than for Golden Age painters. Such sympathies, still unusual today, were precocious then:

> The Silos of Burgos, father and son, were likewise excellent sculptors and architects. Gil, the first is chiefly known for his stately tombs of King Juan II, and the Infant Don Alonso, erected in the Chartreuse of Miraflores, by orders of Queen Isabella, in which the most fantastic imagination has found hands to work its wildest will, and alabaster has been moulded like clay, or trained and twined like the green osier, and where the Gothic genius of Spain flashed with dying splendour.[34]

The *Annals* are exceptional too for their emphasis on patronage and collecting. As Stirling was writing, the German art historian Gustav Waagen was touring British country houses gathering material for his monumental inventories.[35] But Waagen did not see art and politics like recto and verso. By contrast, Stirling was the first to understand their indivisibility. Such was the importance Stirling attributed to the taste for art of the Austrian Habsburgs, he suggested it all had adverse effects: it beggared the exchequer as it distracted the king. The priority Stirling gave to art as an element of policy was progressive and precocious for its time – not until the late twentieth century have historians done the same thing for Charles I of England. We are told by Stirling that the acquisition of works of art 'was the chief pleasure of Philip IV', just as it was the only business in which he displayed earnestness and constancy. Much has been made recently of Philip IV as the pre-eminent royal collector in early modern Europe.[36] None of this is new, since Stirling said it all back in 1848:

> Rich as were the galleries of Philip II, his grandson must, at the least, have doubled the number and value of their contents. His viceroys and ambassa-

dors, besides their daily duties of fiscal extortion and diplomatic intrigue, were required to buy up, at any price, all fine works of art that came into the market. He likewise employed agents of inferior rank, and more trustworthy taste, of whom Velasquez was one, to travel abroad for the same purpose, to cull the fairest flowers of the modern studios, and to procure good copies of those ancient pictures and statues which money could not purchase. The gold of Mexico and Peru was freely bartered for the artistic treasures of Italy and Flanders. The King of Spain was a collector with whom it was vain to compete, and in the prices which he paid for the gems of painting and sculpture, if in nothing else, he was in advance of his age.[37]

It may be significant that it was while Eastlake's career at the National Gallery was temporarily interrupted that the Gallery was to acquire the single most famous Spanish painting of nineteenth-century Europe, a picture which had epitomised for the French Romantics the horror of Spanish Catholicism. This was the *St Francis in Meditation* painted by Zurbarán *c.*1637 – before, that was, the artist had been forced to temper his austerity with the softer face of Catholicism which Murillo had offered Seville from the mid-1640s. Of the 446 paintings which had constituted *Le Musée espagnol* in 1838, the National Gallery's *St Francis in Meditation* had caused most interest. Thus its acquisition for London at the Louis-Philippe sale in 1853 had been a considerable coup. In France the *St Francis* had always provoked an impassioned polemical response. Théophile Gautier, the most brilliant of the French art critics, was deeply drawn to a fundamental contradiction between the ambience of the cold and silent cloister evoked by the brooding shadow of the background and the waxen corruptibility of the figure. The almost intolerable physical presence is insisted upon by dirty nails, flesh as yellow as a church candle, and a open wound of a mouth surrounded with a halo of stubble anticipating the panic of a Francis Bacon.

Romanticism never had the hold in Britain that it had possessed in France. Thus, although the purchase of the *St Francis* provoked a furious controversy, the argument was not to do with what the picture might say about the nature of extremism, the tension between flesh and immortality, or how Zurbarán represented the character of the Spanish nation, all of which had exercised French critics. Rather, in London, problems centred on the formal impression the canvas made. The strongest criticism came from William Coningham, a left-wing MP for Brighton and discerning collector who showed an unusual taste at that time for Mantegna; he owned the *Agony in the Garden*, today in the London National Gallery. In the space of seven or eight years, Coningham had built up one of the finest collections in Europe only to sell it a few years later.[38] Such a dramatic and unexpected dispersal was the result of a severe illness which created another reversal – it prevented him going with Ford and Stirling to Spain.[xxxix] That invitation may well have been extended because Ford thought Coningham something of an expert on Spanish art. If so, this may explain why Coningham decided to take on The National Gallery over what he claimed to be a deplorable acquisition in a rebarbative letter to *The Times*.

In Britain as in France, the fanaticism of Zurbarán was understood but at the wholesale neglect of his serene religiosity, something which is seen today as more characteristic. Zurbarán's quiet piety was well epitomised in the narrative histories painted at the celebrated royal house of St Jerónimo at Guadalupe, which for our generation has been singled out as a site of singular importance to the understanding of the painter. These histories depicted didactic works of charity, created for the edification of the brotherhood. But although Guadalupe had been to the Spanish crown what the shrine of St Augustine at Canterbury had represented for the British monarchy – in the words of Ford it had 'once [been] the richest and most venerated convent in Spain' – the royal monastery was rarely visited by foreigners during the nineteenth century. Neither Zurbarán's powers of narrative nor his limpid quietism, curiously reminiscent of Fra Angelico, was appreciated by the Victorians. But his love of picturesque vernacular costume certainly was.

Both British and French commentators wrote about the filth and colour of the country. They were fascinated by regional costume. If travellers made sketches, and few did, they favoured ethnic dress. These amateur artists would make bright watercolours of an embroidered jacket or skirt, but often with no comment on the church or the Moorish arch which served as a frame for their *tableaux vivants*. Zurbarán had often clothed St Margaret or St Catherine in contemporary costume to update the witness of the saints for a provincial Spanish city. That had served the purposes of the Counter-Reformation, but by the nineteenth century these eccentric-looking paintings had quite other attractions for British collectors, for whom Zurbarán's virgins recalled the beauty of Spanish women and the picturesque romance of their equipage.

Nevertheless, Zurbarán remained the poet of 'cold and silent cloisters'. Twenty years before the notorious *St Francis* had reached Trafalgar Square, Richard Ford had returned from Spain in 1833 with a Zurbarán of *St Serapion* (Wadsworth Atheneum) as part of a small but distinguished collection largely dispersed within five years. In the painting, Serapion is presented full-frontal in serene acceptance of death. The body of what is hardly more than an adolescent is suspended from the wrists into which heavy ropes cut as the corpse rests against a wall. Details are depicted with a hyper-realism which would make Salvador Dalí warm to Zurbarán as Manet had to Velázquez. The *St Serapion* was kept in Ford's house in Mayfair, but had it been in a public collection, it would have provoked as much of a *frisson* as the *St Francis*. It was either another version of the *St Serapion* or some other icon to a tortured faith by Zurbarán which surely inspired homage to a dead Republican hero of the Spanish Civil War. Between Zurbarán's painting of 1636 and Xavier Bueno's commemoration of a Republican martyr killed in the defence of Madrid in 1938 (Musée Goya, Castres), little has changed beyond the substitution of a rifle for a rosary.

Eighteenth-century sensibilities had found it easy to accommodate Murillo, though it was only in the nineteenth that Zurbarán began to be noticed in Britain. However, there were other major Golden Age painters whose reception in Britain remains to be assessed. Of these, one who attracted much critical attention was Jusepe Ribera, or, 'Lo Spagnoletto', so called because he spent his working life in Naples. If Murillo looked like an Italian though he was not, how then did people respond to Ribera, professionally speaking wholly Italian but, paradoxically, a painter whose work looked more Spanish than that of Murillo? Stirling entered appreciative comments about Ribera in his Italian Diaries but it was Francis Napier, a fellow Scot and close friend of Stirling's, who made of Ribera a special study.

Francis 10th Lord Napier of Merchiston (1819–1898) had a hugely successful career as a diplomat. He was ambassador first to St Petersburg and then to Berlin, British envoy to the Unites States, six years governor of Madras, from where he corresponded with his old friend Florence Nightingale, whom he had known since their Crimea days when Napier had been secretary to the embassy in Constantinople. She told him how best to relieve famine and improve hygiene. In 1872 Napier became Viceroy, between the assassination of Mayo and the arrival of Northbrook, a post in which most felt he should have been confirmed, but it did not happen. He returned to Britain and a glittering diplomatic career was over. In his native Scotland Gladstone asked him what to do with the crofters.

Napier's first posting to Naples back in 1846 had developed his eye for painting. As a keen student he admired the *Annals*, but he had his reservations. Perhaps it was because he and Stirling had been at university together that Napier felt he could be so disarmingly frank, though he always had the capacity of the well-bred for rudeness. Napier had no scruples about telling the author just how irritating he found aspects of his book. These centred on what Napier considered to be the sycophantic way in which Stirling had referred to Ford, whose *Handbook* (1845) had become the accepted authority on Spain by the time the *Annals* had appeared in 1848. It was when Napier was telling Stirling what he thought of the Scotch antiquary James Dennistoun's *Memoirs of the Dukes of Urbino* (1851) that he went on to disburden himself in robust terms:

> Dennistoun's zeal is not so sentimental and vaporous as Lord Lindsay's, who in my poor judgement is the worst writer on Art I know, except Ruskin, and whom Dennistoun raises to the skies. This reflection leads me on to one on

yourself. I have been reading over a great deal of your book and you offend me by repeated compliments to Mr Ford. It almost amounts to adulation. Surely one or two favourable notices of the Handbook would have been sufficient. But you pursue him with a fire of pretty phrases from beginning to end.[40]

Despite such grapeshot the two remained friends. They had much in common, not least a shared enthusiasm for Ribera. In Napier's case this developed as a result of his appointment in July 1846 as Secretary of the Legation in Naples. It was a posting which opened Napier's eyes to Ribera, who had been the dominant artistic presence in the city two centuries before. Napier had started a diplomatic career under Palmerston, whose belief in the merits of gun boat diplomacy may have encouraged a certain sang-froid in his protégé: Napier had not been in the city long before he found himself on board HMS *Bulldog*, aptly named as an instrument of Victorian foreign policy. The *Bulldog* was standing off Naples, from where Napier explained to Lord Minto that '[w]e are now here for refuge, having been shelled for several days (a man killed in our house) – and a leader of the people having made known violent threats against the English, in consequence of this vessel not having prevented the atrocious bombardment'.[41]

Threats notwithstanding, Napier was in no doubt as to where his sympathies lay: 'The Revolution of Palermo has been a daring, stainless and glorious effort. The mob has given proofs of both courage and abstinence ... Sicily is free.' A fortnight later he was commissioned by the King of Naples to 'employ my good offices in framing an armistice between the contending parties [in Palermo]'.[42]

Before the tumults, Napier had been in the habit of taking the Legation carriage into the city, to ferret out Riberas gathering dust in silent oratories. His letters give a vivid sense of his excitement:

> I have visited every picture by Spagnoletto in every Church in Naples except one which is said to be in a Chapel opened only twice a year. The number is not great. Several indicated in former times are gone, others are injured and dark. Only yesterday I ferreted out an obscure St Diego in the altar of an ancient Spanish Family Chapel. Those in private hands are too often doubtful. I only know of one of unquestionable authenticity and perfect preservation, with the name of the painter at full length, for sale. I lust after its wrinkled and macerated subject, but possession is still denied, I cannot have my hermit for less than £50: The seductive solitary was drawn by myself from the obscurity of a family chapel at Sorrento.[43]

A promised monograph on Ribera never materialised. But while on leave the Napiers took a holiday at Trouville made famous in windy little pictures by Boudin. Victorian patriarchs did not enjoy sand, and Napier was no exception. As his wife Nina promenaded, Napier contented himself with working on a slim volume about contemporary Neapolitan painters. The frontispiece was to be designed by Stirling, who all his life remained as absorbed by the art of the book as by that of painters. Napier survived revolution in Italy to enjoy the major collections of Germany and Russia, from where he wrote to Stirling about a famous Murillo which had recently been acquired at a Paris sale: 'The Murillo is unpacked and hung on an easel in the middle of a room at the Hermitage. It is covered with restorations as big as the top of your hat and is a mediocre work at best, they have an old Murillo a *Jacob's Ladder* which is a pearl indeed. But of the pictures more anon.'[44]

Despite demands as ambassador, Napier remembered what was happening in the galleries, what was hung up, and what restored. He kept careful notes of purchases the Russians were making – particularly of Spanish pictures. These he later communicated to Stirling when on leave at Thirlestane Castle, Selkirkshire, his ancestral seat in the Scottish Borders. His letter refers to West, a copyist who was employed by Stirling: 'I sent you a couple of letters for West this morning. I hope he will make a good excursion. Tell him that besides the Murillos in the gallery at the Hermitage, there are one or two in the private apartments of the Winter Palace which I never saw but which are said to be excellent. The only one in a private house I remember is at Mr Davidoff's.[45]

Prior to Russia and when still in Italy, Napier had been alert to Spanish paintings on sale. Unable to afford them himself, repeatedly he would try to bully the wealthier Stirling to acquire these. On several occasions he urged the merits of an 'undoubted' Velázquez'; sending Stirling a water-colour sketch which still survives among the Stirling papers:[46] 'Carelli bids me assault you again about his full length Philip IV. It is a thousand times finer than anything you got in London. The best judges declare it to be Velasquez. I think I sent you a drawing of it before. If you felt inclined to deal and would like another drawing say so. The price is high but open to reduction. Say what, about what, you might be inclined to give.'[47]

Stirling could not be tempted. Why is not clear, though it could hardly be because of a shortage of funds – a steady income derived in equal measure from West Indian sugar and Scottish coal meant that Stirling was pleasingly prosperous. But what is certain is that no Spanish painter provoked more imaginative myths and wilder misattributions than Velázquez, and so perhaps Stirling was doubtful.

Just how much fantasy Velázquez could provoke became clear to both Ford and Stirling as a result of an argument which was aired in the columns of a provincial newspaper. In 1847 Ford became embroiled in an acrimonious debate with a Reading printer who claimed to have discovered the portrait of Charles I when Prince of Wales by Velázquez, a claim which he confided to the obscurity of *The Reading Mercury*. Snare, the Reading printer, came to believe that his picture was nothing less than the famous Velázquez which the painter's father-in-law Francisco Pacheco stated had been painted in 1623 by Velázquez during the six months

Charles and Buckingham were pursuing the 'Spanish Match'. No one suffered fools less gladly than Ford, and contempt for a relentless bore was compounded by the early encouragement he had given the printer to forget Van Dyck, his first notion, and pursue instead Velázquez. No sooner had Ford mentioned the name Velázquez than Snare became convinced that what he had was none other than the famous missing portrait. So sure had Snare then become that he moved on from the humdrum context of a provincial newspaper to the more elevated platform of a privately printed pamphlet. Ford felt cross enough about the whole business to insert a passage into the 1855 edition of his *Handbook* in which he rejected the idea that somehow, after centuries, a lost portrait of an English prince by the prince of painters had suddenly emerged: 'The 'Fife' daub recently exhibited in London as this missing sketch is a complete snare and delusion: if it be a Spanish picture at all, which is very doubtful, it is certainly not by Velazquez'.[48]

By contrast to how Velázquez was viewed, other Spanish painters were regarded as benighted prisoners of Catholic bigotry, with the exception of Murillo to whom a partial dispensation was granted. The delusions of Snare apart, many thought they could detect a parallel between Velázquez, courtier of Philip IV, and Van Dyck, privileged servant of Charles I. A contact at the embassy in Vienna wrote to Stirling about the group portrait by del Mazo, then regarded as by Velázquez and the equal of if not superior to *Las Meninas*: 'Velasquez like Vandyke had something in him which guarded him against the over-materialism of their great master Rubens – and it is interesting to see how they touch each other from north and south' opined Stirling's correspondent.[49] Having delivered himself of this somewhat sententious generalisation, the writer then got down to the del Mazo, the description of which was the primary purpose of his writing to Stirling. Here significantly he couched his enthusiasm in Flemish not Spanish terms: 'It is a delightful family picture recalling Vandyke's most beautiful and graceful children – each face is a gem, sparkling and lively'. To the modern eye, the children in the Vienna canvas seem about as vivacious as pepper pots. Nevertheless, what is incontestably an ambitious group portrait was hugely admired in those days before anyone had much of a clue as to what was a Velázquez. There were other ways too in which the greatest of all Spanish painters was found a home safely on this side of the Pyrenees. Velázquez and Van Dyck had been exact contemporaries and both pre-eminent as portraitists. It was easy enough to make these two supremely gifted portraitists surrogate historians at a time when for the first time the importance of painting for a reconstruction of the past was noticed.

Nineteenth century historians believed in the centrality of the portrait to an understanding of the Golden Age. Hence it comes as little surprise to find that a Velázquez portrait, or to put it more accurately, what people then understood to be a Velázquez portrait, was a much sought-after commodity. The American historian Prescott, like Stirling, was rich. Both could afford the services of an extraordinary amanuensis, the remarkable Spanish antiquarian and historian Pascual de Gayangos. For years, and on behalf of Anglo-American writers, Gayangos was happy to truffle for rare books and unknown manuscripts all over Spain. It was Gayangos who discovered an important letter addressed by Titian in 1545 to the Emperor Charles V begging him not to allow any Spanish painter to touch up his royal portraits.[50] It was as well a happy manuscript find by Gayangos which settled once and for all the question of the death of Don Carlos, a famous Romantic subject celebrated on stage and opera by Schiller and Verdi. Gayangos's researches were able to establish the part played by Philip II in that real-life drama. Gayangos not only ran a document-finding service for Prescott, but also a kind of research institute of an altogether more ambitious nature. He hunted down portraits for conversion into steel engravings to decorate histories of the Austrian Habsburgs. As work ground on at Simancas, the repository of the Spanish royal archive, letters exchanged between Gayangos and Prescott ranged widely, from the death of Don Carlos to a suppositious portrait of Columbus, then regarded as more important to the founding myths of America even than George Washington. Prescott came to believe that a portrait in Naples was of Columbus. He had it engraved and he made it a frontispiece. But the painting has nothing to do with the man Washington Irving believed to be 'the most important figure in history'. The subject, now residing in Naples, turns out to be of Gian Galeazzo di S. Vitale, a portrait painted – after the death of Columbus – by the Italian Mannerist Parmigianino. That is too bad: he *should* have been Columbus, because he is so romantic, so good-looking. But then why did Prescott think otherwise? On one level the answer is simple. As a historian whose poor eyesight had always precluded any claims to connoisseurship, sensibly enough, he deferred to received opinion. But then there was a more telling point, and it was this: Prescott was determined to see this vibrantly handsome man as a compound of the hero of Irving's *Columbus* (1828) and the same character who appears in his own *Ferdinand and Isabella* (1837).

Prescott and Stirling never met, though they sustained a good-natured epistolary rivalry. They were united in their belief that a good portrait was an invaluable historical document. Thus, while Prescott and Gayangos worked together to provide what would later turn out to be fanciful images of New World conquerors, Stirling was no less eager to identify heroes of the Old. In 1853 Stirling received a letter from Fletcher Norton whose mother, Caroline Norton 'the Byron of poetesses' and muse for Millais' *Justice*, would later become Stirling's second wife shortly before her death. At this earlier juncture, Fletcher was in Naples with Ford's son Clare, who was pursuing 'indecent antiquities' while Fletcher haggled with a Neapolitan painter over a copy of a portrait of Don John of

Austria. Of this, report was sent back to Stirling, then engaged in research on the hero of Lepanto:

> The artist appeared to have attended more to the general effect than to the minute details, which struck me as a mistake as I think you want it to engrave from. His excuse was want of time. I told him to get some tracing paper and trace through carefully a few inches square of the richest part of the armour, which I will send you in a letter. From this the engraver can very well supply the rest as the whole coat is of the same pattern.[51]

No one did more than Stirling to further an appreciation of Velázquez, the greatest Spanish portraitist of the Golden Age. It is therefore something of a mystery, and it is certainly an irony, that Stirling never owned a genuine portrait by this pre-eminent Spanish portraitist. In this context Stirling was the fallible art connoisseur not historian, since Velázquez lived after the period of Stirling's own chosen field of political history. Velázquez alone was to emerge from the 1,400 pages of his *Annals* to receive an augmented volume – what Stirling had had to say in 1848 was issued as a separate book under the title *Velázquez and his Works* (1855). This pocket volume was embellished by a woodblock frontispiece, consciously archaic decoration chosen to suggest an early modern Spanish book. Here Stirling's reader was regaled with a distinctly piratical Velázquez, degenerate version of the artist of *Las Meninas*. The head is framed by stylised links of a gold chain, suggestive of how Stirling saw Velázquez as courtier first. Such a priority was noticed by Prescott who thought the book contained 'rich and racy pictures of Spanish character'.[52]

Although Stirling's contribution to Golden Age history centred upon Charles V, not Philip IV, his first love had been for Spain in the seventeenth century. At Cambridge he had been part of a circle nurtured by that notable polymath William Whewell, Master of Trinity, and a pioneer in the understanding of Gothic vaulting systems. But it was antiquarian books not architecture which had first absorbed Stirling. At Cambridge Stirling had been able to indulge a taste for collecting Jacobean dramatists. With interests centred on the early Stuart period, it required no great leap to move to contemporary Spanish playwrights. There was a certain logic in turning from Spanish literature to Velázquez; from acquaintance with the poetry of Luis de Góngora to the painter of that poet. Stirling's early love for the Jacobean dramatists drew him by osmosis into the life blood of the Golden Age.

El Greco was the last Golden Age painter to be recognised in both Spain and Britain. Indeed it was not until Spain suffered humiliation at the hands of the United States with the loss of Cuba in 1898 that most writers turned to that idiosyncratic artist whom many then began to think of as the mystic of Toledo. The timing of this interest was no coincidence. The Spanish 'Generation of 98', as El Greco's Spanish admirers were called, needed to find someone or something which could be used to salvage national dignity. So El Greco was recruited in the rehabilitation of a country stripped of the last of its imperial possessions. That El Greco did not happen to be Spanish was no impediment to those who wished to see him as the quintessence of a nation which had produced Cortez, Charles V and St John of the Cross.[53] However, while El Greco's life and personality no less than his oeuvre underwent forensic scrutiny in the country of his adoption, the more discerning of British critics had long been aware of a painter about whom they had distinctly ambivalent feelings. The sense of displacement and disorientation which El Greco's pictures induced in his British critics is clear enough from the *Annals*.

The life of 'the Greek', as Stirling refers to El Greco, opens with an engraving of a self-portrait of what the reader takes to be an *hidalgo*, not a mere painter – a member of the minor nobility who might have been associated with one of the pious secular confraternities which then flourished in Spain but who certainly never flourished a maulstick. This is emphasised in the illustration by El Greco's black dress and extended ruff. The most revealing suggestion of the fastidiousness of the artist, however, is his right hand. It holds a brush between thumb and forefinger as delicately as if the painter were sipping chocolate from a Meissen cup.

Stirling's El Greco was a very different historical character to the one favoured by Spanish critics. Whereas Stirling saw El Greco mingling imperceptibly with the brotherhood in the *Burial of Count Orgaz*, the Generation of '98 recognised a very different person. For the intellectuals who were to appoint themselves as saviours of Spain, El Greco was a tortured mystic whose vision of a spiritual realm spoke to the troubled soul of the country as his canvases began to inspire the Expressionists. Exactly fifty years earlier, and in another country, Stirling had felt that although El Greco had certainly been eccentric, he had prospered materially to become a pillar of Toledan society, hence our vision of the 'Greek' as Spanish knight.

Stirling earned his position as the foremost authority in Britain on Spanish art without ever darkening the doors of an archive, just as Prescott became the historian of Spanish kings without setting foot in the country. Some of the important facts which Stirling harvested from his extensive searches in secondary literature on El Greco were later proved wrong. It is therefore something of an irony that much documentation subsequently unearthed supports Stirling's broader view of El Greco as worldly, ambitious and materialistic – characteristics delineated by Stirling based on his own misapprehensions.

Stirling's life of El Greco is an important staging post to modern understanding, however unreliable it may be in detail. Stirling himself owned at least one superb El Greco, now in the National Gallery in London – the *Adoration of the Name of Jesus* – as well as the intriguing portrait of a woman still at Pollok House which may or may not be by El Greco.

Stirling could forgive, even if he could not overlook, the perversities of the Greek's style, as is clear enough from his choices as a collector, and the positive remarks he committed over the years to the privacy of research notes and travel diaries. As for his published views of the artist, he manoeuvred around this most difficult to situate of Golden Age painters. The following passage in the *Annals* typically swings one way then another, between Stirling's frank acknowledgement of his admiration and yet his distaste for excess. So much for the art historian. Yet there was also the writer as historian whose integrity demanded that subjective arguments about taste should not occlude what the secondary sources said. These made it abundantly clear that to Stirling, El Greco had been very successful in his own lifetime:

> The fine portraits of Tavera and Palavicina were painted in or about 1609, which is also the date of his delightful 'Holy Family' and his offensive 'Baptism of Christ' at the Toledan Hospital of St John the Baptist. In the latter picture, the narrow draperies, and the gleams of light, thin and sharp as Toledo sword blades, produce effects not less unpleasing, than difficult to be described intelligibly to those who are unacquainted with the Greek's style. He might have painted it, by the fitful flashes of lighting, on a midsummer night, from models dressed only in floating ribbands. In the Louvre we find near his excellent portraits, an '*Adoration of the Shepherds*', in his most extravagant style, in which the lights on reddish draperies and dark clouds are expressed by green streaks of so unhappy a tint, that those harmless objects resemble masses of bruised and discoloured flesh. Yet the perpetrator of these enormities sometimes painted heads that stood out from the canvas with the sober strength of Velasquez's, and coloured figures and draperies with a splendour rivalling Titian. With all his faults El Greco was a favourite artist in Spain, and his pictures were highly valued.[54]

This is Stirling at his best, but it is not original; it is borrowed light from Gautier, whose unrivalled account of Spain had appeared conveniently enough in 1845 as *Voyage en Espagne*. Gautier gave Stirling some of his similes, describing El Greco as 'an extravagant and singular painter who threw onto his canvases touches of incredible impetuosity and brutality, with slender, steely lights gleaming through the shadows like sabre blades whilst his extravagances and caprices shine in intermittent flashes'.[55] Stirling does not appear in anthologies – he was no Gautier, nor even as good as Prescott, but he was pre-eminent as English historian of the Austrian Habsburgs. However, it is as a biographer of Spanish painters that Stirling is remembered today. So what, then, was important about this book?

As a prosperous landowner, a Member of Parliament and a man much seen at Royal Academy dinners, Stirling was never inclined to get dust on his cuffs. The archive was not for him. Primary material does not appear. But then, the *Annals* are original in important ways. Emphasis on the interconnectedness of art and history, and the value Stirling put on context, were critical for the future development of art history. Priority given to history and milieu was something quite new in writing about art, so all this represented a permanent legacy. But although Stirling's account of the art of Spain has an abiding place in British historiography, his most celebrated work had had a complicated start. Ford regarded Stirling's appearance in his field as distinctly threatening. He was not impressed by an early draft of the *Annals*, feeling it needed major revisions if he were to support its publication. Disappointment was followed by bad luck. The *Annals* was turned down by Murray who was to publishing what Coutts was to banking. Murray rejected the manuscript, for he had just agreed to publish another account of Spanish art. That was, however, only half the truth. What was unlucky for Stirling was fortunate for Murray who had been told by Ford that the manuscript which Stirling had submitted in 1845 was no good. The author of the book Murray had been prepared to take on was Sir Edmund Head, quondam Fellow of Merton College, Oxford, whose idea of a happy retirement would be to translate Icelandic sagas. The fearsomely intelligent Head much impressed George Ticknor, then the world authority on Golden Age literature, who happened to be in London in 1857 when Head was on leave as Governor-General of Canada. Ticknor wrote: 'he is one of the most accurate and accomplished scholars I have ever known. He has been a good deal in Spain, and has some curious Spanish books in his large library, over which we have had much talk. I think he can repeat more poetry, Greek, Latin, German and Spanish, than any person I ever knew'.[56]

Ticknor went with the Heads to the *Art Treasures of Britain* exhibition held at Manchester in 1857. Head had got to know his Spanish pictures back in 1833 when he had been befriended by the Fords in their rented apartments in the Alhambra. There Head had become close friends with both Ford and the painter David Roberts, the former much impressed by the quality of Head's intellectual range and facility with languages. Then Andalucía was threatened with a cholera epidemic and Ford had warned his new friend before enthusing about the art of the south: 'I was sure you would like Seville and its painters. You see the Seville School in its glory and quite a different and higher class of art, than as seen at Madrid. You see Murillo pure untouched and unvarnished instead of the glazing and scrubbing the Madrid pictures have gone thro' in the restauracion as much a restauracion as a restoration is in Politics'.[57]

Head's most prominent contribution to an appreciation of Iberian painting was his account of the Spanish School, a complement to Kügler's *Handbook of Painting of the German, Dutch, French and Spanish Schools*. Head's book came out in 1848 and represented a fuller and more considered view than the article which he had contributed to the *Foreign Quarterly Review* back in 1834.[58] That short but pioneering essay had been an important milestone, anticipating Ford and Stirling by a full decade. Nevertheless, Head's book, a fuller and more academic offering than the earlier article, was really something for the reference section of a museum library – not, like Ford's and Stirling's, an accessible introduction to the Spanish School.

There was a rash of publications on Spain during the 1830s and 1840s, many of which were anticipating a market for travel which it was thought would develop once the political situation calmed down after the death of Ferdinand VII. This never happened. The expectation had been that a British readership would start to visit the country in sufficient numbers to give authors a decent income. However, with the exception of Ford and possibly Stirling, no one made money out of the country. One of many disappointed authors was Commodore Samuel Cook RN, whom Ford always insisted on calling 'Captain Cook'. Ford was the most impatient of men, and probably he mocked Cook because of a sardonic nature bordering on the cruel. Might there, however, have been a residual fear of a rival who threatened Ford's self-appointed position as *the* authority on Spain? Ford was understandably uneasy, since Cook actually knew the country better. Accordingly Ford mixed honey and vinegar in a letter in which he told his friend Addington, then British ambassador in Madrid, of Cook's publication: 'You should look at Captain Cook's book: Sketches in Spain ... dry, painstaking and accurate, better than I had expected by far. He understands the people better than the pictures. There he breaks down lamentably. But he is without taste, and does not know a Murillo from a mainmast.'[59]

It is hard to know whether Ford was being fair. Sooner or later every connoisseur gets paint on his face, and it was entirely predictable that two such opinionated men would disagree. Cook certainly thought that a picture acquired in Spain was that improbability, a Velázquez landscape. Cook sold it in 1836 to his old acquaintance John Macpherson-Grant, who had been secretary to the British Legation in Portugal. By the time Cook started negotiating about the painting, Macpherson-Grant had left the diplomatic service to live at his ancestral seat, Ballindalloch Castle near Elgin. It was over Ballindalloch that Cook cast his fly:

> It occurred to me that if you want more pictures you might not dislike a landscape by Velasquez. I have one in the Claude manner which are exceedingly rare. I never saw but the two. I bought this from Serafin before that which is hanging up came in the way. There are 3 figures one on horseback which is Velasquez himself and two on foot to which he is speaking ... It is a warm glowing picture. The price is 15£. It wants nothing.[60]

It is clear that this picture never had anything to do with Velázquez. But though Cook may have been a bad judge, he was a plausible salesman. What could be more seductive than to be offered a picture by Velázquez with aerial perspective in the style of Claude whose canvases had been metamorphosed into the green lawns and stone temples of England? Macpherson-Grant was merely doing what others had done, buying what was regarded as an important Spanish picture because it reminded him of something wholly alien to Spain.

It cannot be assumed that Ford was right in claiming Cook did not know a Murillo from a mainmast. When Cook first saw the *Rokeby Venus*, now one of the greatest treasures of the London National Gallery, he responded with huge enthusiasm. Some years later, Ford also found himself at Rokeby where he heard about Cook's visit, by then something of a legend. He rushed to tell Stirling a story which reduced his rival to a salacious voyeur:

> We made an excursion one day – a van full of silk and satin and bursting with Walter Scott – to Rokeby where Mr Morritt took us over the sites of Bertrams doings: *my* object was to see the Alva Velázquez *Venus* who would have thought that she should waste her sweetness in this secluded spot. old Morritt by the advice of Sir Th Lawrence bought the picture for £500.
>
> It is very fine indeed. it is painted in a free and darkling manner, and admirably composed. She is lying at full length and wears not even a fig leaf. She exhibits a portion of her person which in Billingsgate euphemism is desired by such gents to be kissed – but which in the beso los *pies* land, might be done without degradation and disgust. This Callipygean Damsel reclines on a tenderly painted *purple* sheet, which is coloured somewhat after the favourite tint of Zurbarán but fainter. She only shows – you will say she has shown enough – her profile. Here, as in the Hilanderas is another instance of how Velázquez felt his inability to do justice to the charms of the *face* female, however powerful and potent a posteriori: a little cupid with a purple sash, kneels at the foot of the concub and holds up a black framed looking glass in which the full face and the reclining nymph is reflected, not however very clearly or successfully: behind the cupid hangs a rich crimson velvet satin curtain: near her, Velázquez has introduced a bit of *green* veil; why I cannot tell except to give morbidezza to the flesh – excuse all these dry details, which may interest you. But before 2nd Edition [of the *Annals*] go and see it yourself and if you doubt do as Thomas did with probing finger: by the way to lard all these cold blooded criticisms let me tell you what befell our good friend Capt Cook. We know that he is the simplest most serious and sagest of men.
>
> When first he went to Rokeby, and this Eve spread her charms before him, he jumped on a table opposite to her, and as chance would have it placed himself exactly in the *middle* of the picture: he immediately began touching and rubbing just where he had better have left friction and manipulation alone; in due time his excitement became ungovernable and he exclaimed aloud – There was a large party and principally ladies – ' What a gem but how dirty' – I leave you to fancy the faces of the fair audience conscious of their own charms, better indeed concealed and more conversant with Castille soap: I have another anecdote which I can only tell viva voce dicendum non.[61]

Many who worked in the embassy in Madrid besides Macpherson-Grant became keenly interested in Spanish art – some as collectors, others as speculators hoping to relieve inadequate salaries by supplying the London art market. At the highest level, there was Villiers whose dealings with the redoubtable General Evans featured in Chapter 2 of the present volume. Though adventurous in his tastes, Clarendon was interested in furnishing houses, not in writing art history – unlike Sir Austen Henry Layard (1817–1894), the most indomitable, energetic and opinionated of all his successors at Madrid (Figure 9).

9 Ludwig Passani, *Sir Austen Henry Layard*

In 1839, the year Villiers finally left Madrid, Layard and a friend had started a walk to India but, parting company in Persia, the former had returned to Constantinople. The ambassador, Sir Strafford Canning, an amateur archaeologist, had then sent Layard into Mesopotamia where, at the modern-day city of Mosul, he came to play a famous, if exaggerated, part in uncovering the civilisation of ancient Iraq – sufficiently exaggerated, indeed, for his epithet 'Layard of Nineveh' to be wide of the mark in more senses than one. In truth, Layard was involved only in the excavation of peripheral sites rather than what had come to be identified as the centre of a fabled city of biblical renown. But such a romantic sobriquet did Layard no harm, as well he knew. Although less central to the discovery of Nineveh than he liked history to believe – he was quite unable to read cruciform script – as cultural adventurer, he certainly caught the imagination of those for whom the Great Exhibition opened new worlds. In 1846 he had the great sculptures now in The British Museum dug up, floated down the Tigris and sent by ship to London. The gateway stone figure of a colossal winged human-headed lion from the palace of Assurnasirpal II, King of Assyria (883–859), created a sensation. For that matter so did Layard with books like *Nineveh and its Remains* (1847–1849), fruits of his gunboat archaeology. Immediately the University of Oxford conferred on this fearless explorer their Doctorate of Civil Laws; five years later followed the Freedom of the City of London. In 1851 an abridgement of *Nineveh and its Remains* was published for the railway bookstalls under the title *A Popular Account of Discoveries at Nineveh*. But not everyone was convinced and certainly not Motley, the American historian of the Dutch Republic, whose refinement and deep culture was repelled by a man he regarded as a mountebank:

> Layard is short, square, hirsute and taurine of aspect, as befits the Nineveh bull, but he is a bull without wings. Not that he is slow in reality, for the world knows well enough the indomitable energy and rapid intelligence of the man. Moreover he has rushed all over India in an impromptu manner and incredibly short time, for the sake of investigating matters there and tossing the Ministers with his horns when he returns, and he is now delivering lectures upon the subject'[62]

Layard entered Parliament and he entered the Government. He served in the Foreign Office under Lord Clarendon, the former ambassador to Spain, to which post Layard would himself be appointed in 1869. There he remained until March 1877 when Disraeli, always the romantic, unwisely transferred him to the embassy in Constantinople; influenced by what he knew of Layard's youth in the Middle East. Turkey was locked in crisis with Russia, and Layard succeeded only in transforming a stand-off into a war. His conduct was perceived to have been transparently biased in favour of Turkey; it was alleged that he had promised that if Turkey went to war with Russia, it should receive material help from Great

Britain. It declared war, but help was not forthcoming. The Foreign Office took the view that it was impolitic encouragement from Layard which had pushed Turkey into hostilities. Layard challenged all this in the most strenuous terms but his career was finished. There was nothing for him but to retire. He chose Venice and the small palace, Ca' Capello on the Grand Canal, which he had acquired in 1874. There his notable collection of art treasures assuaged some of his bitterness at what he regarded as a career choked off before it had reached its full promise. Lady Layard busied herself in good works. As hostess she presided bossily over an entourage of gossiping ex-patriots and connoisseurs come to admire exceptional paintings like Gentile Bellini's *Sultan Mahomet II*.[63] Some of the pictures the Layards had acquired while he had been ambassador in Madrid.

The moment Layard arrived in Madrid he had begun bullying Spaniards about what he saw as their disgraceful neglect of national treasures. He thrust open the doors of the Prado, believing himself to be invested with a natural authority in matters of art through his trusteeship of the London National Gallery; unusually, he remained a trustee while serving in Spain. But he also saw himself as a favourite disciple of Sir Charles Eastlake, who had represented the type of the museum director at its most formidable. Layard consulted the spirit of Eastlake through the medium of a regular correspondence with the latter's widow. He had arrived in Madrid without having quite finished an appreciation of his mentor destined for *The Edinburgh Review*. Layard sent it to Lady Eastlake for her approval, with a covering letter in which he stated how Eastlake's career had not only been an inspiration to him but should be an example to all: 'I have endeavored to put forward the character and mental training of Sir Charles as one deserving of imitation and to point out how such a man raises the standard of his profession and gives it the claims that it ought to have upon the public respect'.[64]

Over the next seven years Layard relied heavily on Lady Eastlake, during what can best be described as a cultural crusade to bring the riches of Spain to the notice of a museum-going public in England. Once Layard knew of his appointment to Madrid, he had pressurised Sir Henry Cole into coming out. 'Old King Cole', as Sir Henry came to be known, was a colossus of Victorian public life; the first and still the most famous Director of the Victoria and Albert Museum. Cole's visit was a triumph. Although both Eastlake and his successor at the National Gallery, Sir William Boxall (d.1879), had visited Spain, neither had made purchases. This is somewhat surprising, at least in the case of Boxall, since in his previous incarnation as a society portraitist, he had once painted the poet Landor who had anticipated George Orwell by going to fight for the left in Spain. However, whatever chances the National Gallery may have missed, by 1870 Prince Albert's mission for a museum of the decorative arts to transform taste was an article of faith to which all subscribed in the most catholic way. Much besides money, therefore, was invested in Cole's expedition to Spain. This Layard explained: 'I think that Cole's visit will be useful – as he has purchased a few interesting things and is going to have casts and reproductions made of others, which will give the English public some idea of Spanish art, Spain being very poorly 'exhibited' at South Kensington.'[65] Six months later Layard was busying himself tracing the origins of Spanish painting. By then his mission had become to prod the *Fomento*, or Ministry of Works, into creating a dedicated room at the Prado for the best of the primitives in which he had become interested:

> I have been looking up, as far as materials and opportunities will allow me, the early Spanish schools. They are interesting and very little known. There is a very curious altar-piece signed and dated, of the early part of the 14th century in the Academy of History – and in the churches of Toledo and Seville I have found some interesting early work ... I had hoped to be able to write something about all this for the 'Quarterly' but the war and constant occupation here have otherwise engaged my thoughts, and I have not yet, moreover, been able to collect sufficient materials. I am endeavouring to persuade the authorities to make a selection from the vast collection of early works from the Convents and Churches now crammed into the Ministry of Works ('Fomento' where the magnificent Van Eyck hangs) and to have a room in the Gallery for the illustration of the history of Spanish art. I trust that this will be done. Since I have been here I have not seen a picture worth a shilling on sale – so that I have not added to my small collection.[66]

Layard charged about all over Madrid and southern Spain showing an interest in aspects of Spanish art which few English critics had noticed. What did unite him with earlier devotees of Spanish culture, however, was that both they and he undertook field-work in an atmosphere of political violence. This reached a moment of peculiar crisis shortly after the arrival of Layard in Madrid when General Prim, a soldier of particular political skill, was assassinated on the day that a fresh king of Spain, imported from Italy, arrived in the country for the first time. Layard was better equipped than most to cope. He carried on as best he could. He continued to pursue early Spanish painting with more enthusiasm than research. He spent time not only looking, but ferreting out documents for others who had more patience for scholarship. Layard was fortunate enough to be present when the coffin of Charles V was opened:

> I looked upon the body of Charles V in his marble coffin and compared him with Titian's portraits. The chin and scanty beard are still there – but it was a stretch of the imagination on the part of a friend present to recognise the dried body from Titian's delineation of the live man. Had not Prim's death and other things occurred to occupy my thoughts I should have written an account of my visit to the Escorial. I may drag it in somewhere some of these days.[67]

Gradually Layard became interested in Goya, stating his new-found admiration in a way which characteristically did not invite debate: 'Goya would have been a distinguished painter had he lived at a good time. His frescoes in a small church here show that he had good stuff in him'.[68] He told his old friend Giovanni Morelli of how he had just been to see some Goyas and of how he detected parallels between Goya and Rembrandt. With the passage of time, Goya came to mean more to Layard who – though always dogmatic – had generous tastes. Shortly after his arrival in Madrid, there had been modified enthusiasm, and then only for San Antonio de la Florida (1798). The frescoes in that church may have appealed because they seemed retrogressive with their *allegro moderato* suggesting Goya's festive style of the 1780s. Some two years later, however, Layard seems to have been coming to terms with Goyas of a much later period – only late works would seem to make sense of his comparison of Goya with Rembrandt. Morelli was told of how Layard had seen 'un fort beau portrait de Moretto ... et aussi d'admirables toiles de Goya, qui s'approchent de Rembrandt. C'était un vrai prince de peintre original et bizarre'.[69] Was Layard here paying Goya the ultimate compliment of equating his achievement with that of Velázquez, the 'Prince of Painters'? The correspondence does not say.

Although Layard was conspicuously a man of action in the nineteenth-century scramble for culture, he wrote a lot, not least as contributor to the quarterlies which were so much more decisive than books for the creation of opinion. He was well aware of the importance of archival evidence for the documentation of an artist's career. So John Murray had turned to him for a revision of Ford's *Handbook*, while acknowledging how much Layard had done to provide documentation for Crowe and Cavalcaselle, whose two-volume life of Titian remains as essential to an understanding of the Venetian painter as Justi's monograph of ten years later for Velázquez.[70]

Layard was fascinated by Velázquez. He doubted one of Velázquez' most important early works, *Christ at the Column* (National Gallery, London), claiming 'entre nous', as he coyly put it, that no one in Madrid believed in it. Such a view contrasted sharply with that of Eastlake who had seen the picture in Madrid in 1859.[71] The canvas, in a beautiful state of preservation, had just been acquired by the little-known collector John Savile Lumley. Lumley appears to have been a man of exceptional responsiveness to pictures. His long letter to Stirling, in which he describes his appreciation of the *Christ at the Column*, stands as the most sensitive of all reactions to the painter encountered within the time frame of this book. On seeing that picture in Lumley's rooms in Madrid in company with painters the Madrazo brothers, Eastlake had made an offer there and then on behalf of the National Gallery. Although that institution would indeed eventually secure it, Lumley refused. As for Layard, he was clearly mistaken in dismissing this great example of an early to mid-period

Velázquez. Layard was much keener on a manuscript which had come to his notice and which, he claimed, had been written by the artist himself. He wrote excitedly to Morelli at the end of February 1873 about how he was going to send Morelli 'un travail curieux' by Velázquez on the paintings which had existed in the Escorial when Velázquez was alive. Layard told Morelli that he intended to publish the manuscript, not least because in it Velázquez had interesting things to say about several Titians which, at the time Layard was writing, had disappeared. Today there is neither trace of this priceless manuscript, nor indeed Layard's commentary. So much the worst, for surely it is hard to imagine a more ingriguing document in the history or art than 'Velázquez on Titian'.[72]

It says much for Layard that he should have sustained the regard not only of Lady Eastlake but of the still more remarkable Giovanni Morelli. It is difficult to exaggerate the importance of Morelli to the development of art history. Morelli had trained as a scientist in the 1830s. Thereafter he had tried to promote in art historical studies the 'science of connoisseurship', the scrutiny of minute particulars such as an anatomist would use for taxonomy. It was Morelli who famously reattributed the *Dresden Venus* to Giorgione and it was his book on connoisseurship which Layard had had translated; adding his own fulsome introduction.[73] Without Morelli there would have been no Berenson, whose fundamental work in sorting out the Uffizi drawings would have been unthinkable without his inspiration. Freud too was much encouraged in his forays into art criticism with his essay on the 'Moses of Michelangelo', in which the Morellian method is used by Freud as apologia for trespassing into the field of art history.[74]

Morelli too was bullied into visiting Madrid. He and Layard enjoyed themselves rummaging in neglected storerooms to bring out remarkable early Netherlandish holdings after centuries of neglect. This was consistent with Layard's attempt to make sense of the beginnings of painting in Spain, and with his understanding that much of the impetus for what had been painted in Spain had come from the Netherlands. Layard was in part responsible for the decision by the Spanish authorities to dedicate rooms in the Prado to work from the court of Burgundy and the Spanish Netherlands, a whole dimension of European painting largely ignored since the opening of the museum in 1819. As for Morelli, Layard credited him with sorting out the amalgam of hands in an important work by Jan van Eyck:

> Yesterday I was able to show Morelli the fine picture ... attributed to Van Eyck ... Morelli maintains that the whole of the lower part of the picture which is marvellously fine, is by Van Eyck, and the upper by a weaker hand – probably by his sister –Margaret. This picture, with a splendid Roger van der Weyden (only recently discovered) and about a hundred more of the Flemish and early Spanish schools have been removed from the 'Fomento' to the Gallery – where they will ultimately be hung and be a great addition to it.[75]

The two discussed Velázquez at great length. Layard thought him inferior to Titian, declaring that 'I place Velasquez in the very first rank for his technical skill and the power of perfect representation. But the want of the very highest quality, imagination, places him far below Titian and the greatest painters.'[76] Morelli had an instinctive dislike for generalisations: for him, what mattered was attributions. He might not have understood what Layard was getting at, since his priority was brushwork, though Layard did claim that while Morelli 'was charmed with Velasquez' he agreed with him in 'thinking that he is a dangerous guide for a young painter'.[77]

Layard was unique: no British admirer of Iberian culture was more effective in making Spaniards aware of their patrimony. Nevertheless, what Layard did to encourage a taste for Spanish art in Britain is still more important. As someone who had thought nothing of sawing through Assyrian sculptures the size of a small house, the idea of decorating subordinate parts of Wren's interior at St Paul's with decorative work inspired by Spanish *azulejos* seemed entirely appropriate. Layard in Spain received a letter from an artist who had gone ahead of him to take details of tile work which could be used for decoration in St Pauls. The writer was in Spain looking at Spanish tiles (*azulejos*) because Layard was anxious to know whether they might prove appropriate as a covering for some of the subordinate vaults of the Cathedral.

> At Seville there was so much to see that I find I did not make many sketches one at St^a Paula and some detail of the *Ayuntamiento* being pretty nearly all I have to *show*. But I found an immense deal to study. The *azulejos* especially – Because there is I think a great disposition to try something of this kind in *subordinate* parts in St Paul's and I was glad to have the opportunity of making myself fastidious in this material. I imagine that the *azulejos* of St^a Paula and the kiosk of Ch.V in the garden of the Alcazar are very different from the painted china which Mr Ayrton and Mr Cole are driving at. But for the important parts of St Pauls Mosaic is a necessity and I think that all the Executive Committee feel this. According to Salviati's estimate it would cost about £30,000 to fill the dome of St Paul's. I think it would be one of the most desirable things to begin with and there is almost money enough already to do it.[78]

Although the original intention of Wren had indeed been 'to have beautified the Inside of the Cupola with the more durable Ornament of Mosaic-work, as is nobly executed in the Cupola of St. Peter's in Rome', fortunately perhaps, this did not happen.[79] Fortunately too, Layard was not to be given free rein, since the firm he favoured, Salviati and Co. of Venice, had been partly responsible for the disasters perpetrated in the city and its islands during the mid-nineteenth century – campaigns of transformation described as classic instances of 'falsification in the cause of notional integrity'.[80] But then, Layard shared to the full the Victorian commitment to the improvement of public taste and this was to have been done by acquiring facsimiles of all that was best in the art of the world. He was an apostle of *The Arundel Society*, a body of worthies dedicated to the chromolithographic reproduction of iconic works for the edification of the Victorian schoolroom. Layard had hardly been in Madrid a year when Cole wrote to thank him for 'stirring up the Spanish Government' into sending a selection of the best of Spanish decorative art. Thus encouraged, Layard laboured mightily to bring the finest aspects of Spanish design to South Kensington through casts of iconic works. No one in the world of British museums did more than Layard to create an awareness of Spain, so it was therefore gratifying for him to be told by the Council of Education at the Kensington Museum: 'We are very proud of the Spanish contributions'. Of one thing we can be quite sure: Layard would have been proud of himself as he read that letter. In Britain, Spanish art – defined in the broadest and most generous terms – had at last begun to be noticed.

Notes

1 For Ford as historian of Spanish art, see Robertson, *Ford*, passim. For Stirling: Hilary Macartney, 'Sir William Stirling Maxwell: Scholar of Spanish Art', *Espacio, Tiempo y Forma*, Series 7, *Historia del Arte* 12 (1999), pp. 287–316.
2 Sir William Eden, 'Journal in Spain', 1788–9, BL Add. Ms. 34464, fol. 8r.
3 John Pemble, *Venice Rediscovered* (Oxford: Oxford University Press, 1996), p. 167.
4 Grantham to Lady Pelham, Madrid, 12 April 1779, BL Add. Ms. 33099, fol. 385v.
5 Grantham to Thomas Pelham, Madrid, 6 February 1775, BL Add. Ms. 33099, fol. 107v.
6 For Grantham as a connoisseur of Spanish painting, see Glendinning, Harris and Russell, 'Electric Eel'.
7 Thomas Pelham to Lady Chichester, Madrid, 21 December 1775, BL Add. Ms. 33126, fol. 232v.
8 Thomas Pelham to Lord Chichester, 'Aranques', 2 June 1776, BL Add. Ms. 33126, fol. 383v.
9 Antonio Ponz to Thomas Pelham, Malaga, 14 August 1776, BL Add. Ms. 33100, fols 22–25v.
10 Thomas Pelham to Lady Chichester, Cariñena, 27 September 1776, BL Add. Ms. 33127, fols 67v and 68v.
11 Thomas Pelham to Lady Chichester, 'S. Ildephonso', 9 September 1776, BL Add. Ms. 33127, fol. 53v.
12 Grantham to Thomas Pelham, Madrid, 13 January 1777, BL Add. Ms. 33099, fol. 240r.
13 Thomas Pelham to Grantham, Rome, 2 August 1777, BL Add. Ms. 33127, fol. 287v.
14 Grantham to Thomas Pelham, Aranjuez, 27 May 1777, BL Add. Ms. 33099, fol. 269v.
15 Grantham to Thomas Pelham, Aranjuez, 29 April 1777, BL Add. Ms. 33099, fol. 262v.
16 See Ian Robertson, *Los Curiosos Impertinentes: Viajeros Ingleses por España 1760–1855* (Madrid: Editora Nacional, 1976).
17 Carlyle, *Life of Stirling*, p. 77.
18 In 1826 the Faculty of Advocates in Edinburgh had acquired a significant part of the celebrated library of the Marqués de Astorga which had come to London and been broken up at auction.
19 *The Athenaeum*, no. 390 (30 May 1835), p. 417.
20 E. Davies, *The Life of Bartolome E Murillo* (London: Bensley and Son, 1819), pp. 50–1.

21 Ibid., p. 84.
22 Ibid., p. 92.
23 Ibid., p. 4.
24 MLG T-SK 31/30–34, 'Notes and Notices not already used in the Annals of Artists of Spain 1848', Escazena to Stirling, 12 February (n.y.), 27 Edwards St. Portman Sq: 'Have you ever seen the Real order of Charles the 3rd of Spain forbidding the extraction of pictures from Spain, particularly Murillos? I think it is a curious document, as in it is shown how early his works were sought after by foreigners you find this document in Ponz Viage de Espana in the 10th vol: I think at the end it is the volume where he describes Seville.'
25 John O. Hagan (ed.), *William Wordsworth*, Poems, vol. 1 (Harmondsworth: Penguin, 1977), p. 298.
26 I am grateful to Gabrieli Finaldi for this suggestion.
27 Graham Parry, *The Trophies of Time: English Antiquarians of the Seventeenth Century* (Oxford: Oxford University Press, 1995), Chapter Five, 'James Ussher', pp. 130–56.
28 Francis Haskell, *History and its Images* (New Haven and London: Yale University Press, 1993), pp. 4–6, 50–1, 67–70.
29 Richard Ford, *A Handbook for Travellers in Spain*, 6th edn, 2 vols (London, 1882 [1845]), 1, p. 50.
30 A separate appendix was published by Nicolaas Henneman who worked with Fox Talbot. The plates illustrated some of the Spanish material discussed in the three-volume text. These constituted the first photographs ever to be used in an art history book.
31 Stirling, *Annals*, p. 34.
32 Ibid., pp. 421–2.
33 Ibid., p. 57.
34 Ibid., pp. 88–9.
35 Gustav Waagen, *Works of Art and Artists in England*, trans. From the German by Hannibal Evans Lloyd, 3 vols (London: 1838), and *Treasures of Art in England*, trans. from the German by Lady Eastlake, 3 vols (London: John Murray, 1854).
36 Jonathan Brown, *Kings and Connoisseurs* (New Haven and London: Yale University Press, 1995), Chapter III, 'The Greatest Amateur of Paintings among the Princes of the World', pp. 95–147.
37 Stirling, *Annals*, pp. 522–3.
38 For Coningham as collector see Francis Haskell, *Rediscoveries in Art* (Oxford: Phaidon, 1976), p. 141.
39 Coningham to Stirling, 26 Sussex Square, 28 February 1849, MLG T-SK 29/5/105: 'Nothing could have given me so much pleasure as an expedition, with yourself and Ford, to Madrid. But alas! I fear health and strength will be wanting to enable me to journey so far. My illness has been a very severe one, and I am shaken and reduced to an incredible degree by so short an indisposition.'
40 Napier to Stirling, Thirlestane, Monday, [n.d. but May or June 1851], MLG T-SK 29/6/13.
41 Napier to Minto, Naples, 21 January 1848, NLS, Ms. 12076, fol. 23.
42 Same to same, 3 February 1848.
43 Napier to Stirling, Naples, 29 May [1851], MLG T-SK 29/6/12.
44 Same to same, St Petersburg, 4 November [1852], MLG T-SK 29/28/30.
45 Same to same, Thirlestane, Selkirk, 22 May 1856, MLG T-SK 29/7/145.
46 The Napier picture may be the full-length studio version of *Philip IV Hunting*, now at the Musée Goya at Castres.
47 Ibid., Naples, 28 May [1851], MLG T-SK 29/6/12.
48 Ford, *Handbook*, 1855 edn [1845], 11, 689.
49 Erskine to Stirling, Vienna, 20 June 1846, MLG T-SK 31/32.
50 Layard to Morelli, Madrid, 12 December 1872, BL Add. Ms. 38966, fol. 179. The letter to which Layard was here referring was written by Titian to Charles V from Venice on 5

October 1545, and is transcribed in: Ugo Fasoli (ed.), *Tizian Le Lettere* (Belluno, 1977), Letter 63, p. 83.
51 Fletcher Norton to Stirling, Naples, 27 April 1853, MLG T-SK 29/28/45.
52 Prescott to Stirling, Boston, 12 November 1855, MLG T-SK 29/7/161.
53 For the posthumous reputation of El Greco see J.Brown, 'The Man and the Myths', pp. 15–33, in *El Greco of Toledo*, exh. cat., Madrid-Washington-Toledo (Ohio) Dallas, 1982–1983.
54 Stirling, *Annals*, pp. 286–7.
55 Théophile Gautier, *A Romantic in Spain*, trans. Catherine Alison Phillips (Oxford: Oxford University Press, 2001), pp. 35–6.
56 Ticknor to the Hon. E. Everett, Niagara Falls, 22 August 1859, in George Hillard (ed.), *Life, Letters and Journals of George Ticknor*, 2 vols (London: Sampson, Low and Co., 1876), 1, p. 424.
57 Ford to Head, [Granada], 'Sat^y' [31 August or 7 September 1833], MLG T-SK 29/57/97.
58 Edmund Head, 'Noticias de los Quadros', *Foreign Quarterly Review* 26 (1834), pp. 237–72.
59 Ford to H.U. Addington, 26 March 1834, Rowland E Prothero, *The Letters of Richard Ford* (London: John Murray, 1905), p. 140.
60 Cook to Macpherson-Grant, 3 March 1836, NRA (S) 0771, TD 1999/31/ Bundle 132.
61 David Howarth, 'Mr Morritt's *Venus*: Richard Ford, Sir William Stirling-Maxwell and the "cosas de Espana"', *Apollo* (October 1999), pp. 37–45.
62 Curtis, *Correspondence of Motley*, 1, p. 227.
63 For the Layards in Venice, see, Pemble, *Venice Rediscovered*, pp. 34–6.
64 Layard to Lady Eastlake, Madrid, 4 February 1870, BL Add. Ms. 38972, fol. 4.
65 Same to same, Madrid, 23 April 1870, BL Add. Ms. 38972, fol.7.
66 Same to same, Madrid, 23 October 1870, BL Add. Ms. 38972, fol. 10.
67 Same to same, Madrid, 1 February 1871, BL Add. Ms. 38972, fol. 14.
68 Same to same, Madrid, 23 October, 1870, BL Add. Ms. 38972, fol. 10.
69 Layard to Morelli, Madrid, 27 February, 1873, BL Add. Ms. 38966, fol.182.
70 J.A. Crowe and G.B. Cavalcaselle, *Titian: his Life and Times*, 2 vols (London: John Murray, 1877); Carl Justi, *Diego Velázquez und sein Jahrhundert* (Bonn:1888).
71 For the purchase of this picture by Lumley in Madrid in 1859, see Hugh Brigstocke, 'El Descubrimiento del Arte Español en Gran Bretaña', in *Torno a Velázquez* (Oviedo: Museo de Bellas Artes de Asturias, 1999), note 80.
72 Layard to Morelli, Madrid, 27 February 1873, BL Add. Ms. 38966, fol. 182.
73 Giovanni Morelli, *Italian Painters: critical studies of their works The Borghese and Doria-Pamfili Galleries in Rome*, Trans. From the German by Constance Jocelyn Ffoulkes, with an Introduction by The Right Hon. Sir A.H. Layard, G.C.B., D.C.L. (London: John Murray, 1892).
74 James Strachey (gen. ed.), *The Penguin Freud Library*, 15 vols, 14, Albert Dickson (ed.), *Art and Literature*, trans. from the German by James Strachey (Harmondsworth: Penguin, 1985), 'The Moses of Michelangelo', pp. 249–83.
75 Layard to Lady Eastlake, Madrid, 17 April 1872, BL Add. Ms. 38972, fol. 23.
76 Same to same, Madrid, 23 October 1870, BL Add. Ms. 38972, fol. 10.
77 Same to same, Madrid, 8 May 1872, BL Add. Ms. 38972, fol. 23.
78 Francis Penrose to Layard, St Paul's Chapter House, 12 January 1871, BL Add. Ms. 38999, fol. 23.
79 From Wren's *Parentalia*, quoted by Peter Burman, *St Paul's Cathedral* (London: Bell and Hyman, 1987), p. 99.
80 Pemble, *Venice Rediscovered*, p. 129.

6
Collectors

The purpose of this chapter is to look at collectors of Spanish art. We shall be concerned with the acquisition of famous pictures, but also with why and when Spanish art became noticed in Britain. Charles I lived well before this period, and he was drawn to the culture of Spain for reasons which had more to do with self-image than with any liking for Spanish art. Famously, Charles had spent six months in Spain from March 1623, and that constituted the first record we have of an English collector staying in Madrid. He was there to acquire a bride, not pictures, but although he failed as matchmaker he was much consoled as art lover.[1] The royal collection was enriched, though not by anything Spanish. Pacheco, the father in law of Velázquez, tells of his-son-in law painting the future British king in Madrid. But supposing what Pacheco said was true, it is most unlikely that Charles would have taken an active interest in the portraitist at this early stage. Velázquez was transforming himself from a purveyor of *bodegones* into a court portraitist. To his sitters, Velázquez would have come across as powerful but austere. The contrast between what Charles might have seen in 1623 and what could have been available had he returned to Madrid in 1633 constitutes one of the most exciting transformations in the history of portraiture. Colours of sand and leather had by then been exchanged for a spangled skein of silver and carmine in pursuit of a new type of Spanish portrait which looked backward to Titian and ahead to Whistler. But Charles could never have seen these recollections of Titian, much as they would have appealed. Charles in England was not able to follow Velázquez' portrait style, though he liked to hear about Spanish artists. Why then did he take what might be termed an 'epistolary interest' in Velázquez and his contemporaries?

Sir Arthur Hopton, ambassador to Spain, mentioned Velázquez in letters while acting as a conduit for Spanish paintings. Hopton presented his predecessor Sir Francis Cottington with still-lives by Juan Labrador which soon found their way into the English royal collection. Charles I's interest in what was happening artistically in Madrid had less to do with pictures, however, than with a fascination for the Habsburgs as patrons. This is suggested by the presence in Madrid for much of the 1630s of the modest English artist Michael Cross who copied Titians under the supervision of Hopton. It is odd that Cross should have been doing this, since Charles had a sufficiently representative Titian collection. The truth was that Charles did not need anymore. Had Charles got bored with his own Titians, there were many superb examples at hand: *The Flaying of Marsyas* at Arundel House, *The Vendramin Family* at Van Dyck's. Indeed what was then available in London could have made a better exhibition than any recent Titian show in Britain. As for Cross, he was merely a copyist and so today not a single work by this nonentity can be identified. The copies were always flat and listless, as Charles I would have noticed with his well-attuned eye. Yet these pedestrian images were genuinely valued because they alluded to the most famous creative partnership of early modern Europe – Titian's special relationship first with Charles V and then with Philip II.

It was only the Titians in Spain that were copied for Charles – nothing Spanish was recorded, as far as we know. This was because Charles I was trying to get closer to the famous personality of the Emperor Charles V, a personality best understood by the most discerning connoisseur ever to sit on the British throne, through 'Spanish' Titian. Hence for Charles, both Titian and Spain were means to an end. But then Charles was also keen to learn from his contemporary, his 'cousin' Philip IV and his entourage. Charles followed the career of Philip IV's chief adviser on the arts, Giovanni Battista Crescenzi – an Italian by birth, like so many important creative figures in Spain. It is known that Crescenzi turned down an offer of employment at the court in London.[2] Rumours of a deal between the king of England and a servant of the king of Spain gave the great English dramatist and poet Ben Jonson welcome but unlooked-for ammunition in an assault on the architect and theatre designer Inigo Jones. Jonson's poem entitled *To Inigo, Marquess Would Be, a Corollary* is a sardonic attack on Jones, the opening lines of which refer to Crescenzi having been created a Spanish nobleman, as the Marquess de la Torre:

> But cause thou hear'st the mighty king of Spain
> Hath made his Inigo marquess, wouldst thou fain
> Our Charles should make thee such? 'Twill not become
> All kings to do the selfsame deeds with some!
> Besides his man may merit it, and be
> A noble honest soul! What's this to thee?
> He may have skill and judgement to design
> Cities and temples: thou a cave for wine
> Or ale! He build a palace thou a shop
> With sliding windows, and false lights atop!
> ... for all thy work is show:
> But when thou turns't a real Inigo;
> Or canst of truth the least entrenchment pitch,
> We'll have you styled the marquess of Newditch.[3]

Crescenzi's letter turning down the offer of employment was dated 28 January 1631 – that is, between the occasion of two masques, *Love's Triumph through Callipolis* performed on 9 January of that year *and Chloridia* seen at court on 22 February. It was rows over who should have precedence in claims for the 'invention' of just these two masques which caused the final breakdown between Jonson and Jones. That in turn provoked the Jonson poem. Jones, it would appear, was something of a social snob, a leaning which habitually annoyed Jonson, who appears to have always been much more independent of the court than his collaborator. Now the threat that Jones was to be superseded by Crescenzi, who had already been ennobled by the king of Spain, may have brought matters to a head and inspired Jonson's malevolent muse. Jonson's wounding assaults on Jones were of such a barbed nature that it permanently destroyed their working relationship. They would never collaborate again.

This spat in London developed while Velázquez – who, we may be sure, knew nothing about it – was in Italy. But it is no coincidence that it was from the time that Velázquez returned to Madrid, just when Van Dyck joined the English court, that Charles I began to receive intelligence about the king of Spain's premier portraitist. Charles I wanted to know about Velázquez because he wanted to know about how Spain used its artists to its best advantage. But Charles I was not just interested in painting – he was eager as well to learn about the Habsburgs as builders. The mystique of the Escorial fired his imagination as it did all monarchs at that time. John Webb, the star pupil of Inigo Jones, played with sketches for a gargantuan new palace on the Thames.[4] These never got very far, though there is enough in them to reveal the influence of the Escorial.

How Charles I engaged with Spain anticipates ways in which later generations connected with the country as they too would pursue preoccupations which also only impinged on the Peninsula adventitiously. As was to be the case with many of those who would later become involved with Spain, Charles had looked through Spain in pursuit of something else: to acquaint himself with the legends of the Habsburgs as he tried to construct a Spanish-style self-identity. Turning now to the period with which this book is primarily concerned, we consider some of the more celebrated collectors of Spanish painting, to observe how, in their turn, many had decidedly mixed motives for their pursuits.

Grantham's eighteenth-century passion for Velázquez featured in the last chapter. He commissioned copies of the portraits perhaps because he could not collect originals. His priority was to understand the secrets of the brush. Accordingly, he is better placed among writers and art historians than among collectors. For Victorians Velázquez eventually came to mean more than any other Spanish artist. This was for his painterly qualities admired by artists such as Sargent, Whistler and Lavery, none of whom ironically was actually English, though all benefited from English patrons. But why did it take so long for a painter like Velázquez, who owed so much to Titian – always revered in Britain – to come into his own in this country? It was because his paintings were almost all in Spain and very few people visited. When a few intrepid souls did venture there from the 1820s, it was never very easy to see Velázquez. Although the Prado opened in 1819, the chaotic administration which characterised the early decades of the Spanish national gallery militated against 'discovery'. Furthermore, Velázquez produced relatively few portraits compared with the output of his great contemporary Van Dyck. Historically too, a higher proportion of Velázquez portraits were of royalty than was the case with those of Van Dyck, whose courtiers were scattered all over England. Spain had almost no surviving noteworthy aristocratic collections and most Velázquez paintings were secreted in royal palaces as mournful as the shadows of *Las Meninas*. The 'old buffoon' Ferdinand VII was heard to declare that those who were interested in his pictures could do what they liked with them because he preferred a nice wallpaper. Such wholesale indifference at the highest level hardly encouraged a European reputation for the artist. The evident philistinism of Ferdinand could not have been in greater contrast to the passion and discernment for pictures manifested by Ferdinand's exact contemporary, the English king George IV. Further discouragement followed. Madrid in the 1830s could be dangerous. Carlistas threatened a sack, and so it seemed something of an indulgence to wander about looking for pictures. But access was not the whole story. Part of the slow appreciation of Velázquez was because of the mood of his images. Velázquez and Philip IV conspired to create a royal image which promoted distinction through the paradox of ordinariness. There has never been a portraitist who has relied less on charm, and for most English visitors to the Prado the contrast between Velázquez and Van Dyck could hardly have been more marked. Although some were intrigued by what they saw as an affinity between the two painters, for most a typical Velázquez sitter was alone, austere, intense. By contrast, Van Dyck's were flamboyant, distracted, theatrical. The distinction mattered. For the English, Van Dyck was British portraiture, and so Velázquez could be ignored because his works did not conform to their preconceptions.

By contrast, Murillo, or the 'Spanish Van Dyck' as Britons often referred to him, was of real interest even in his own lifetime.[5] Two copies of his so-called 'beggar boys' belonged to the MP Sir Ralph Bankes (d.1677). It has been suggested that the marriage of Charles II to a Portuguese princess – a union which gave Britain Tangier, a land base within sight of Cádiz – increased interest in Murillo, then at the height of his powers and living in Seville and Cádiz. The Godolphin family had long-standing connections with Spain which may have induced Sidney Godolphin to pay the notably high sum of eighty guineas for some

Murillos. By the eighteenth century, Murillos could be found in the grandest houses. Marlborough came by two 'beggar boys' painted by the associate of Murillo, Villavicencio, probably acquired because of the disruption caused by the War of the Spanish Succession (1701–1713). Such means anticipated what would happen a century later when Wellington became the beneficiary of French looting of churches and monasteries. Blenheim and Apsley House grew splendid through the accident of war, not the exercise of a positive taste for Spain.

The Treaty of Utrecht ended the War of the Spanish Succession in 1713. Thereafter Britain and Spain grew closer. The British South Sea Company was a powerful trading force in the southern hemisphere with strong commercial links to Seville. The partial dismantlement of the Spanish Empire following the end of the War of the Spanish Succession had given Britain Gibraltar and, much more lucratively, the *Assiento* – the sole right of supplying black slaves to South America. There was much to encourage a British presence in Andalucía, much to encourage an appreciation of things Spanish within the British mercantile community, whose warehouses were divided between Cádiz and Seville. Nathan Wetherhall, the eighteenth-century British merchant and antiquarian who still lingered in Seville when the Hollands visited, did his best to gather up archaeological litter neglected and strewn all over Italica, Spain's most extensive ancient Roman site and the birthplace of the emperors Trajan and Hadrian. Before Wetherall, such visitors who did come to Andalucía might well have run into William Dalrymple who, as the younger brother of a baronet, had left Scotland to divide a forty-year working life between Rotterdam and Cádiz. Upon finally returning to the United Kingdom in the 1780s, Dalrymple had remembered Spain, writing to his brother: 'I am looking about for a Painter who for about 10 Guineas will draw my Picture in the Spanish Stile which will be send[t] down'.[6] That is the last we hear of the picture; it would be fascinating to know what Dalrymple thought a 'Spanish' as opposed to an Italian portrait looked like.

With an increase in the presence of the British in southern Spain came growing sympathy. It was a sympathy which extended north to Madrid, where William Stanhope (*c.*1683–1756), 1st earl of Harrington, presided as ambassador. During that time (1720–27), Stanhope proved to be a good friend and apologist for the country. After returning to England, he remained strongly committed to an entente between the two countries, negotiating the Treaty of Seville (1729). This put matters on a new level of cooperation and good will. Stanhope had always been warmly sympathetic to Spanish Catholicism, and this may explain why he had returned to London in 1727 with three altarpieces by Murillo. Stanhope also appears to have been one of the very few Englishmen to acknowledge the great antique heritage of Iberia. There are records of his bringing home antique inscriptions from Tarragona.[7] In short, Stanhope was a student of Spain whose broad sympathies for its culture would repay further investigation.

Sir Robert Walpole, the first Prime Minister of Britain, had a favourite client in the political jobber Sir Benjamin Keene, who was rewarded with the embassy in Spain from where he supplied Walpole with no fewer than five Murillos. These formed the backdrop to the political gatherings at Houghton Hall, the magnificent Walpole country seat in Norfolk. There, an ensemble of pictures which later came to form the Hermitage in St Petersburg did much to influence the development of collecting in mid-Georgian England. The Walpole Murillos, at the time the largest cluster in Britain, had nothing to do with the exercise of choice by their owner. They owed their presence at Houghton to calculations by Keene as to how best to keep things sweet with his political master. Nonetheless, they certainly encouraged an interest in Spanish painting in those who were hoping to run Britain. Walpole managed politics for the Hanoverians, but there were a considerable number of their enemies the Jacobites, who identified with Spain, not just with its pictures. Among these were the Arthurs, Sir Daniel and Francis, who were conspicuous then though not now: little evidence has survived to tell of a group of Catholic Hispanophile collectors who seem to have circulated around the Arthurs. By 1728 they had formed what has been described as 'one of the most impressive [collections] to be imported from Spain in the eighteenth century'.[8] Besides a number of 'beggar-boys', the Arthurs also possessed the remarkable Murillo *Self-Portrait* (National Gallery, London). The family were Catholics, and to acknowledge their commitment to Spanish culture is to recognise the place of co-religionists in developing a taste for Spanish art, attracted to Murillo because his sweet Madonnas sustained their faith. However, while Murillo Virgins may once have been a matter of piety, later they became secularised, even eroticised as 'Gypsy Madonnas', until everyone, Gainsborough and Reynolds included, became mad for Murillo.

Prosecution of a successful campaign against Napoleon by combined British and Spanish armies demanded a new interest in the topography of the country. Prolonged periods spent in the Peninsula by well-educated Englishmen with a liking for pictures stimulated a taste for collecting. Toward the end of the campaign, Wellington received perhaps the finest of all *bodegones* by Velázquez, *The Water Carrier of Seville*. When eventually it found its way to Apsley House it was catalogued as a Caravaggio. That was not as foolish as it might seem, since there has long been a debate as to what if any knowledge Velázquez may have had of the Italian painter. Furthermore, of all the Velázquez *bodegones*, the *Water Carrier* is his most Caravaggesque. This came with a whole lot more Spanish paintings which had been retrieved from the baggage of the retreating French armies after the battle of Vitoria. The spoils had then been given by the Spanish government to the British hero. Wellington was embarrassed and made serious efforts to return them but the Spanish authorities were not having it and he was obliged to keep them. Clearly there was no sense in which Wellington had chosen these paintings: he may have grown to like them but there is no evidence whatever to suggest that he responded positively to art in Spain, nor indeed does he seem to have added a single Spanish picture to what had been a famous tribute from a liberated nation. The French historian of Spanish art, Louis Viardot, related an anecdote of how the Field Marshal had offered a great deal of money for the famous Murillo *St Anthony* in Seville Cathedral but provided no documentary support for his assertion. For his part Ford considered the tale stuff and nonsense; writing to Stirling in characteristically dismissive turns about someone he thought a fool: 'Viardot is a sad ass, with his *intuitive* nonsense and idle tales about Wilkie and the Duke's "bid" for the St Antonio at Seville.'[9]

By 1800 there was no competitive exam for the services. The army was heavily staffed by aristocrats who had bought their commissions – officers brought up in houses filled with family pictures. One such was Sir William Napier, amateur artist and friend of the Royal Academician George Jones. Jones had enlisted for the Peninsula, and after the end of the war made a good living from stirring reconstructions of the great battles. Years after the Peninsular campaign, Jones recalled how

> Will Napier told me that when he was with the army in the Peninsula he carried cakes of Water colours, in the curls of his hair which at one time were magnificent – his great desire was to draw well, but his tendency to extravagance under the impression of grandeur, led him into error, and prevented the attainment of truth, he had a good idea of Chiaro Scuro but he had not time or opportunity to mature his perceptions.[10]

General Sir William Napier, as 'Will' eventually became, had served with distinction in the Peninsular War of which he was to write a famous history. Eighteen months before Wellington died, the Field Marshal asked Napier for his portrait to help recall Spain in the way he best liked:

> I wish very much to have a good picture, of yourself in the first place, and of your brother Sir Charles, to put in the room with the other soldiers of the Peninsula. Alas I much depend on search for one of Sir Charles, but I want you to permit Gambardella to paint a picture (a head merely and it shall not give you much trouble) of you and He will paint it at your own house, or everything shall be done to suit your convenience.
>
> I have bought a picture of you but I don't like it, and our friend Roebuck has added to my discontent.
>
> I recollect those early days and wish you and your brother both in that room for posterity's sake.[11]

Wellington and his officers remained bound together, reminiscing at anniversary dinners of heroic exploits before Salamanca and on the field of Waterloo.

However, Spain had been invested not just with redcoats, and there were large numbers of civilian dependents and hangers-on – diplomats, victuallers, medical men, camp women and even the feckless tourists, all of whom tottered behind the vigorous step of the British army.

One who came to see what was up was the life-long friend of Byron, William John Bankes (1786–1855); of him, Samuel Rogers had said that when on form, he could eclipse even Sydney Smith with the brilliance of his repartee. In August 1813, and at the very end of the Peninsular War, Bankes had visited Galicia where he had roughed it on the straw of monasteries. He then traversed Spain to accompany Sir Henry Wellesley to Valencia to see the deposed Ferdinand VII. Bankes remained in Spain until 1815 while Wellington remained his hero. Bankes played a central role in furthering the career of the sculptor Baron Carlo Marochetti of Vaux (1805–1867) who, with his encouragement, designed the equestrian monument to Wellington in George Square, Glasgow. After Spain, Bankes spent much time in the Middle East pursuing what it has been assumed was the opportunity to practise his homosexuality without the risk of a scandal. Unfortunately a return to London and an indiscretion with a guardsman in Hyde Park suddenly made the Continent compellingly attractive. That was unfortunate. Europe was a relief, but it was also a wrench because in 1835 Bankes had inherited Kingston Lacy, where he had hung an extraordinary collection of Spanish art. From 1838 until his death in 1855 and from Venice, Bankes orchestrated a campaign of decoration to embellish the 'Golden or Spanish Room' at Kingston Lacy.

Bankes was different, not only for his sexual proclivities but for his attitude to Spanish painting of which he seems to have been peculiarly fond. Bankes noticed painters wholly ignored by others. For example, he was the only person before Ford to comment on the Zurbaráns at Bishop Auckland: 'There are [?fine] pictures of ye 12 tribes by a Spanish Master unique in England'. Stirling would devote his best labours to an encyclopaedia of Spanish art, but before then – and in the same spirit of comprehensiveness – Bankes tried to create a representative account of Spanish masters, not in print as with Stirling, but upon wood and canvas.

Bankes made up with enthusiasm what he lacked in discrimination. Although he accepted the attribution to Velázquez of Gentileschi's *Finding of Moses*, a mistake now utterly incomprehensible, he transformed a Caroline house into a temple to Spain. The work had begun fully twenty years before Bankes inherited that property in 1835 – that is to say, when he had been with Wellesley in Valencia. By October 1814 he had sent three cases of Spanish pictures to London. Examples of the then unfashionable Espinosa and Ribalta had been dispatched earlier. A year later Bankes was instructing his father from Cairo, encouraging him to look for work by Juanes in Paris, an artist of whom Bankes was especially fond. Bankes represented an early instance of someone trying to acquire examples of a 'rare' master rather than simply filling his gallery with established names.

It has been argued that he was trying to exhibit representatives of the different Spanish Schools, or of the Spanish School in general. Whatever the truth, improbably enough, it was in secluded Dorset that the rarest Spanish masters were to be best appreciated at the end of the Georgian era, including painters whose work was nowhere else to be seen in England. But there was one exception: El Greco remained unrepresented at Kingston Lacy. Here Bankes may have depended upon his books, upon the eighteenth-century authority on Spanish art Palomino, who persisted in regarding that artist as ridiculous.

The climax to the display at Kingston Lacy was the 'Golden' or 'Spanish' Room, an echo perhaps, of a similar chamber dedicated to the painting of Spain which Bankes could have seen in the Peninsula itself, where he may have visited the house of Richard Wall, a former Prime Minister of Spain. In old age Wall had sequestered himself along with his pictures in Andalucía where he welcomed British visitors, among whom Grantham's protégé Lord Chichester had certainly been one. The Spanish Room at Kingston Lacy was alleged to contain five pictures by Velázquez, of which only the portrait of Camillo Massimi is now thought to have been genuine. One such always created a buzz of excitement. Then it was said to be the preliminary sketch for *Las Meninas*, but now it is thought to be by del Mazo, the son-in-law of Velázquez himself.[12]

Did such Spanish pictures affect taste? It is difficult to say but if so, the most likely classroom would have been Apsley House. Scholars today estimate that there is certain record in the world of ten *bodegones*, either in the form of autograph paintings by Velázquez or copies after lost originals. Of these, two autographs are in the Wellington collection: *The Water-Carrier of Seville* and *Two Men Eating at a Table*. But the early nineteenth century was too soon for any real appreciation of the Velázquez of Seville as opposed to the court painter to Philip IV. Here it is as well to recall that *The Water-Carrier*, the greatest early Velázquez, was taken to be a Caravaggio by the connoisseurs of London, and was published as such in the first catalogue of the Apsley House collection. Only later were the *bodegones*, the creation of Velázquez' Sevillian years, taken seriously. Promotion of abstraction by a post-Impressionist generation, the importance of the still-life in twentieth-century aesthetics, and an admiration for Spanish still-life painters like Gris, Picasso and Miró, all may have contributed to opening the eyes of critics to the significance of the fish, the lemon and the pestle.

But as for the portraits of Velázquez, that was an entirely different matter. In addition to the *bodegones*, Wellington owned three: one still accepted as autograph, the others as 'studio' and 'ascribed'. Intriguingly he also possessed a fully worked-up copy by Goya of a head of Innocent X by Velázquez. All were admired by Richard Ford, who would emerge as the most influential British critic of Spanish painting. After Waterloo,

Ford developed a kind of adulation of the Duke, whose military genius appealed to the romantic in him, as the Duke's profound conservatism spoke to a natural reactionary. Wellington's Spanish paintings may well have been important for Ford before he went to live in Spain in 1830. However, the Wellington Collection mattered not just for Ford. At a later stage, Stirling certainly became attracted by the portraits: Pope Innocent X; the scholar, lyricist and satirist, Francisco Quevedo; and José de Nieto, Chamberlain to Margarita María of Austria, whose mysterious silhouette is framed by the door in *Las Meninas*.

British thinking about Spain inevitably involved France; as indeed had Wellington's unwitting acquisition of a great collection of Spanish pictures. French writers were well in advance of their British counterparts in commenting on the Spanish school: as has been remarked in Chapter 5, Stirling had to plagiarise Gautier when challenged by the difficulty of describing late El Greco. So too, Moorish Spain attracted French artists and antiquarians well before their British counterparts. The net effect was to reinforce a marked antipathy frequently encountered in British writers on Spain. Richard Ford's generation were brought up to define Britain by its antipathy to France and to Jacobinism. Part of the interest people took in Spain was that Spaniards had been such heroic opponents of French tyranny. In Britain Spain was admired because it was not France.

Rapacious French collectors had goaded the British into being more ambitious. The most notorious of these was Marshal Soult, whose unpleasantness of character is well captured in a portrait at Apsley House. Soult had been utterly ruthless. After the defeat of Napoleon, he installed himself and his famous Spanish pictures in a magnificent *hôtel* in Paris. Soult's compatriot Baron Taylor was another who was watched with competitive unease by the British in Spain. Taylor, a naturalised Frenchman of Irish extraction, was sent by Louis-Philippe to acquire the largest number of Spanish pictures in the shortest possible time. Between 1835 and 1837, Taylor took advantage of the 1835 suppression of religious houses to amass a holding of 446 Spanish paintings. As an ensemble in Paris, this was to become known at its opening in 1838 as *Le Musée espagnol*. Although the *Musée* was dispersed fifteen years later, it had at once established itself as the most spectacular holding of Spanish art outside the Peninsula.[13]

By contrast, appreciation of Spanish art in Britain was at best intermittent, the occasional flurry of interest but not more. There were moments when Spanish painting became fashionable and prices went up, though much longer intervals when no one seems to have bid very much at the sale rooms. Insofar as there was a sustained commitment to collecting, it was almost exclusively made by those who had lived long periods in Spain or its colonies: ambassadors, consuls, retired military men and doctors. A constant were those hoping to make their fortunes by importing pictures from Madrid, Seville, Cádiz and even Peru. Although Spanish art never attracted the interest in London which Italian, Flemish and Dutch pictures induced, there was a paradox: London was frequently awash with some of the greatest paintings ever produced in Spain. But this had little to do with either recognition of the painterly merits of the school or a perception that there was a strong market in England. Whereas British dealers had seen the disruption of the French Revolution as a chance to get rich from British clients, the great dispersal following the closing of the monasteries of Spain was not regarded in anything like the same light. Rather, the presence of wonderful Murillos and Zurbaráns in London sale rooms between 1848 and 1855 had more to do with violence and the desire to make money than with a taste in Britain for things Spanish. Spanish pictures from French collections came over as asylum seekers following the revolution of 1848 when Louis-Philippe was deposed and the famous *Musée* dispersed – the most concentrated holding of Golden Age painting ever assembled in one place cast adrift in less than a decade.

Who then in Britain was committed to Spanish art: whether because they really appreciated it, or because they hoped to make good profits by buying cheap in Seville and selling dear in Sothebys? One of the most fearless venturers into Golden Age painting was Sir William Eden, a wealthy baronet from Co. Durham and dedicatee of Ford's *A Handbook for Travellers in Spain*. Metaphorically the Eden house, Windlestone, had been made of coal: erected upon the profits of local mines and reported to have cost £100,000. Eden liked to winter in the south and, in 1832, this happily coincided with the Fords then living at the Alhambra. Ford reported how they went on shooting parties and that: 'We are crazy here about pictures, such buying and selling. By the time Maecenas Standish and that eminent connoisseur, Captain Cook, arrive, the market will be cleaned out'.[14] But then Ford implied that they were paying far more for their pictures than they could possibly hope to recoup in London. Whereas Ford came to sell his pictures within five years of returning to Britain, whether at a loss it cannot be said, Eden hung on. The year after having the gratification of being presented with the *Handbook* dedicated to himself, Eden wrote warmly to Ford, as well he might have done:

> I send you a hasty catalogue of my pictures. I wish you could see them with this bright morning sun on them they look very handsome ...
> Spanish Pictures belonging to Sir Wm Eden at Windlestone Co: Durham *Virjen de la Manzana* and *Virjen del Rosario* both full length sitting figures. The first is in Murillo's early manner – but by no means *hard* and is I think, the best Virgin and Child that I have ever seen she has so much dignity as well as gentleness of expression and is not the mere pretty looking girl who is so often painted for the Virgin. The child is also a *real* and not a *fancy* baby in a white shift and holding an apple in its right hand.
> The upper dress of the Virgin is of a Brick red colour and the lower green not blue-

The *Virgin del Rosario* is the one mentioned by Ponz as being in the Carmelite_Convent at Seville he calls it ' *Bellisimo* a todo ser lo' [In another hand is written *La Porciuncula*]

3rd The *Vision of St Francis*. St Francis on his knees – The Saviour with the Virgin appears above surrounded with Angels scattering flowers – This picture is in Murillo's strongest and darkest style. These three I bought of Don Julian.

4th a Picture on wood by Juan de Juanes, bought in 1831 of the Barbero at Valencia – It represents St Joseph and the Virgin and the little St John on their knees behind the Infant Saviour who is reaching up to a small cross fixed on a tree his right foot resting on a skull – behind St Joseph and the Virgin stands Mary Magdalene holding the crown of thorns and an alabaster box – the background is a river flowing thro a mountainous country – This picture is beautifully finished and very fine colouring – and the faces full of expression – far superior to the general run of what are 'called' early Raphaels – it is the next best picture to that of the Last Supper at Madrid by Juanes, that I know by that master.

5. A large picture of the *Last Judgement* by Ribalta – a vast number of figures the colouring quite Venetian

6th A picture of a Spanish cavalier presenting a painting to a Spanish Lady – the portrait of the man is superb! I conceive it to be by the same master as the above. It formerly belonged to Mr Tupper. I bought it at Valencia in 1831

7 3 *Angels* by Espinosa This is a remnant of the large *Assumption of the Virgin* wch was in the Dominican convent at Valencia and was destroyed by a shell in the attack by the French in 1809?

No 5 and 7 I bought out of a palace in which there were several other good pictures, wh I now regret I did not also acquire.

8. The *Angel of the Passion* a half length figure holding a glass in the right hand this is doubtless part of a picture-I saw an original sketch by Alonso Cano in wh this very angel – was above looking down on our Saviour on his knees – the sketch belonged to Don Julian. The picture I bought of the linen draper at Seville in 1832[15]

Eden lived in easy retirement, watching his Murillos fade in the sun. But there were other busier men whose professional commitment to Spain allowed them to develop a real respect for the art of the country. Of these, two whose careers in the Peninsula were bound together were George Villiers, from 1839 4th earl of Clarendon, and his private secretary Henry Southern. Their case histories are interwoven, though each considered separately provides a marked contrast – the one was a collector for posterity, the other a dealer in desperation.

Henry Southern had a good mind but little money. After leaving Cambridge he had made an important contribution to English letters as co-editor of *The Westminster Review*, founded by Jeremy Bentham in 1824. Southern and Villiers had then become friends despite marked difference in station. It was as a result of an intimacy established in London that Southern had first come to Spain, invited by Villiers as his secretary. There Southern did well – well enough for Palmerston as Foreign Secretary to promote him to the post of permanent attaché to the British Legation in Lisbon. But although Southern was good at his desk, he was disastrous with money, hobbled by acute financial worries during an age when a well-off aristocrat might be appointed to a foreign posting so London did not have to pay. It was because Southern had never had landed rents that in Spain, battling with a low income and encumbered with a large family, he decided to chance his arm with pictures, fervently believing that financial salvation was to be gained through the merits of painted saints.

If Villiers was Southern's *padrone*, Southern appears to have been the ambassador's Leporello. Strikingly handsome like the Duke of Wellington, Villiers, like the Duke too, was fond of sex. He was never discreet, proclaiming loud and clear how he admired Spanish women for their attractiveness. At first Villiers's devotion to the bedroom was treated light-heartedly enough – on one occasion, Southern informed his superior: 'I had yesterday a visit from another lady on y^r account, the sister of Mme Perez she brought me a little girl which you seem to doubt about being y^r daughter. I beg you to dismiss all such doubts: for there never was parentage so clearly legered'.[16]

But then Southern became rather less easy-going when one of Villiers's conquests grew tiresome. There was talk of blackmail. In similar circumstances, Wellington had famously declared, 'publish and be damned'. By contrast, Southern counselled Villiers to seek the advice of his brother-in-law, a top London lawyer. Hereafter the records are silent. In any event, in 1839 Villiers had left Spain, its women and the distracted Southern, who not only had to protect his master from former indiscretions but was charged with seeing to the despatch of an exciting medley of paintings acquired by Villiers for the embellishment of The Grove, his country house in Hertfordshire. The Grove grew resplendent. The work of Brettingham and Taylor in the eighteenth century, by the middle of the nineteenth the mansion had been extended by Edmund Blore who added a grander ground floor and main staircase to make space for the earl's Spanish pictures. When sold by the Villiers family in the 1920s, the Grove was described as having been 'One of the great political houses of the 19th century'. In 2004 The Automobile Association named it 'Hotel of the Year'.

Villiers has long been acknowledged as a pioneer collector of Spanish art, though enthusiasm and a degree of naiveté may have outstripped discernment. Ostensibly it would seem that Villiers was markedly progressive.[17] Once domiciled in Madrid, he had quickly spotted Goya, or at least what he took to be Goya. He wrote to Holland about a double portrait in such terms as to suggest that there was more early appreciation for the Spanish painter than has been thought. But then the Villiers letter reveals not only enthusiasm for a specific canvas but respect for the greatness of the man. It is an important document, provocative for what it implies about the critical reception of Goya, and important for encouraging a revisionist view of the Hollands as patrons of the visual arts:

> I have long been waiting for an opportunity to send and beg your acceptance of a picture wch I think will be interesting to you.
> It is of Florida Blanca and the architect Castro, and painted, as you will at once see, by Goya of whose works I know you are an admirer – they are daily rising in esteem and becoming more prized here – I have directed the picture to the care of John Bidwell together with a lithograph of Goya done by his daughter from a portrait by Lopez wch is esteemed by all who knew him as an excellent likeness.[18]

Here Villiers may be referring to a second version of the so-called *Count Floridablanca and Goya* now in the Banco Urquijo, Madrid. However it is more likely that he was actually looking at a copy painted possibly by Rosario Weiss, the woman to whom Villiers refers in the letter above as 'Goya's daughter'.[19] The original of the *Floridablanca*, an imposing canvas of 1782, had been Goya's first important official commission, a triple portrait, and a critical picture in the oeuvre.[20] However, for all Villiers readiness to look at contemporary or near-contemporary Spanish art, there is a parallel here with the British responsiveness to Velázquez. As has been noted, British views as to what constituted a Velázquez were wildly idiosyncratic and usually wrong. So too with Goya, Villiers fondly believed he was acquiring originals. But in reality, none of his so-called Goyas has in fact been positively identified as authentic, although his *Attack on the Coach* may be so.[21]

Villiers was briefed about Spain by the Hollands, and it was surely then that he discovered the progressive tastes of this extraordinary couple who, at Holland House in Kensington, presided over gatherings by turns exhilarating, unpredictable and terrifying.[22] Villiers discovered before going out that Holland himself had collected Goya prints when travelling in Spain twenty years earlier: in a rough notebook of purchases by Holland, there are references to '*Grabados por Goya y Castillo*' and '*Siete Estampas de los Caballos de Velasquez*'. We cannot be certain which of Goya's *grabados* Holland may have had, though it seems likely that the *siete caballos* were prints after Velázquez' equestrian portraits of Philip IV and family which Goya had made in 1778.[23] But it is necessary to be cautious here. Holland must not be credited with seeking the artist out in the recesses of his studio, a kind of prospecting which never happened. Holland's real love for Spain was a literary, political and cartographic affair. Although it does indeed appear that Holland was more 'visual' than has been thought, in no sense was he an apologist for Spanish art. These sets of etchings were readily available for purchase in the *Calografía Nacional* in Madrid in the late eighteenth and early nineteenth centuries.

Villiers might have seen at Holland House either of two portraits, by unknown artists, of Holland and his children which had been commissioned in Spain.²⁴ But then, as with almost everything done at Holland House, such appreciation of Spanish art as there was represented a shared enthusiasm. In December 1838 Villiers wrote to Lady Holland giving her a progress report on some topographical views which she had commissioned from the Spanish painter Carderera. She had been importuning Villiers with characteristic peremptoriness and he felt obliged to fend her off:

> I fear you must think that I have forgotten your commissions but I assure you I had not been here 24 hours before I set about *endeavouring* to execute them. Carderera the painter was not here and has only lately returned. He is now occupied in doing for me the exterior and the inner Court of Infantado's Palacio at Guadalahara but neither he nor one or two others to whom I have addressed myself have any sketches of the Palaces at Buitrago and Lerma and as they are said to be both in ruins now I fear that part of your commission is unexecutable, but I shall continue trying.²⁵

Villiers became the leading collector in Britain of images of a painter whose reputation Ford was to make blacker than the *Black Paintings*. But Villiers did not confine himself to Goya. After Villiers had departed Madrid, Southern tried to sort out what exactly Villiers had bought and what if anything he owed to a man often referred to in the Southern-Villiers correspondence as Serafín. The latter was Serafín García de la Huerta, the sharpest dealer in Madrid, and well known for handling imitations and copies of works by major artists.²⁶ Of this Southern was aware:

> Serafin is a particular old Scoundrel. I have not settled with him yet. He refuses the Titian – and says that it was all conversation – he will not take back the pictures and pleads length of time and that they were never his – all this is however capable of composition and after a few more interviews we may come to terms. He has lost his memory and ventures the most extraordinary pretensions – claiming as the grand merit that he put it in y^r way to purchase what he calls y^r three grand pictures – the first is the Murillo *St José y Niño* (w^h Costanza has) the portrait of Becerra by himself (the Velázquez of D. Luis) and the *Baccanalia* of Carreño (w^h belonged to the Doncel collection and also the first mentioned) from these disparates you may judge how low the poor man is tocando al bajón.²⁷

For his part, Southern was a great admirer of Spanish paintings but could not afford them nor indeed, as he would later discover, to speculate in them either. From Lisbon he suggested Villiers buy a picture long coveted but out of reach:

> Ever since I was at Seville in 1835 I have desired a picture that Williams has – a Cano –in his fine Italian style –Virgin and St Joseph full length. I made him

promise not to part with it without giving me the option – He renewed the promise as I passed through – and said that when he parted with it I should have it for what he gave for it inclusive [of] the interest of the money. He has now resolved to sell all his pictures and has kept his word by offering me this – the price is 10,000 reales – It is a grand and magnificent picture – in the most perfect state of preservation – Would you like it? I cannot even buy it to sell again – much less to keep it – for I am living upon £500 a year minus commission – with a wife – a house and five servants – w^h are necessary in this idle country a mile and a half from the markets of Lisbon.[28]

Although Villiers had affected to despise Spain, he had a generous feel for Iberian culture which extended beyond its historic painters. Patron of contemporary Spanish artists; promoter of scholars working on Spanish literature; avid purchaser of furniture, tapestries and textiles – he was one of the most receptive ambassadors to the glories of that country. But then all these enthusiasms went hand in hand with that marked contempt for the Spanish character frequently encountered among Victorians. This would be distilled most destructively in the corrosive prose of Ford, whose unflattering animadversions on the Spanish character would cause the famous publisher John Murray to cancel the first edition of the *Handbook,* on the grounds that it was likely to have caused an international incident. By contrast, Villiers had been diplomat enough not to stamp his thoughts in metal. Nevertheless, within the discreet confines of private correspondence, he expressed a mass of contradictory responses to a country at once intensely frustrating but vivid and exciting. He had written to Lady Harriet Baring, a close confidante:

> As for Spain even the most remote corner of it – I could not advise my bitterest enemy to come to me nobody who has not been here can have the slightest idea of the inconvenience and dangers wch it entails, at this moment in particular – The civil war wch is more or less *exhibiting* in every part of the country furnishes every Spaniard with a pretext for indulging the darling passion of his life – marauding – and the roads everywhere are lined with banditti. Barcelona is a beautiful town and the climate is delightful but the people are more ferocious than in any other part of Spain – a whim takes them or an act of revenge is considered necessary and then there is no stopping their sanguinary atrocities – the road from Perpignan to Barcelona is completely occupied by Carlist bands and malheur to the Gentleman and more particularly to the Lady who falls into their infernal hands – You may easily suppose that if it had been in any way decent or practicable I s^{hd} have asked for leave of absence before this time and gone to see my kindred but I know it is not, and for the present I abandon the idea of leaving Madrid. I have never even been able to get away long enough for a journey to the South, and I can assure you that the life of a *Dip* here is very different to the joyous role they play in any other country. Here there is no amusement or relaxation of any kind – no society – no able men – I can't say there are no pretty women for there are – no learning – no literature or books or instruction or arts – the detestable climate – the environs such as one might expect at Timbuctoo, and

one lives in the midst of villainies and low intrigues – having passed 2½ years in hot water I almost feel boiled down. Still however I like being here exceedingly and w^ld scarcely change any other D^ipt post in Europe for mine – there is more to do in the way of business here more to learn of human nature more influence to be exercised in a week than at any other Court in three months. This is owing to the particular circumstances of the country but it is in these circumstances of daily hourly excitement in wch I find myself, and wch suit me so exactly that I never give a thought to the local desagremens.[29]

Villiers, apparently punctilious member of the British aristocracy, thought nothing of breaking Spanish laws. This he did blithely enough while busy upholding justice for British subjects. This amiable contempt for Spaniards is nowhere better illustrated than in his uninhibited correspondence with Palmerston, as Foreign Secretary, his master in London. Evidently a man of style, Villiers was fond of indiscretion and disposed to boldness. So it was that while he had been ambassador, he had responded *con brio* to Palmerston who sounded him out as to the feasibility of buying the best of the Escorial pictures for the newly founded National Gallery. The contrast between Villiers and his predecessor of half a century before, Lord Grantham, could hardly have been more marked. Grantham had come to admire the Escorial so deeply that he had been moved to make a unique gesture for a Briton in Spain: he had donated a painting. But in 1837 Villiers became wildly enthused with the idea of running off with the Escorial 'Raphaels' which included the *Madonna della Perla*, so called because Philip IV had regarded it as the pearl of what in 1650 was the greatest collection of pictures in the world. Villiers responded to Palmerston who tentatively enquired whether it was true that the Spanish government, as always bankrupt, was ready to let pictures go – 'especially the Rafaels of the Escorial'.[30] Villiers replied in June 1837:

> You can hardly suppose that I have not long had my eyes upon the magnificent pictures both here and at the Escurial with a view to transferring them to our National Gallery. Four or five months ago I took the opportunity when Calatrava was in the depth of despair at the emptiness of the treasury to insinuate that he might become a second Aladdin and convert old canvas into solid gold – but he was so horrified at the idea and swore so often that he would sooner sell the shirt off his back than part with a single one of the pictures which the nation valued as the apple of its eye that I have not ventured to renew the subject with him.[31]

Much to Villiers's chagrin, eventually the whole idea had to be dropped. When Calatrava had been approached again, he 'nearly cried with despair' at the idea of Spain losing the only treasure it had left.[32] That excitement was then replaced by watching the Russian ambassador who it was feared might be trying the same thing. Villiers disabused Palmerston, assuring him that there was no Russian in Madrid in treaty for pictures. But he took the opportunity of saying that if Britain did not get the Escorial pictures nobody else would. Whereas it now appeared there was no realistic chance of carrying off the royal patrimony – either to London or to St Petersburg – a real opportunity had been lost following Mendizabal's dissolution of the monasteries. That had happened in 1835 when something really could have been done. Britain had been outsmarted by Baron Taylor working for Louis-Philippe:

> I am in the way of knowing all that passes in the picture dealing world, and I have heard nothing of an agent from Nicholas being here for the purpose of buying pictures of which the Government has the disposal, and I am certain that none is in treaty with the Government. The Russian consul at Cadiz was here two years ago buying pictures from private collections for the Emperor, but the greater part of what he sent to Petersburg was looked upon as rubbish. Spring Rice ought to have sent out some really good judge here to pick up the splendid pictures that were to be found in the convents. Louis Philippe did so and his agent has carried off some prizes.[33]

Frustration at the missed opportunity of walking off with the Escorial 'Rafaels' seems to have provoked Villiers into boasting to Palmerston how he snapped his fingers in the face of authority. After reporting that the government pictures were not going to be disgorged, Villiers continued:

> I wish my patriotism moved me to cede to the National Gallery three pictures by Herrera (the master of Velasquez) which I got privily from Seville and which have been diligently searched for by the authorities of that place and by the Government ever since, but although my treasury is in a most Spanish condition I should, like Calatrava, prefer a state of shirtlessness to parting with them. I merely mention the subject to shew that valuable pictures may be got here in spite of both Government and authorities – indeed it is the best or rather the only way of going to work in Spain. A thundering royal decree was published a short time ago against foreigners who were robbing the national pictures, and the Queen's authorities were enjoined not to suffer one to leave the country. The week afterwards I exported a case 14 feet square full of pictures without let or hindrance either here or at Santander.[34]

Villiers may have been pleased with himself but his manipulative methods of bagging pictures certainly did not please patriots such as the painter José María Escazena. Years after, Escazena, writing to Stirling with amendments to the *Annals*, remembered what Villiers had done. Escazena still recalled with evident bitterness how between them, Williams and Villiers had stitched things up. Referring specifically to the coup which had yielded the Herreras, Escazena used Villiers's unscrupulousness as an example of how foreigners could smuggle patrimony out of the country:

> I cannot forbear to mention how these three pictures by Herrera el Viejo came to the possession of the Earl of Clarendon, because it is a good instance, illus-

trating how the good pictures of Spain belonging to the extinct convents have come out of that country. Mr W^ms of Seville, that successful dealer in pictures, bought these pictures from the friars of San Buenventura of Seville just before the government laid hold of the Church property. It was ascertained by the "fuenta Artistica" that Williams was in possession of those pictures and he was pressed by the authority to give them back to the Nation but W^ms would do no such thing, for as the refra[i]n says "la sardina que se lleva el gato nunca vuelva al plato" [the sardine that the cat takes away never comes back to the plate]. He could not keep them but send[t] them to Madrid to the then British Minister there, the present Lord Clarendon, who of course covers them with his protection and nobody dared to say a word more about them. I cannot say whether W^ms sold them to Mr Villiers or made a present of them to him.[35]

Although Villiers thought the Spaniards absurd, he relished the opportunity Madrid provided of doing what he liked. In Madrid, he was a law unto himself. Throughout his time as ambassador he encouraged faithful Southern to circumvent all and any rules against the export of pictures, as the letter below vividly suggests:

By the Convoy thirty one cases were dispatched the day before yesterday to Cadiz – they contain all your books and pictures and Spanish wine and are sealed by the Custom House here: so they will not be opened until they arrive in England. A little difficulty arose with the Vista and the Academician whom the Custom House sent to see if there were pictures. The difficulty was overcome with money. The pictures are all in false bottoms, but the officers wished to see the cases re-packed. Raymond acted with great advantage and proved that he understands a thing or two.[36]

Southern's letter is a little smug. Not only had he greased the necessary number of palms, but he had even outwitted the crafty Serafín. Southern extracted what belonged to Villiers from Serafín and made him deduct nearly half of a bill because six pictures had been returned. Suddenly too Serafín had disgorged two fruit pieces which Southern greatly admired. A *tallador de madera* had been sent off into 'Old Castile', to acquire seventeenth century furniture, whilst the fashionable Villamil, Spain's most successful topographical artist, and who was to make a fortune plagiarizing Roberts, 'very conscientiously touched up all the little views and costumes'. Southern consoled himself for not being able to purchase on his own account, by commissioning contemporary Spanish artists on behalf of Villiers. It would appear too that his *tallador* (furniture maker) had been successful: Spanish chestnut furniture came to decorate The Grove. Two enormous rosewood chairs particularly appealed. They made Southern think of the seventeenth century and of how the first great Lord Clarendon might have sat in them.

The marked presence of Iberian decorative art at The Grove suggests that the 'Spanish' country house in Victorian Britain may have been more of a feature of the architectural scene than has been appreciated. At the least it is something worth exploring further. In any event, Villiers's mansion certainly had surprising reminiscences of Iberia both inside and out: Portuguese velvet in the library, Spanish pigs in the fields, Spanish plants in the flower beds, and even something out of Don Quixote in the form of a 'monstrous fine ass' whose priapic disposition caused a certain amount of mirth. After his return from Madrid Villiers had been told that for £5 he could have an animal with as distinguished a provenance as any of his paintings: 'It was the Queen's and had been in the habit of carrying her so you may conceive the beast's force: She had it sold I understand for its amorous propensities. The Swedish chargé d'affaires bought it and he tells me he must part with him for the same reason. I could send him in a fruit vessel.'[37]

So much for ambassadors and foreign secretaries. There was much activity at a less elevated level. Despite the excitement of being involved with playing for the highest stakes, Southern, Villiers's eyes and ears, was borne down by money worries. These he thought to alleviate through playing the art market. Southern's position was more precarious than that of most of his colleagues in either Madrid or Lisbon: Lord Hervey, with whom he worked in Lisbon, was the son of the Marquess of Bristol while his former colleague John Macpherson-Grant, who had enjoyed organising cricket matches when the Spanish court was on tour, could afford to retire from the service. He simply reinvented himself as Sir John Macpherson-Grant of Ballindalloch when, upon the death of his father, he inherited a baronetcy and much of Banffshire. Early retirement was not an option for Southern and so he got into the business of buying and selling, though not before he had petitioned Villiers with requests for promotion to a post outside Europe. With something in the colonies, Southern calculated, he would not be expected to sustain the sort of expenses which went with an embassy in Europe. He told his friend that he would be prepared to do a twelve-year stretch in somewhere like Mauritius or Trinidad. In either place he would get up a valuable description of the country with the help of naturalists and artists whom he would assemble. Here spoke the erstwhile editor, open and curious about what was new. But such a posting would never achieve salvation or solvency. Southern ended his days as Minister in Rio de Janeiro, but not before he had had to resort to selling Spanish pictures. During service in the Peninsula, he went into partnership with López, who may have been the fashionable portraitist in the service of the Queen of Spain. In the spring of 1841, the two had amassed sufficient paintings for what they hoped would make a prominent sale in London. Soon it became clear, however, that restoration, shipment, viewing and a host of other vexatious details were creating enormous complexities. Tensely, Southern wrote to Villiers of this 'vital affair to me', as he enlisted what he considered would be the invaluable assistance of the ex-ambassador. Whatever Villiers did by way of a puff, sufficient interest in Spanish art does not seem to have materialised. A poor reception given to Southern's pictures by experts did not help and the sale was a disaster. This became all too clear when Southern ruefully apologised for continuing to ask help from Villiers: 'which sprang from the sense of helplessness and anxiety caused by the blow which the utter failure of the picture speculation has given to my circumstances. I will quietly submit and wait the result of time and chance ... I am now endeavoring to invent some method of disposing of the pictures with the least loss to all parties.'[38]

Then Southern fell out with López, who started to demand money. Southern told Villiers that he was going to make another attempt to offload his pictures, perhaps interesting politicians when Parliament reassembled. If that failed, then he might be forced to chance a 'sale in Mexico or South America. The difficulty in the latter case would be I fear the small chance of finding an honest agent'.[39]

Wisdom was not the fruit of experience. Southern tried the picture business again. Three years later, operating from Lisbon and with different pictures, he thought he had made a good sale to the rich City of London traders, the Bicknell family. Elhanan Bicknell the Elder had become the patron of Turner, having hit upon the happy idea of turning whale spermaceti into wax candles. It was through the intervention of the Bicknells – whose son, also a patron of the arts, had married the daughter of David Roberts – that Southern was confounded. Roberts was called in and the pictures were returned. This was decidedly unwelcome, not least because of complications involving Southern's brother-in-law, the lawyer once recommended to Villiers when in a spot of difficulty with Spanish ladies:

> It was with great pain I saw that some one had given you to understand that your name had been used in any transaction of mine with respect to pictures. I presume allusion is made to Mr Bicknell a city merchant and friend and client of my brother's for whom I bought four of Madrazos most highly prized pictures: two[of] Vandykes portraits [of the] Marquis de Moncada [and the] Duchess of Croy; Rubens's head of Philip IV and Murillos'original sketch of Villavicencio's famous sketch of boys playing which is in the Museum at Madrid. He appeared to be much pleased with these at first and I bought some more for him – but the connoisseurs got about him and the pictures were condemned and the others I had not sent I took myself, offering to take the whole and pay him by instalments
>
> How the matter was ultimately arranged, I do not exactly know but I believe I am to pay him a 1000 as I can: and he is to return the pictures ... This is one of the debts hanging over me and which has always made me so desirous of getting some post in which it was possible to lay something by annually in order to extinguish [it]. I would sacrifice my life readily for this: if that sacrifice would bring only a very few years of gain.[40]

Southern failed to create a market because of the mixed quality of what he was offering; but then, a sustained appetite for Spanish art did not exist in Britain. Had Southern indeed tried South America, his pictures might have crossed with those of a Scot who had spent many years working in Peru where he had formed a collection. Archibald Brown was busy freighting South American treasure because he too was hoping Britain would become El Dorado.

Dr Brown of Lima sounds like the title of a Sherlock Holmes short story. However, Brown first appeared not on the door step of 221b Baker Street but at the Edinburgh address of William Stirling, where he called because he wished to sell what he believed to be a Velázquez of Mariana of Austria. This was part of a collection Brown claimed to have rescued from 'the gorgeous temples of Lima' during many years' practice as a doctor in Peru. It is not certain that Stirling took the bait but he kept in touch. The provenance which Brown claimed for his pictures suggests that some at least may have been of real quality:

Belshazzar's Feast by Pereda
A Lady at lace work and all decorated with red ribbons by Diego Velasquez
A large Donkey with Mary and Infant attended by Joseph by Zurbaran or his pupil Sarabia
Two flower pieces by Juan de Oreleña
The Preparation of the Martyrdom of St Sebastian (by Spagnoletto) signed
A full sized lady in 'Capilla' with consoling Angel by Moya
Two pictures representing stages in the progress of the Prodigal Son probably by Mazo Martínez
A snow piece by Barolome Vicente
Murillo's fruit boys
An Immaculate Conception by Murillo
A large Adoration of the Shepherds by Murillo
A large Adoration of the Shepherds by Jose Ribera, date 1638. This is different from that in the Louvre – tho' similar in some respects and especially in the feeling and expression of Mother and Child – it consists of 10 figures in all, besides cherubs and a dogs head.
The Raising of Lazarus by J Ribera date 1635 on copper
A head and bust of Christ (viz an Ecce Homo) by Luis de Morales
A Dead Christ supported in the arms of his sorrowful mother. N.B. Both these pictures by the Divine Morales are on panel and represent the two styles of this painter. The Ecce Homo was the gift of Charles II of Spain to the Mausoleum of St Francis in Lima.
The head of St Francis – it is a fine picture of a sweet and placid death. I think it may with great propriety be ascribed to Navarette.
The Judgement of Solomon It is somewhat smoky looking but a sweet picture, painted by Alonso Cano 1661, as signed.
A St Jerome by Zurbaran – the gift of Charles II of Spain to the Mausoleum of St Francis in Lima about the years 1672–1678
An Adoration of the Kings

The circumcision of our Lord
Christ as a boy found by his parents (These Zurbarans may have been copies of the series which Zurbaran painted for the Holy Trinity, Seville in 1629.)
The Flagellation of Christ by Roelas.[41]

What can be said of Brown's wares? If the attributions were correct, then this surely represented a remarkably comprehensive gathering of much that was best in seventeenth-century Spanish painting. But doubts begin to creep in, as indeed they did for Stirling. The supposed comprehensiveness of the Brown collection may in itself have been too neat, too didactic an exposition of the Spanish School, given the decidedly uncertain grasp in Britain of what was what in Spanish painting. Rather, it seems that Brown's pictures may have been embroidered as richly as the dress of Santa Rosa. Certainly Brown seems to have encountered real difficulties in selling, though it has to be said he did better than the hapless Southern. The Scottish painter Nöel-Paton, famous for *faeries*, was recruited to shift this cargo. Favourable views were passed to Stirling via Brown who told him that Nöel-Paton had seen his pictures at the 1857 Art Treasures Exhibition:

> Many connoisseurs, and some professed artists have passed an hour or two in viewing them with apparent interest. Among others Mr Noel Patton was particularly taken with the still-life picture on the first floor, with fruit, game and the lobster etc. He had just returned from Manchester and seemed full of Diego Velázquez. He frankly said *he did not like Murillo*. He felt quite satisfied, if not absolutely certain, that the still life picture I alluded to was an early work of Velázquez – the detail was such as his early works exhibited his taste and skill for ... It is now time for me to say in conclusion, that I should not have imposed on your endurance the perusal of the above remarks, nor written so fully, were it not that this may be my last opportunity of speaking of these pictures *as an interested party*. I have too many and cannot well spare the room they occupy, tho' they have served to wean me from my former habits of active out-door occupation. I know pictures in the hands of a man without great name, are a bad stock on hand: there is a *prima facie* prejudice against a person of my station holding genuine property of this sort in England. But were my Adoration of the Shepherds by Spagnoletto exhibited in Manchester under some noble patron, the Marquis of Hertford's Murillo on the same subject would not be there without a rival. Indeed Murillo's composition is only a slight modification of Spagnoletto's.[42]

Stirling does not seem to have been persuaded. He liked to be able to associate a picture with a particular building, a person famous in Spanish history or a document from the hand of greatness before he was prepared to acquire something for himself. However, some pictures do seem to have impressed others as Brown, perhaps angry at Stirling's dismissal, was determined to make clear:

I left London without calling on you to take leave, or leaving as much as my card in token of respect. But I do not the less feel your kindness. After you left me at Christie and Manson's with the Jew Benjamin, I looked round the room for you – but you were gone. After a while Benjamin returned, and asked me if I would take £100 for the Adoration of the Shepherds that you redeemed. I do not know if he would give this money, but he looked as if he would. The picture which, but for its inconvenient size, Mr Christie told me would have sold well, is with the Pereda, the Circumcision by Zurbaran (which was hung too high to be seen to any advantage by Mr Ford, but which, in itself, is an excellent specimen that drew your own attention in my house) and the Luca Giordano with St Jerome, I sent to my brother Duncan Smith, of the firm of Messrs Charles Tennant and Co. Glasgow. The Lady at Lace, or the so called Velázquez, fell into the hands of a Mr (W.S.) Lindsay, a MP and friend of Mr Dalgliesh. It fetched £46.

I have really had a lesson *in the large Devotional Picture Way*. But in other things I have been much pleased ... I have several other copper pictures quite equal, we think, to these; and they seem to show, as do our Italian frames, with engraved ivory facings etc that really good paintings and works of art were conveyed and caressed in Peru. In Truxillo – the first Peruvian town built by Pizarro – there were up to the Revolution of the War of Independence, pictures carried there by the soldiers of the Adventurer who had been present at the Sack of Rome by Chas the Vth – I have, since my return home, sent up the Picture of the Immaculate Conception (Maria la Blanca) to be cleaned and slightly restored by Messrs Seguir and Smart 3 Russel Court St James's. They write me it is a *picture of Great Merit*. It is about a Yard Square, exhibiting the Fathers of the Western Church, the *blond* Virgin floating in air, and surrounded by 16 cherubs etc The Father, and Spirit in shape of a dove witnessing the Miracle from above. This you'll recollect you thought was by Murillo or the younger Herrera, I believe by the former [43]

Who then might have been bidders? Although clearly the stuff was not easy to shift, there was a small coterie of enthusiasts for Spanish painting, notably the Marquess of Hertford and Lord Ward. Further down the scale were the likes of Ford, and Stirling himself who owned one or two exceptional Spanish pictures each. But they did not have the indecent wealth of either Hertford or Ward. Furthermore, Britain would never have an apologist for Spain like Henry Huntingdon whose Hispanic Society of America was to be founded at the turn of the twentieth century. That remains today what it has always been – the most evocative holding of Spanish material culture outside the Peninsula. Huntingdon brought Toledo to New York as Isabella Stewart Gardner transported Venice to Boston. But then, there has never been that urge to build cultural sets in Britain as has prevailed in the New World with its yearning for the Old. Most of the really knowledgeable British collectors of Spanish art lived in Seville as ex-patriots

One of the most colourful of those domiciled in southern Spain was Frank Hall Standish. Standish longed for social acceptance. He might have stepped out of *The Pickwick Papers*: a social snob, 'a sad pudding headed fellow', he was a bad poet whose delusions had once induced him to ask David Roberts to collaborate with Wilkie on painting scenes from Standish's collections of poetry entitled: *The Maid of Jaen* and *The Bride of Palencia*. Roberts wisely declined.[44] Standish was devoted to poetry but also to the baronetcy which he believed should have been his, together with Duxbury Hall near Chorley inherited on the death of a cousin in 1812. The recipient of a fortune by the early age of twelve, Standish spent most of the rest of a short life in Europe before settling in Seville. He died in Cádiz in December 1840, his early end perhaps brought on by disappointment in not having being able to climb into the British aristocracy. During the previous decade he had tried to use wonderful pictures acquired in Seville as a softener to persuade the British government to transform him into 'Sir Frank Hall Standish'. In 1830, had the British Government agreed to revive the family title, the National Gallery could have had the lot, but the request had been turned down. Standish was not pleased. Having it seems developed a rare enthusiasm for the French monarch Louis-Philippe, Standish then began to think of giving all to 'the Citizen-King'. In hindsight that may appear to have been a somewhat redundant gift given the size and richness of the Spanish holdings already housed in Paris. However, Standish felt that there had been tensions between Louis-Philippe and Baron Taylor over the creation of *Le Musée espagnol* and may have felt his gift was going to make up for whatever inadequacies and frustrations Louis-Philippe had felt when presented with the fruits of Taylor's Spanish campaign. Standish told the painter David Roberts all about this when he wrote to him in England from Cádiz in 1838 as thoughts turned toward France as the eventual recipient of his Spanish paintings: 'Louis Philip[p]e is not I believe pleased with Baron Taylor's purchases. He did the best he could but was not long enough in the country and made too much noise to buy cheap.'[45] Before then, however, and indeed ever since his first approach to the British government, Standish came to enjoy what prima donnas have always relished: he kept everyone guessing. He repeated his offer to Britain in 1840 on the same terms as in 1830 but now using Villiers as his conduit in an approach to the Prime Minister, Lord Melbourne:

> Should the Ministry grant me the Hono[u]r of the Baronetcy I will immediately pass over to such persons as they may appoint the whole of my Collection of Spanish Paintings for colocation in the National Gallery. They are upwards of one Hundred in number and as you are aware such as a Nation may be proud to possess. Most have passed through the hands of Mr Dunford of London of Great Newport Street, Leicester Square to whom they were consigned from abroad, and He will assist in pointing them out to the Commission from the other Paintings as the diversity of styles of Murillo in particular would probable puzzle them.
> I could also send a list as far as my memory serves to assist. There are

upwards of thirty Murillos perhaps Twenty Zurbarans, Six or Eight Cano with his own Portrait, as many of Velázquez, and a due proportion of other Spanish Masters. Some are old and others require cleaning, but almost the whole are fit for immediate hanging.

You would be happy to hear that I am now considered out of danger, but my recovery till of late was almost hopeless.[46]

Viscount Melbourne, Prime Ministerial survivor of the consensual European *ancien régime*, might have been susceptible to a discreet arrangement. But matters were no longer conducted as they had been. This Melbourne ruefully admitted when in less than a month the Government said no. Villiers received a courteous rebuff:

This will never do – It would be neither more nor less than buying the Pictures with a title – All the Governments of Europe used to raise money by selling Honours – I don't know that it was a bad thing ... But it would not do now assuredly whatever he is ... By what I hear and read lately I think that both Louis Philippe and Theirs are anxious to find a way out of this affair – It seems to me that the former is desirous to induce the Council to make some proposal that shall have this effect.[47]

That was that. Standish gave the lot to France and was dead by the end of the year. France already had the largest holding of Spanish paintings anywhere outside the Peninsula, and with the arrival of *Le Musée Standish*, the French obtained some more of the best Spanish pictures in the world – though, as with Bankes of Kingston Lacy, Standish too had his fair share of fanciful attributions. Nevertheless, many had been acquired from Julian Williams (d.1866), honorary vice-consul in Seville and pre-eminent among connoisseurs of Spanish art.

Don Julián Williams went native as no other British resident in nineteenth-century Spain. He had a wonderful collection, including Zurbarán's *S. Serapion* which Ford acquired from him in the early 1830s. He had owned what was almost certainly the largest and most important collection of Spanish drawings ever assembled privately. Some of these Ford had managed to buy but evidently not enough; he regretted not having got more. This he confessed to Stirling, for whom in the three-year interval between the appearances of the *Handbook* and the *Annals* he acted as a modern-day supervisor would to a Ph.D. student: 'I would also send you *the* etching of Murillo, that you might swear to having seen it; I *have seen* but time not preserved the signature of Murillo. the Standish drawings are genuine: they were sold to him by Williams who got them from the Curious collection of the conde del Áquila who was murdered. I have some out of the volume which I foolishly did not buy.'[48]

Williams regarded himself as the undisputed authority on Spanish art, and did not like to be challenged. This was perhaps why he told Ford that he thought Widdrington – or Captain Cook as he was also known – 'had an organic capacity to misunderstand Spanish pictures'.[49] Williams was the most generous of hosts – generous, that is, to those who did not dispute with him as an authority on Spanish art. When interrogated, Williams could be dismissive; when acquisitive, dishonest. He thought he had seen the chance of purloining one of the few Murillos still left in that famous shrine to the painter, the Monastery of the Caridad in Seville. The best had been forcibly removed by Soult, carried away to Paris where they came to treasured as supreme examples of the work of the only Spanish artist who had never lost his popularity:

> It was about the year of 1825, that Mr Williams of Seville succeeded in taking to his house under pretence of making a copy, a very small tablet from the sacristry of the Caridad of Seville, on which tablet there is a light sketch of a man bur[y]ing the dead, by Murillo – a thing, which very likely has escaped the observation of every body. The object of Mr W^{ms} was to keep the original and send the tablet back with a copy instead of the original sketch and to bribe the Sacristan for the change, which no body would have found out. I myself made the copy which being fixed up on the old tablet was taken back by Mr Williams who offered to the beggar-looking Sacristan ... eight dollars to hold his tongue, but the honest man strictly refused the bribe and Mr W^{ms} had to give up the original sketch, much to his great disappointment ... Those times are now over and the Murillos in the public buildings are, I believe, quite safe.[50]

The Williams–Standish collection was inventoried in Paris in 1842: 144 paintings and 213 drawings.[51] There was a *Self-Portrait* of Murillo and also, it was claimed, a portrait of the artist's mother. There were 4 autograph Velázquez besides pictures attributed to him. What purported to be genuine were: an *Angels appearing to the Shepherds*; a *bodegón*; a *Child eating a pastry* and a portrait of *Balthasar Carlos*. Predictably enough the artist to whom the largest number of drawings were attributed was Alonso Cano, though it was claimed that there were also 4 of that extreme rarity – drawings by Velázquez. In addition there were 20 drawings by Murillo.

No one had had a more elevated sense of the worth of that bequest than Standish himself. As he moved toward favouring the French not the British, he had fired off obsessively detailed letters to ensure that he had the competitive edge over rivals. David Roberts would receive mixed orders for new paintings with pride for old: one dated December 1836 had begun in an irritable vein. Standish wanted Roberts to paint the Alhambra but 'not to put in Weeping Willows as Mr Lewis does where they were never known to grow'.[52] He then moved on to a discussion of one of two extant *Self-Portraits* by Murillo. Evidently at this stage, this was not part of the Standish collection and Standish was afraid that Williams was going to offer it to Baron Taylor:

> I had heard that Mr Williams had sold the Portrait of Murillo to Baron Taylor for the French Government some days ago ... I wrote last night to Williams as I understood I was to have the refusal of the Picture which he would not sell some time back requesting he would name a price for it and shall consequently know more by his answer ... I have had great opportunities here of getting paintings which would not have been ventured in sale to a Spaniard or the Baron but now almost all the convents are emptied and only an occasional picture finds it way into the market and then the prices are so high that no private collector can venture on them. The list of Murillos from Williams's which I have given you cost me only 2400£ and he certainly has been very liberal for you have no paintings in England of superior quality ... but I confess I shall scold him if he has disposed of his portrait without letting me know. It must have been at some very high price.
>
>   P.S. I have omitted to mention that I possess the whole collection of the Murillo and other Spanish Drawings of Mr Williams as well as his prints.[53]

Standish bought great pictures because he loved Spanish painting and they gave him some status in the British expatriate community of Andalucía. But he also fondly hoped that possession of more than thirty Murillos and ten Zurbaráns would do things for him back home – not just as a Lancashire landowner but within the privileged world of London. To argue this is not to doubt Standish's genuine enthusiasm for art. Rather, it is to suggest that Standish was trying to manipulate Spanish culture to gain access to a reserved aspect of British life. He thought he had something special to offer. Perhaps if those great Spanish pictures had been Italian, in fact those Raphaels from the Escorial which Villiers had targeted, then Melbourne might have seen a way of gratifying this absurd individual.

British critics thought the Seville School – the pride of the Standish collection – represented Spanish painting at its best. Seville had always been a much more vibrant and cosmopolitan city than Madrid. Most commentators found little to relish in the capital. The *Palacio Real* was something of an embarrassment, the *Buen Retiro* had been blown up, and such monuments as the capital could offer were eclipsed by the Burkean sense of awe induced by the Escorial, easily reached in a 'dilly' (for 'diligence', a type of public stage coach much used in Spain). The Escorial and the Alhambra were the two great monuments of Spain, as they have remained to this day. The first was the most sublime building in Europe, the second the most romantic. They were the two poles which induced a current in everyone who visited them. The Escorial was a Piranesi dungeon erected from stones of horror, and Stirling himself was inspired to one of his more memorable periods when describing its relationship to its creator, Philip II:

> With the Escorial is blended much of the history of Philip II ... From the Escorial, too, he issued the decrees which were law on the banks of the Po,

and the shores of the Pacific; and here in a little alcove adjoining the church, – on the wall of which hung a grim allegory of the Seven deadly Sins, by Jerome Bos – amidst the solemn sounds of the organ and the choir – and clasping to his breast the veil of our Lady of Monserrat – he died. The Escorial is, without doubt, one of the most interesting edifices in Europe ... In point of size it will bear comparison with the mightiest works of the Pharaohs or the Caesars, with Karnak and the Colosseum; and it is probably the greatest architectural undertaking ever conceived by one man ... No great structure was ever more strongly stamped with the character of its founder, and the spirit of his age. Seated amidst the rocks and deserts of the Guadaramas, it was the fitting abode of the austere brotherhood of St Jerome; and its dim halls and cloisters are the scenes which imagination most loves to people with the ecstatic monk, and the iron-visaged inquisitor, and the dark and terrible figures of ancient fanaticism. The cheerless prison-like palace seems adapted solely to shelter the old age of that relentless prince, who, in the prime of his manhood, welcomed to Spain his young and beautiful bride, Isabella of Valois, with fire and faggot, and the human sacrifices of an Auto-da-fe. Where is the mind in which the very name of the Escorial does not awaken thought and evoke high associations! For the student of History it stands like a land-mark on the hills of Castile; a relic of the days that are gone, when it was the pride of the Spaniard and the envy of the foreigner; an outward and visible type of the glory and pre-eminence of Spain.[54]

For critics of painting there had been no such thing as a Madrid School. It was quite another matter with the painters of Andalucía, Valencia and even Aragón. It was in pursuit of the relics of the Sevillian School in particular that Stirling emerged as in many ways the most original collector of Spanish art in the Victorian era. It was not just that he had an unusual understanding of and sympathy for the cultural relic in the form of the image. He was also progressive and knowledgeable in various branches of Spanish painting. It has been seen that as far as Goya went, Villiers had enthusiasm but lacked discernment. This was not the case with Stirling, who came to appreciate Goya years before any other Englishman. Furthermore, as one who was deeply interested in the history of the book, Stirling was peculiarly sensitive to graphics of all sorts. It may have been Stirling's love of the printed image – and he came to own one of the finest collections of emblemata in the world – which made him naturally sympathetic to Goya as a printmaker. Whatever the truth, Stirling's collection of Goya prints was outstanding at the time in Britain. This may explain how he came to possess what may have been the best private holding of Goya prints ever to have existed in Britain. As for Goya oils, these were real as opposed to much of what was to be found hanging in Villiers's mansions.

Ford could not abide Goya, because he saw him as dangerous radical. But although this was a blind spot, he had a better eye than Stirling, something tacitly acknowledged when Ford acted as scout for Stirling at major sales. But then they were not after the same things. Stirling had a quite idiosyncratic approach to the remains of Spanish culture. This set him apart. He was a cultural anthropologist, buying paintings as an archaeologist gathers axe heads. He wanted to reconstruct the tribal customs of a society to whose mores a Scot did not normally warm. But then Stirling was never pious, always a latitudinarian, respectful of a society where religion was as integral to the community as fluting is to a pillar. Stirling was a Scottish plutocrat who prided himself in keeping abreast of new technology. Yet he was improbably tolerant of an alien culture.

Stirling's collections were notable for the high proportion of images which had relatively modest artistic merit but were of real value for the light they threw on priority and prejudice in the Golden Age: the Immaculate Conception; the rosary; St Ildefonso, supreme apologist of a Spanish Virgin Mary; *conquistadores*. History was more important to Stirling than art; indeed art was history. Here there is an irony. The appearance of The *Annals* had at once made Stirling father of Spanish art historical studies, though it is more accurate to see him as more than this. He was a pathfinder for Hispanic Studies in Britain. It was as historian not art historian that Stirling had set out to write the first synoptic account in English of Spanish art. But for all the ground-breaking importance of that book, the author remained dug-in in a narrow trench which gave him partial sight – he never challenged the conventional view which always had it that Spanish painting was a subset of Italian art. Nor indeed did Stirling diverge from an Italian way of doing things. It is ironical that Stirling's methodology was profoundly conservative, however novel subject matter may have been. It was Vasarian, it was Italian, it was not Spanish. Ford, who was more attuned to Spanish painting, might have given greater prominence to a framework of regional schools, rather than adopting Stirling's road of progress defined as a march toward an ever greater grasp of realism.

Stirling was appreciated by Thomas Carlyle, who was to history for Victorians what Ruskin was to art. Carlyle treated Catholic imagery with as much caution as scientists handle bacilli at Porton Down, but he chose Stirling who revelled in incense, to lobby for a Scottish National Portrait Gallery. This Carlyle did because he recognised how Stirling regarded painting as no less valuable than documents as historical evidence. Here a brief exchange between Stirling and Ford is revealing. In 1853 Stirling had just acquired an attractive full-length of a Spanish ecclesiastic by Eugenio Cajés (d.1634) (Pollok House, Glasgow). Ford had deciphered the iconography, something which the two had not known when Stirling bought it. The subject was S. Julián of Cuenca. This Ford had discovered when mousing in his library. Ford's books told him of the Spanish legend which had it that S. Julián used to raise money for charity by making and selling baskets for the poor of his diocese.[55] Both Ford and Stirling had enjoyed the intellectual challenge of deciphering the iconography as much as what the picture told of the Spanish mind, and the information it provided of Cuenca.

The staircase at Pollok House, now the home of what is left of the Stirling collection, has portraits of people prominent in Golden Age Spain. Of these, the most suggestive – though far from the best painted – is a half-length of Philip IV, set in an elaborate architectural, garlanded frame with its illusionistic swags and cherubs. Today this would not be given wall space in a national museum. But Stirling treasured it because this was the very painting which had hung above the Presidential chair of the *Academia de Las Bellas Artes* in Seville. To those who confined themselves to the narrow approach of the connoisseur, such a modest image would have been an object of indifference. But for Stirling, it had abundant imaginative possibilities: a likeness of a great man, a part of the fabric of a famous building, and a monstrance displaying the *zeitgeist* of seventeenth-century Seville.

It was not until the very last years of the nineteenth century that the National Gallery in London effectively acquired its first Goya oil painting. But for all the tardiness of official encouragement, there had been a sustained period of nearly 130 years during which Spanish painting had impinged upon the British imagination. Visitors to Trafalgar Square may have searched in vain for a Goya, but in the Regency and Victorian periods the British contributed in important ways to an appreciation of the Spanish School of Painting.

Notes

1 For a summary of what happened in Madrid see John Elliott, 'A Troubled Relationship. Spain and Great Britain, 1604–1655: The Prince of Wales's Visit', in Jonathan Brown and John Elliott, *The Sale of the Century* (New Haven and and London: Yale University Press, 2002), pp. 23–8.
2 Paul Shakeshaft, 'Elsheimer and G.B. Crescenzi', *Burlington Magazine*, September 1981, pp. 550–1.
3 G. Parfitt (ed.), *Ben Jonson: The Complete Poems* (London: Harmondsworth, 1988), pp. 347–8.
4 See John Harris, Stephen Orgel and Roy Strong, *The King's Arcadia: Inigo Jones and the Stuart Court* (London: Arts Council of Great Britain, 1973), cat. No. 261.
5 See Xanthe Brooke, 'Seville and Beyond: The Taste for Murillo's Genre Painting across Europe', in Xanthe Brooke and Peter Cherry (eds), *Murillo: Scenes of Childhood* (London: Dulwich College Picture Gallery), 2001.
6 William Dalrymple to Sir Hew Dalrymple, Union Temple Bar, 10 May 1781, NRA (S), GD 110/965/52.
7 NRA (S), GD 18/5032.
8 Xanthe Brooke, 'Seville and Beyond', p. 61.
9 Nicholas Tromans, 'Wilkie and Spain', University of Birmingham, Ph. D. 1995, p. 59; Ford to Stirling, Hevitre Exeter, 26 November 1846, MLG T-SK 31/30.
10 Bod. Lib., Ms. Eng. Letters d. 296, fols 152–4. These are Jones's undated reminiscences about Napier after the latter's death.
11 Wellington to Sir William Napier, London, 18 April 1851, Bod. Lib., Ms. Eng. Letters c. 252, fol. 150.
12 For Bankes and Spanish art, see Kathleen MacLarnon, 'William Bankes and His Collection of Spanish Paintings at Kingston Lacy', *Burlington Magazine*, February 1990,

pp. 114–25; and, same issue, Enriqueta Harris, 'Las Meninas at Kingston Lacy', pp. 125–30. For a biography of Bankes see Anne Sebba, *The Exiled Collector: William Bankes and the Making of an English Country House* (London: John Murray, 2004).
13 See Ilse Hempel Lipschutz, *Spanish Painting and the French Romantics* (Cambridge MA: Harvard University Press, 1972), Chapter 4, 'Louis Philippe's Musée espagnol', pp. 123–41; also Geneviève Lacambre and Gary Tinterow (eds), *Manet Velázquez: La manière espagnole au XIXe siècle* (Paris and New York, 2002–2003).
14 Ian Robertson, *Richard Ford*, p. 91.
15 Sir William Eden to Richard Ford, Windlestone, Rushyford, 22 October 1846, MLG T-SK 29/56/1.
16 Southern to Villiers, Madrid, 27 July 1839, Bod.Lib., Villiers Ms. Deposit, c. 526/1.
17 Nigel Glendinning, 'Goya and England in the Nineteenth Century', *Burlington Magazine* (January 1964), pp. 4–14.
18 Villiers to Holland, Madrid, 3 April 1835, Madrid, BL Add. Ms. 51617, fol. 3.
19 For light on the role of copyists – specifically Rosario Weiss – and the complexities of assessing the reliability of Clarendon and his art advisers as connoisseurs, see José Álvarez Lopera, *La carrera de Rosario Weiss en España: a la busqueda de un perfil, La Mujer en el arte Español* (Madrid: Jornadas de Arte, 8, Centro de Estudios Históricos. CSIC, 1997), pp. 313–18.
20 Pierre Glassier, *Vie et oeuvre de Francisco Goya*, trans. Juliet Wilson as, *Goya: his Life and Work* (London: Thames & Hudson, 1971), Cat. No. 203.
21 For the early reception of Goya see Nigel Glendinning, 'Spanish Inventory References to Paintings by Goya, 1800–1850: Originals, Copies and Valuations', *Burlington Magazine*, February 1994, pp. 100–10.
22 For an account of what it was like to dine with the Hollands, see Claudia Heide, Chapter 2, 'A Place at the Table', in *The Many lives of Pascual de Gayangos (1809–1897)*, University of Edinburgh Ph.D., 2005.
23 BL Add. Ms. 51629, fol. 50v.
24 Ibid., fol. 48v.
25 Clarendon to Lady Holland, Madrid, 15 December 1838, BL, Add. Ms. 51617, fols 78r and v.
26 For Serafín, see references in Glendinning, note 21 above.
27 Southern to Villiers, Madrid, 20 April 1839, Bod. Lib., Villiers Ms. Dep., c. 256/1.
28 Same to same, Lisbon, 19 October 1840, Bod. Lib., Villiers Ms. Dep., c. 526/2.
29 Villiers to Lady Harriet Baring, Madrid, 18 February 1836, NLS, Ms. Acc. 11388/49 (unsorted envelope).
30 Palmerston to Villiers, Foreign Office, London, 29 June 1837, Palmerston Papers, p. 671.
31 Villiers to Palmerston, Madrid, 8 July 1837, ibid., p. 675.
32 Same to same, Madrid, 15 July 1837, ibid., p. 678.
33 Same to same, Madrid, 8 July 1837, ibid., p. 675.
34 Same to same, Madrid, 8 July 1837, ibid., p. 676.
35 Escazena to Stirling, memorandum [n.d.] contained within package entitled 'Notes and Notices not already used in the Annals of Arts of Spain 1848', MLG T-SK 31/30-4.
36 Southern to Villiers, Madrid, 15 June 1839, Bod. Lib., Villiers Ms. Dep., c. 526/1.
37 Same to same, Lisbon, 13 March 1845, Bod. Lib., Villiers Ms. Dep., c. 527/2.
38 Same to same, Lisbon, 19 July 1841, Bod. Lib. Villiers Ms. Dep., c. 527/1.
39 Same to same, Lisbon, 19 July 1841, Bod. Lib., Villiers Ms. Dep., c. 527/1.
40 Same to same, Lisbon, 21 March 1844, Bod. Lib., Villiers Ms. Dep., c. 527/2.
41 The inventory with covering letter and short essay entitled: '*Some Brief observations on the works of art in Peru viewed under the auspices of the Spanish Kings and Viceroys*' are contained in MLG T-SK 31/4–18.
42 Archibald Brown to Stirling, 2 Manor Place, Edinburgh, 28 August 1857, MLG T-SK 29/28/112.
43 Same to same, 2 Manor Place, Edinburgh, 3 March 1858, MLG T-SK 29/28/114.

44 Standish to Roberts, Duxbury Park, 22 June 1838, NLS Acc.11760 (unsorted envelope).
45 Standish to Roberts, Cádiz, 10 September 1838, NLS Acc. 12158 (unsorted envelope).
46 Standish to Brackenbury, Cádiz, 31 August 1840, Bod. Lib., Villiers Ms. Dep., c. 525.
47 Melbourne to Villiers, Windsor Castle, 17 September 1840, Bod. Lib., Villiers Ms. Dep. c. 525.
48 Ford to Stirling, Hevitre, Exeter, 26 November 1846, MLG T-SK 29/4/128.
49 Robertson, *Richard Ford*, p. 233.
50 Escazena to Stirling, undated memorandum, MLG T-SK 31/30–4.
51 For an inventory of the Standish bequest see Lipschutz, *Spanish Painting*, pp. 225–8.
52 Standish to Roberts, Cádiz, 17 December 1836, NLS Ac. 11760 (unsorted envelope).
53 Ibid.
55 Ford to Stirling, 123 Park Street, 22 June 1853, MLG T-SK 29/57/60.

7
Picturing Spain

How the history of Spanish art came to be written and who bought what Spanish pictures has been addressed. It remains to consider the dialogue between British artists and Spain. This chapter begins with a consideration of that supposed natural affinity which many felt existed between the British and Spanish schools of painting. The story starts with David Wilkie, the first and most distinguished painter to engage with Spain. When in Spain – a country Wilkie famously described as 'the wild unpoached game-preserve of Europe' –between October 1827 and May 1828, he tried to understand the technique of Velázquez, wanting to imitate the style of a painter of whom he had long been in awe.[1] Wilkie's intense interest in both Velázquez and the Spanish school had been stimulated by an earlier unforgettable experience in Paris. In 1821 he had been shown round the Soult collection, then the best holding of Spanish art outside the Peninsula. Wilkie had been captivated quite as much by the attention Soult paid to him as by the pictures:

> His manner to me was exceedingly good humoured and when he spoke to me even familiar. I was nearly two hours in his Hotel during which time he was always by, particularly when I came to the leading pictures. He would lead me by the arm to look at another picture, and though there were people by who could interpret[,] he seemed to prefer having me explain what I thought of the pictures as well as I could myself ... there was a deference shown by those about him that kept me in mind that I was all along in the presence of the great opponent of Wellington[2]

But it was to be another six years before Wilkie got to Spain for what was to be his single brief visit. He was frustrated to find the Prado closed while the Dutch and Flemish paintings were hung, though he did manage to get in on Wednesdays when he would stand for hours transfixed by brown and sand-coloured impasto with which Velázquez had painted *Los Borrachos*. But he was busy too with other things. He enjoyed flirting at the Russian legation where the ambassador, Prince Dolgorouki, orchestrated Murillo tableaux so that girls in the party could play the Virgin. What part Wilkie took is not clear, though had he transformed himself into Murillo that would surely have been right; he was then working on an ambitious quartet of 'Spanish' pictures which were to be bought by George IV. By May, Wilkie was described as the 'Lion of Madrid': the sobriquet because the capital came to observe progress on the most famous picture of this quartet, *The Maid of Saragossa*.

But although Wilkie had a well publicised love affair with Spain and the place of his visit has been seen as critical, his response was as complicated as his experience was equivocal. It has recently been suggested that the impact of the visit on his subsequent painting has been exaggerated.[3] The truth is that Wilkie never did succeed in penetrating the secret of Velázquez; perhaps because his head was full of Van Dyck. He had come straight from Genoa where he had been buying portraits for the future Prime Minister Sir Robert Peel. Van Dyck apart, he also visited Spain too late – early fluency and easy accomplishment had become stalled by a life of increasing personal unhappiness. But then, for years he had been paying theoretical tribute to Velázquez, sensing how this painter could provide much-needed fresh impetus. Wilkie, Sir David Wilkie no less, had long been an influential seer. He had a permanent platform from which to deliver sententious apothegms on the nature of his profession, and he fully subscribed to the views of the quarterlies. They habitually responded by declaring how Velázquez was an entirely appropriate model upon which to form a modern British school. But there was that perennial problem: what did a Velázquez actually look like? There were of course the royal portraits in the Prado, but the *bodegones* and the mythologies, so important for attempts today to unravel this most inscrutable of painters, were then yet to be excavated. Williams, to whom even the supercilious Ford deferred, did not know a Velázquez from a Veronese: not one Williams Velázquez is accepted today as genuine, and Williams was acknowledged by all to have been the pre-eminent judge of Spanish art. It was only with the publication of Karl Justi's monograph *Diego Velázquez und sein Jahrhundert* (1888) that a relatively objective understanding of the artist could be made. This was followed eight years later with the appearance of *The Art of Velasquez* (1895) by Robert Louis Stevenson's cousin, R.A.M. Stevenson.

Stevenson had what might be taken as a painter's understanding of Velázquez because he had been trained by the eminent French artist Carolus-Duran. With Stevenson, and for the first time, a critic at last expressed an appreciation of the artist which is recognizably 'modern'.[4] Stevenson wrote a prose poem about Velázquez' brushwork evoking the magic of the artist which no other critic in any language has since been able to touch. Stevenson too was the first to put it on the line when he stated quite simply that '"Las Meninas" [is] an absolutely unique thing in the history of art'.[5] By contrast, Foucault's take on *Las Meninas* is anything but simple. Surely, however, this ferocious French analyst would have concurred with Stevenson about *Las Meninas* even though Stevenson's approach was so utterly different, guided as he was by his instincts as a painter rather than by the Cartesian logic favoured by this latter-day student of Velázquez.[6]

Nevertheless, although it might be said that the critics had at last got to grips with Velázquez by the dawn of the twentieth century, no artist of comparable stature had to wait so long for justice. However, this did not prevent anyone from having a view. It was Wilkie the art theorist who, early in the nineteenth century, best articulated what was seen as a natural affinity between artists in Britain and Spain. It was a congruity which had intrigued Wilkie for years. Although Wilkie was never able to load his brush with Velázquez, what he had only sensed in London about the affinity between the Spanish master and the British School he grasped fully in Madrid, confiding to his *Journal*:

> Velasquez, however, may be said to be the origin of what is now doing in England. His feeling they have caught almost without seeing his works; which here seem to anticipate Reynolds, Romney, Raeburn, Jackson, end even Sir Thomas Lawrence. Perhaps there is this difference; he does at once what we do by repeated and repeated touches. It may truly be said, that wheresoever Velasquez is admired, the paintings of England must be acknowledged and admired with him.[7]

Wilkie also liked to share thoughts with mentors and patrons. From Madrid a brisk correspondence was maintained with Sir Robert Peel and Sir Thomas Lawrence. The future Prime Minister was shrewd; the President of the Royal Academy, ceremonious. Lawrence was perhaps not entirely happy at having things pointed out to him and, it has to be said, never entirely convinced of the merits of Velázquez – all of which might have accounted for his tone to Wilkie[8]: 'Yes, I fully agree with you in the sympathy of our English pencil with that of Velasquez; but in all the objects and subjects of his pencil, it is the true philosophy of the art – the selection of essentials, – of all which, first and last, strikes the eye and senses of the spectator.'[9]

Philosophy was not one of Lawrence's strengths. Peel was an acute judge of when a painter was working within himself. He was the most discerning collector of Dutch art when it was the height of fashion in England; but although he was not especially interested in Spain, he kept a close eye on Wilkie whom he liked, despite the painter doing his best to ruin much of his work by plastering it in bitumen in pursuit of 'a Rembrandt tone'. Wilkie returned to London with four paintings which were rapturously received by many, though not by all. Peel wrote to the Irish antiquarian Thomas Croker of how he was not happy with what he saw as Wilkie's contrived historicism. More publicly, an art critic of the *New Monthly Magazine* took issue with *The Maid of Saragossa* which had created the biggest sensation when it was unveiled in London: 'The Saragossa picture I think a failure, though you may term it heresy to say so. The figure of Augustina is bad, especially as the picture is most of it fancy. There was no heroine who played Joan of Arc in the way described.'[10]

Au fond, Peel sensed that Wilkie's reach had exceeded his grasp – limitations cruelly exposed by Spain. Wilkie could never be reconciled to the fact that British painters were incapable of creating convincing historical narrative. He could manage the fungal gloom of a Highland cottage, but never the romance of Columbus. Once he strayed from the anecdotal he was lost. But then, difficulties were not simply to do with the story-line but with the very appearance of his canvases as well, technical issues of interest only to a minority of those who visited the exhibitions and who could understand facture. Problems were compounded by state of mind. In Madrid, Wilkie could never banish the thought of Correggio. That mattered, because Correggio managed lights and darks – chiaroscuro – in ways he instinctively warmed to. But then, so what? Velázquez was incomparable: a painter's painter. For that reason alone, Velázquez induced frustration and an inevitable sense of professional defeat in any artist who failed to come to terms with him. The difficulty has been neatly summarised:

> Wilkie's fascination with Velázquez was not of the same intensity as his devotion to Correggio: the Spaniard was lacking those qualities which we have seen Wilkie never ceased to demand – depth and richness. The problem of Velázquez in the eyes of Wilkie was that in terms of his actual application of paint he was too two-dimensional: he did not use glazes sufficiently ('lights and shadows are opaque'), which meant that the warm ground paint was not brought into effect and coldness resulted. This quality of being 'without transparency' set Velázquez apart from what Wilkie considered the essential mainstream of European painting.[11]

Doubts Peel felt about Wilkie were not so much to do with technique as with the sentiments induced by the spectator looking at the finished results. Once Wilkie was back in England, pressure from London clients made him want to be all things to all men. He tried to assimilate Velázquez's methods – something the French painter Manet was the first to do – but in addition, Wilkie was making life especially difficult for himself since he was also attempting to compose histories in the grand manner. That went against the grain. Wilkie felt his Spanish histories not only needed to be stirring stuff, they had to do justice to the vernacular, the ethnic and the picturesque – the very qualities Wilkie had first noticed in Spain, and the first items of Spanish culture he had enumerated in letters home. The heroic and the picturesque were genres which were incompatible even in the most competent hands, but here, the results were distinctly unhappy. This is clear enough in the *Spanish Posada*, or

Guerrilla Council of War. It was in connection with this picture that Wilkie pointed out how 'Spanish regional costumes are brought together in an inn'. It was a pity he did that. A combination of prettiness and brooding drama explains what is wrong. Attitudes are struck, figures isolated, and melodrama ensues. There is a feeling that Wilkie gave up on Spain, perhaps because he went there too late to change habits and preconceptions. This is suggested by his lack of response to an approach made via David Roberts from Standish who was very rich and very keen on getting painters to take him seriously as a writer. Standish asked Roberts and Wilkie to paint scenes inspired by his poems. This he made clear in a letter sent to Roberts by Standish on one of his intermittent visits to his Lancashire property:

> I had rather leave the choice of composition for a Picture to Sir D: Wilkie himself – I have a great deal of Spanish Costumes Edifices and paintings so would as well have a subject of any other kind. However from either of my two little poems the *Maid of Jaen* or the *B. of Palencia* he might extract very pretty scenes. The first w^d present him 'the flight with Gypsies' 'the Meeting with Banditti' and the 'Return' when the funeral is met. The Second 'The meeting of Adela and Philip', 'the Spanish Camp' the 'Bishop judging Adela she lying on the ground' (if this were taken you must paint the Architecture) and the 'scene at the Grace' this w^d also want your help for the accessories. Indeed I should like a joint picture by such eminent Artists and would take another by Sir D. alone – You can shew him this letter and let me know what he says.[12]

Perhaps responding to this letter, Wilkie wrote to Standish in November 1838 to say that 'he will have great pleasure in proceeding with his [own] picture of the Village School for you'. It is surely revealing of Wilkie's defeatist and defeated attitude to the country that he seems to have rejected all the Spanish suggestions which had been made by Standish.[13]

The enduringly vulnerable *Self-Portrait* by Wilkie (c.1804/6, Scottish National Portrait Gallery), so startlingly like Velázquez's *Juan de Pareja*, made clear that Wilkie was going to have trouble in Spain. It is tempting to see graphically etched in Wilkie's haunted face lines of fracture which would never be closed – indeed, would come apart in the massive nervous collapse Wilkie endured in 1824. Wilkie never mastered Spanish painting. But that was not a lone failure. Spain continued to be viewed through an Italian glass, even by David Roberts whose superficial success at capturing a 'British' Spain induced Genaro Pérez de Villaamil, later to become Spain's premier painter of topography, to make a pilgrimage to Seville when Roberts was there, to sit as his feet. William Brackenbury, a kindly and knowledgeable connoisseur of Spanish painting who thought the world of Roberts, wrote to the artist from Cádiz:

My friend Mr Villa[a]mil born and bred a gentleman – an officer in the Engineers of which his father was a Colonel but who has followed the fate of many others in this country, and had recourse to the exercise of his talent for drawing and painting, to aid himself and many others dear to him, has manifested so great a desire to become acquainted with you and your Works – that he goes to Seville, chiefly for that purpose; having requested a few lines of introduction, I could not deny him the gratification he seeks for – and therefore, although I had already given him a letter to Mr Williams requesting him to introduce Mr Villa[a]mil, I beg to present to you, a Spanish Gentleman of Talent and acquirement who I have known for some years and for whom I feel much esteem and in whose welfare I have taken and do take an interest, Escazena speaks in raptures of your production.[14]

Thereafter Villaamil, on visiting London in the summer of 1841, came to ask for Roberts's advice.[15] But although everyone seemed to think Roberts captured 'Spanishness', the Roberts encounter was ultimately superficial. It was not until Whistler got going on Velázquez in the late 1850s that someone working within a British orbit could be said to have had their vision transformed by a Spanish artist.

Ostensibly David Roberts was the most successful British artist to picture the Peninsula. Somewhat improbably, he had begun as a house painter. But the trouble was he had remained one in spirit. Roberts was driven by an overwhelming desire to make money, not to push boundaries. It was said he returned from Spain dripping with honey: he gave clients what they expected, what they understood, and what they wanted. It was observed more than once how Roberts turned the Alhambra into Windsor Castle. In so doing he was by no means the first to transform the 'other', the alien, into something which could be understood by those whose efforts to assimilate Hispanic culture were confined to turning the pages of a travel annual or the plates in a set of bound lithographs. James Cavanagh Murphy, an architect who had visited Spain in 1802, had published his beautifully illustrated book *The Arabian Antiquities of Spain* in 1815. As has been pointed out by Raquejo, the plates detailing the Alhambra translate somewhat prosaic spaces into visions of the sublime such as might have been approved by Edmund Burke, the high priest of that aesthetic theory.[16] Murphy's illustration of the fretted roof of the *Hall of the Two Sisters* makes it part cave dripping with stalactites, part early English cathedral chapter house. What was supposed to have been Murphy's topographically accurate account of the idiosyncrasies of Spanish architecture was actually nothing of the kind. It was a presentation of the iconic buildings of Spain in support of the hoary old theory that the Gothic style of medieval France and England really derived from the Moors who had imported and modified the Saracenic arch. As for Roberts, he vulgarised his subject matter. But it worked. He made a huge amount of money as his Spanish lithographs became extremely popular back home in Britain.

But high vulgarisation was just what Russell Flint did later in a quite different way. Flint was a facile and fashionable twentieth-century British water-colourist, and a hundred years after Roberts, he developed a good line in décolletage Spanish ladies. This allowed visitors to the Royal Academy Summer Exhibitions to enjoy a little mild titillation. Flint has an honourable place in the British proclivity to see Spain as a land of sun, sand and sex, something which has remained an article of faith with the British on the Costa del Sol.

Roberts saw an untapped market in a picturesque country. Accordingly he set out for Spain in 1832 and, largely concentrating on Andalucía, worked up sketches to transform prospects after his return to London in 1833. Once back at home, he turned portfolios into popular prints, releasing visions of Spain as periodical illustrations to four *Landscape Annuals* issued by the successful publishing entrepreneur Robert Jennings between 1835 and 1838. The *Annuals* were a triumph for text and image: Roberts produced romantic plates to complement text supplied by Thomas Roscoe, son of William Roscoe, the famous Liverpool historian of Renaissance Italy. But that was not the only way Roberts gave the British public a vision of Spain: he also aimed at a more exclusive market through the production of 'presentation' watercolours, sometimes on a heroic scale. They were much-sought-after by the grand, though few of Roberts's wealthy buyers were creators of taste. How could they have been? Only a brief acquaintance with Roberts in Spain reveals how he owed more to the past than to the future. Precisely because of their technical brilliance, there is a certain sense of slickness about Roberts's watercolours – a shaft of vulgarity like the sunbeams of his Spanish clerestories – which sets them apart from paintings by Turner, Girtin and Cotman. Roberts pursued wealth, but Turner renounced materialism to maintain that integrity which kept him wholly absorbed with the miracle of vision.

But Roberts worked hard and he took risks – though with *contrabandistas*, not his palette. Populism paid off, and success was achieved by an artful insertion of drama into the quotidian and the topographical. But then, Roberts was nothing if not calculating, and had the good commercial sense to give admirers what they wanted. His clients knew what they were looking for because their prejudices had been formed not by looking, but through reading Washington Irving and Blanco White. Spain came to be appreciated through literature first, and only then through pictures. Roberts himself spent as much time reading White as looking at the Escorial. Plate XIII, entitled, *Chapel of the Nunnery of the Most Pure Virgin at Carmona*, from *Picturesque Sketches in Spain* (1837), played on what people could remember of White's scenes of clerical life in Spain (Figure 10).

Roberts, in Andalucía, had often been helped by John Macpherson Brackenbury and Julian Williams, pre-eminent British connoisseurs. Consuls in Cádiz and Seville respectively, the two were able to penetrate

10 David Roberts, *Chapel of the Nunnery of the Virgin at Carmona*

convents for the salacious gaze of the painter. To his collaborator Thomas Roscoe, Roberts dictated recollections of visits to establishments in Seville and Carmona respectively. The account stands as epitome of the male Anglo-Saxon imagination, deeply ambivalent as it was about the culture of Spain. The painter recalled how he had witnessed the ceremony of the taking of the veil at the Convento de los Rejes on 13 July 1833. The nuns are described as sitting cross-legged, 'another instance of the many Moorish customs still retained' and another instance, for that matter, of the habit then of interweaving Christian piety and Moorish romance like an arabesque of the carnation and the tulip. Roberts recalled the nuns as having been shrouded in long white veils, though the penumbral gloom gave the room the 'appearance of a funeral vault'. Suddenly the victim glided into sight. Immediately there is created an erotic *frisson* as Roberts confessed that 'contrary to what I had been led to expect ... the young lady was pre-eminently beautiful; her age, apparently, hardly exceeding seventeen'. Shrouded sisters strew flowers upon the prostrate body; symbol of her death to the world, after which the 'lovely novice' was led away – though Roberts artfully confided that before leaving the chapel, he was unable to resist looking back upon 'the lovely object' which had knelt before him, a vision which induced a strange sadness piercing the soul. Further reflection had made this Scots Presbyterian shudder at the cruelty committed, the more so because the parents of this damsel who herself would soon be in distress, had witnessed the sacrifice; for all that, they 'seemed proud at the part they bore in the heartless spectacle before them'. Finally, to ensure subscribers could visualise her face, the compilers of this suggestive farrago called in Murillo, the only Spanish artist they could be certain would find a response in the mind's eye: 'As the light from her solitary taper fell upon her exquisitely lovely features, I saw a countenance such as Murillo would have delighted to paint; her eyes were truly Andalusian, – full, round, and dark; the forehead high, spacious, and polished. There was a bewitching sweetness in her smile that was irresistible.'[17]

The onlooker sees presiding over this affecting scene a Virgin of the Immaculate Conception who hovers like a tutelary presence over the Abbess whose nobility of birth is stressed in order to provoke a predictable British response. Spanish society was thought of as innately aristocratic, whether by nature or by nurture. Both Wordsworth and Southey thought they saw an inherent nobility in the roughest Spanish *gitano*, while Roberts relished telling his readership that the abbess was the 'Reverend Mother Donna Maria del Carmen de Rueda y Rueda, Lady Superior of the Convent of the Most Pure Virgin, sister in law of the Marquis de Valle de Reyna'. In another part of the room, a would-be Saint Cecilia, in the hands of a painter always a dangerously erotic figure, raises eyes heavenward, playing the organ with moist eyes and bud-like parted lips.

This was not word play but foreplay, an aspect of that sexualisation of Spain which was such an important part of the pleasures of Andalucía. The power of the Spanish woman had long been legendary. During the War of the Spanish Succession, the earl of Peterborough had implied to the Duchess of Marlborough that his conquests included bedrooms as well as cities: 'The most disagreeable country in the world is Spain; their officers the greatest robbers, and their soldiers the greatest cowards; the only tolerable thing is your sex, and that attended with the greatest danger.'[18]

Over a century later, convent interiors – those Regency and Victorian theatres of artful hypocrisy, though only a small aspect of Roberts – were just one of the ways in which the male gaze was successfully aroused by things Spanish. While Roberts and Roscoe worked on the *Annuals*, William and Edward Finden contrived another profitable publishing venture entitled *Byron's Beauties*. This appeared in 1834. It included prints after drawings by John Frederick Lewis (1805–1876) who was in Spain during 1832/33, that is to say he overlapped with Roberts though, wisely, he avoided subjects favoured by the latter.

Lewis was interested in Spanish painting, Roberts apparently not at all. Lewis began his trip by copying more than sixty pictures in the Prado. There he was so drawn to Velázquez that Ford wrote in late August 1832 of how the artist was in Madrid and 'in love with Velazquez'. Lewis did Spanish interiors too, but whereas Roberts drew cathedrals white and incandescent in dissolving shadow, Lewis favoured the ethnic and what traces could still be found of the exotic. In Andalucía, Lewis explored those languid themes which would develop into the airless and perfumed sensuality of Cairo when, between 1841 and 1851, he came to live in Egypt. In Spain Lewis was drawn to Moorish architecture, ethnic costume and beautiful women. For the Findens's *Byron*, Lewis contrived an absurd image of the Maid of Saragossa whom he transformed from Bellona into Venus. Donna Julia appears as a dark and sultry beauty whose languor suggests a narcotically induced reverie. Such tributes to the hidden charms of Spanish women was identical to the mood created in another drawing by Lewis, made in Granada at the same time, but with an altogether different purpose. It was intended to conjure up pleasing memories for Richard Ford, a huge admirer of the painter and evidently too of this woman. Ford was satisfied, writing on the back: 'The Portrait of Concha Barca una de las mas salerosa Senoritas de Sevilla'. Ten years later, Stirling too was to enjoy what would seem to have been abundant sexual liaisons extended over three separate visits to the country. Although there is no diary of Spanish conquests, Stirling kept letters of friends in which their anticipation of pleasures doubtless stirred memories. One correspondent boasted from Seville that ' it is really wonderful to hear my fluency particularly when I can drag anything like bedroom furniture or the parts of the human body into the conversation: the women here I think the handsomest I ever saw and having succeeded in getting an introduction to an influential pimp here, I have no doubt I shall soon hablo castellana like a native'.[19]

So much for sex. The *Annuals* revealed more transparently the extent to which Spain was special: here alone in Europe, history was alive. This exciting paradox which had been so beguiling to Gautier was because Spain had not been modernised. The vernacular survived in astonishing variety and abundance. In the preamble to the *Landscape Annual* for 1835, Roscoe wrote that 'for the moment, we can live in the Past as though it were our natural home, and regard its legends as things of our own experience'.[20] But then, very few came to see all this for themselves and so it had to be transformed into a language for the drawing rooms. The Alhambra, Spain's most famous building, is overlaid with transparencies which familiarise its features:

> Gather together the square towers of our minsters, embattle them, and dispose them in picturesque clusters, place them on a glorious elevation rugged in its acclivities, its sides embowered and empurpled with the olive and the vine, and in their aggregative form an idea of the *Tower of Cormáres*, add our remaining Norman donjons, massive and square as they are, borrow from the palace and castle of Durham a part of their magnificent outline, let Windsor contribute something of the rounded softness of its principal portions, pile up mountain upon mountain to form a background to the lofty but green and wooded height, to which your imagination has now transferred your gathering of towers, connect their crenellated and embattled walls, and you behold Alhambra in its general aspect, and this again forms but a portion of the line which the city of Granada traces along the horizon.[21] (Figure 11)

Such a recipe represented the most extreme effort at Anglicising one of the wonders of civilisation. At the opposite pole was the work of Owen Jones (1809–1874), for whom the Alhambra was the morning star. Jones travelled the world both on foot and in his imagination, mapping its ornament in all its floral abundance. In Greece, Jones had met the French architect Jules Goury (1803–1834), where they discovered a mutual interest in the use of paint in architectural decoration. Together they had journeyed to Egypt, Turkey and finally Spain, there to undertake a detailed survey of the Alhambra. In 1834 Goury died from the plague, the same outbreak which induced both Roberts and that percipient student of Spanish painting Sir Edmund Head to leave Andalucía prematurely.

Jones mourned his friend and dedicated himself to continuing their joint enterprise. What eventually became one of the great architectural publications of Victorian Britain, entitled *Plans, Elevations, Sections and Details of the Alhambra* (London, 1842–1845, 2 vols) – indeed, what became the finest monument of the nineteenth century to the British curiosity for

11 David Roberts, *The Tower of the Comares, The Alhambra, Granada*

Spain – had a complicated history. The initial publication in 1836/37 was never completed: ten separate issues were planned, only three appeared. But what emerged represented an important moment in the history of printing in Britain, and those three modest issues were the first significant fruits of the newly invented chromolithography process. At this juncture Jones was as interested in printing as in architecture, much as William

Morris, his spiritual son, would be thirty years later. Those three issues were a base camp from which Jones went on climbing, joined for the summit by the extraordinary figure of Pascal de Gayangos. First Jones drew the horseshoe arches and then Gayangos translated inscriptions, to produce their great collaboration on the Islamic word and image.

For Jones, his Alhambra book was not the end of the affair. There was much cultural bullying in early Victorian Britain – there were harsh debates, strenuous and uncharitable, about architecture and its handmaidens, decoration and colour. These had been largely provoked by independent but related societies of fanatics in the two ancient universities: the Cambridge Camden Society and The Oxford Society for Promoting the Study of Gothic Architecture, both founded in 1839. The Cambridge ecclesiologists had been responsible for provoking religious wars about proper design of churches and appropriate use of ornament. Jones, spirited and opinionated, joined in with gusto, spending much of the decade enunciating 'principles' as to the proper use of decorative motifs, diktats later to appear at the front of his *Grammar of Ornament* (1856) like some manifesto dedicated to the liquidation of recidivists. Jones mastered – or thought he had mastered – style as it manifested itself universally. He had seen all or most of it and so felt himself to be qualified to pronounce that no culture had so perfectly understood the correct use of ornament as the Moslems of Spain. The decoration of the Alhambra, even after twenty years of intense research into the other great civilizations of history, remained for Jones without parallel: 'The Alhambra is at the very summit of perfection of Moorish art, as is the Parthenon of Greek art. We can find no work so fitted to illustrate a Grammar of Ornament as that in which every ornament contains a grammar in itself. Every principle which we can derive from the study of the ornamental art of any other people is not only ever present here, but was by the Moors more universally and truly obeyed.'[22]

Jones preached, even in the Court of the Lions, though he could not write to save his life. By contrast, Ford composed passages purple as the iris, one of which remains among the finest descriptions of the Alhambra in the English language:

> Such is the Alhambra in its decayed and fallen state, the carcass of what it was when vivified by a living soul, and now the tomb, not the home, of the Moor. It may disappoint those who, fonder of the present and a cigar than of the past and the abstract, arrive heated with the hill and are thinking of getting back to an ice, a dinner and a siesta. Again, the nonsense of annuals has fostered an over-exaggerated notion of a place which from the dreams of boyhood has been fancy-formed as a fabric of the Genii. Few airy castles of illusion will stand the prosaic test of reality, and nowhere less than in Spain. But to understand the Alhambra, it must be lived in, and beheld in the semi-obscure evening, so beautiful of itself in the South, and when ravages are less apparent than when flouted by the gay day glare. On a stilly summer night all

is again given up to the past and to the Moor; then, when the moon, Dian's bark of pearl, floats above it in the air like his crescent symbol, the tender beam heals the scars, and makes them contribute to the sentiment of widowed loneliness. The wan rays tip the filigree arches, and give a depth to the shadows and a misty undefined magnitude to the saloons beyond, which sleep in darkness and silence broken only by the drony flight of some bat. The reflections in the ink-black tank glitter like the subaqueous silver palaces of Undines: as we linger in the recess of the windows, below lies Granada, with its busy hum, and the lights sparkle like stars on the obscure Albaicin as if we were looking down on the reverse firmament. The baying of the dog, and the tinkling of the guitar, indicating life there, increase the desolation of the Alhambra. Then in proportion as all here around is dead, do the fancy and the imagination come alive. The halls and the courts seem to expand into a larger size: the shadows of the cypresses on the walls assume the forms of the dusky Moor, revisiting his lost home in the glimpses of the moon, while the night winds, breathing through the unglazed windows and myrtles, rustle as his silken robes, or sigh like his lament over the profanation of the unclean infidel and destroyer.[23]

Here is a world of light and dark, silver and black, much closer to the Victorian photographer of Spain, Charles Clifford (1821–1863), than to Roberts and Lewis who certainly laid siege to the Alhambra but never captured it. Charles and his devoted wife and assistant Jane clattered round Spain with mule and cart overloaded with heavy photographic equipment, an improbable pair to be encountered on the dusty highways of the country, calling to mind in their eccentricities Mr and Mrs Vincent Crummles, the endearing if preposterous itinerant actors in *Nicholas Nickleby*. Clifford, 'fotográfico inglés', and court photographer to Queen Isabella II, remains one of the greatest topographers in the genre. But the Cliffords were even-handed: they did not favour Andalucía. They were unusual in valuing those parts of Spain the water-colourists had often ignored: Toledo, Valladolid, Burgos, León among the great historic cathedrals. In otherwise neglected cities, Clifford made darkness visible as he captured the deep shadow of a gothic cloister with as much artistry as he caught the incandescent filigree of an Islamic balcony.

On more Christian if Catholic ground is the treatment given by Roberts to the iconic figures of Ferdinand and Isabella. The frontispiece to his 1837 *Picturesque Sketches in Spain* is a beautiful example of nineteenth-century book illustration, showing the entrance to the funerary chapel of the two sovereigns. But rather more intriguing is how within, and on a separate plate, Roberts manipulates the angles of the tombs. As presented, they serve for a history lesson (Figure 12). Details are arranged so as to insinuate that the Catholic Kings liberated Andalucía from the Moor because of their devotion to Christianity and to that most Spanish aspect of it, the cult of the Virgin Mary. The eye looks over the tombs at an angle of 60° until arrested by the wall of the chapel. In front is an altar dedicated to the Virgin with a forest of guttering tapers. But although Roberts

12 David Roberts, *Chapel of Ferdinand and Isabella, Granada*

shows a good eye for the evocative detail, his presentation fails to deliver. Roberts has chosen to present the tombs of the founders of Spain's greatness, short end on: only the heads of the recumbent effigies in dramatic foreshortening is seen, and even the heraldry which would help with identification, is perfunctory. This is not archaeology but a romance on the clash of civilizations.

The Literary Gazette took the opportunity of reviewing Roberts's work to make portentous remarks about spirituality and creativity. It is declared that

> [e]very artist *quoad* artist, must lament the Reformation. As a man he may be rejoiced at the liberation from superstitions, bigotry, and intolerance of the Romish church, but as a painter, he cannot reflect without regret on its magnificent and picturesque ceremonials, and on the facilities which the noble edifices where these ceremonials were performed afforded for the exhibition of the finest productions of the pencil and the chisel. This is a feeling which the superb volume before us will greatly increase. There is no country in which all the gorgeous pageantry of the Catholic religion has been, and still is, so profusely and ostentatiously displayed, as in Spain.[24]

The article stressed not the timeless magnificence of the Spanish interior, those qualities Cardinal Wiseman would always adore, but the unparalleled opportunity given to artists to depict performance and ceremony. In early life Roberts had done much painting in Edinburgh theatres, and it is his interpretation of the anthropology of worship as theatre which was his abiding contribution to the invention of Spain.

Roberts's interiors of Seville Cathedral seem to give prominence both to the Mass as performance and to the allurements of vernacular costume. Architecture is spidery and schematic. Little attempt is made to convey what was unique to the Spanish cathedral. Space is vertiginous certainly, and that was as it should have been. But then such an effect could have been equally enjoyed from the pencil of Prout at Amiens or Turner at Ely. Roberts ignored that fusion unique to the Spanish cathedral: mascara virgins reflected in pools of black mahogany; *retablos* as high as rookeries; golden lamps and dull refulgent bronze; flaming glass and rivers of silver brocade; macerated hearts in crystal and gem; bishops as withered as salted fish; martyrs in robes of magenta and electric blue. Spain needed John Ruskin with his eye for the kingfisher. But him, it never found.

Roberts engaged with the dramas of space and light, and the theatre of worship but not with materiality. It is no surprise that William Beckford was an admirer: the crockets of Fonthill pierced the clouds of Wiltshire as the eye is lost in the mystical vaulting of a Roberts nave. The interior of the nineteenth-century Spanish cathedral, a crustaceous husk, demanded the brush of Moreau, the surface of whose canvases seem crusted leather. What Roberts gave the British public was Roman: it was Piranesi. Roberts was certainly no ecclesiologist; that would have to wait for George

Edmund Street and Street's passion for the roughage of local brick. Roberts was a *vedutista* who translated conventions evolved for the Colosseum into Spanish.

The extent to which Roberts sacrificed truth for the picturesque is demonstrated in *Part of the High Altar during Mass and the Great Candle in the Chancel of Seville Cathedral* (Figure 13). Here separate tribal customs are run together. In no sense is all this an accurate record of what would have happened during a service. Instead Roberts creates a *mélange* of stages, vaguely reminiscent – but not accurate in detail – of what would have been enacted at different intervals and indeed in different services. In the middle ground, behind the altar, a monk attends to the wick of the famous giant candle which at twenty-six feet was the size of a tree. Roberts responds to this famous attraction with enthusiastic wonderment in the way that a visitor to a Victorian fairground loved to see the strong man hit the bell. The giant candle would not have been lit during Mass. Candle-bearers and acolytes swinging censors, these too would not have been distributed with such artful asymmetry. In truth, mass is not taking place because no priest stands opposite the tabernacle where the host was reserved. What looks like *reportage* is simply the clustering of groups whose presence is demanded by the exigencies of the artist rather than by the tolling of a mass bell.

Integral to the success Roberts enjoyed with Spain was the presence of women in his views of church interiors. It was as if women provided an antidote to what would otherwise have been alien and threatening. Throughout four volumes on Spain, Jennings, the proprietor of the immensely popular *Annuals*, massages the rigours of Spanish Catholicism with the presence of the devout but beautiful lady in a mantilla. The compilers of the texts absolved themselves from any apparent interest in sex by pronouncing that 'the association of women with infidelity of any kind, is revolting to the mind of man'.[25] But such a disclaimer was surely challenged by another aside: witnessing the emotion of a woman at prayer was a substitute for quite other sorts of fervour. Roscoe declares that '[t]he Andalusian beauty, indeed, never looks more lovely and engaging than when she appears at mass'.[26] Here was something of an abiding theme. Twenty years later, the highly sought-after Aberdonian painter John Phillip, whose engagement with the country earned him the sobriquet 'Spanish' Phillip, or 'Phillip of Spain', was well aware of how exciting the assignation between religious observance and the male gaze could be. His painting entitled *Agua Bendita – a Church Scene* shows a man standing at a holy-water stoop while slyly eyeing up two girls whose charms are much enhanced by their fervent piety. Here Phillip was merely exploiting a theme which Edwin Long, a popular if rather vulgar purveyor of historical drama, had been the first to exploit with his own *Agua Santa* of 1859, in connection with which Long had written: 'the custom in Spain of passing holy water by touch, often gives a lover his first opportunity of

13 David Roberts, *Part of the High Altar during Mass and the Great candle in the Chancel of Seville Cathedral*

approaching the object of his affection'.[27]

How ambivalent Victorians felt toward Spain when confronted with performing churches is vividly brought out in Roscoe's description of religious ceremonies at Salamanca where, it is declared, the cathedral would be 'pronounced a huge, ill-assorted, and unmeaning pile ... were it not for the boldness of its nave, the splendour and elaborate ornament of its decorations, assisted by gorgeous show and the pomp of its public worship'.[28] However, there is much evidence to suggest that ephemera and transience caught the imagination of the travelling mind rather more than did vaulting or crockets. Here there was something of an irony, since it was the unchanging nature of the way of life which it was always claimed was what was most remarkable about Spain. The point is made in the most illuminating way when Roscoe argues that 'the loud thrilling music of its admirable choir, especially during the holy week, leaves you little wish to criticise its exterior beauty, or the want of exact symmetry in its parts'.[29]

Ford in prose, Roberts and Phillip in pictures, all expressed a settled condescension toward the Spaniard as a racial type. It was an article of faith that the ordinary Spaniard was mulish, a prejudice which lived on to create the iconic figure of the Spanish waiter whose last and most famous manifestation has been 'Manuel'. He eventually made his way to Britain, where his appearance in *Fawlty Towers* was essential to the creation of one of the most popular and profitable of all British television comedies. Before then, however, the fecklessness of the Spaniard is epitomised by the Roberts lithograph entitled, *Correo de Los Morros Granada* (Figure 14). Much here is provocative. The insistent depth created by the arch serves to frame a painting of *Christ Carrying the Cross* while a proclamation boldly announces 'Granada Cólera Mórbido'. Beneath are slumped picturesque beggars. One of them challenges the viewer while apparently showing complete indifference to the danger of diseases the announcement of which hovers above. Another appears to be the resigned victim of a monk who, it may be imagined, delivers a homily about the deadly sin of indolence. Within the frame of the arch is an '*Obrador de Botas y Zapatos*', and on the side next to the beggars '*José Rodríguez Gallego Abaniquero*'. Here the proprietor sits in the front stall with legs crossed and leaning on his stick. To his left is a woman whose state of *décollotage* suggests a prostitute. The net effect confirms the British view of the street Spaniard as a sturdy beggar.

Surveying the contribution Roberts and other painters had made to the image of Spain, a reviewer in *The Spectator* offered a brief survey: 'John Lewis' had given the British public 'representations of the costumes, people, and manners', while David Roberts had 'delineated the buildings', before a challenge ensues: 'it now remains for some master of landscape to picture the wild mountain scenery'.[30] This was not to be. Although Ruskin had abiding connections with Spain through family involvement with sherry, neither he nor his hero Turner ever visited the country. The

14 David Roberts, *Correo de los Moros, Granada*

Pre-Raphaelites were not interested in Spain. These absences may have had nothing to do with any instinctive lack of sympathy with the sierra but were quite simply the consequence of market pressure. Dealers could sell Andalucía but not Castile. Thereafter the situation did indeed change. British book illustrators and print-makers, together with some painters in oils, do seem to have responded strongly to the character of buildings and landscape in the Peninsula in the last decades of the nineteenth century and the first half of the twentieth. However, that achievement is beyond the parameters of this book.[31]

Although it had been correct to say in 1837 that an engagement with Spanish landscape had yet to happen, it was surely wrong to describe Roberts as having delineated the buildings. He chose only those buildings, whether Islamic or Christian, which allowed the imagination to escape its material prison in pursuit of the Romantic. Rather, it was Roberts's engagement with the context of worship which was his most abiding contribution to an evocation of Spain. The ritual of worship, the equivocal position of the priest in the community, the nun, the tense interplay between Church and State – these were the themes which came to the fore as 'Spanish' subjects for painters of narrative and history, annually offered up at The British Institution and The Royal Academy.

Before then, however, John Frederick Lewis was also creating a synoptic vision of Spain in watercolours of interiors. These were markedly different from those of Roberts. Figures are more important, interiors more closely observed. Lewis paid tribute to his friendship with the Fords, his enthusiastic and generous hosts in Granada. This he did by including the couple in his watercolour *The Celebration of Mass in a Moorish Chapel in Cordova Cathedral* (Figure 15). Here the chapel is a palimpsest: architecture, only generically Moorish, has features taken from cathedrals in both Córdoba and Seville. The setting is reminiscent of the chapel of the *Villa Viciosa* in the cathedral at Córdoba; once the seat of the *kalif* and thus containing the *Al-koran*. But it is not an accurate reconstruction. Lewis is trying to create an epitome of what interested the British visitor to Andalucía with much the same sleight of vision as a Dutch flower painter included the narcissus with the rose. There is the profile of an Islamic arch whose deep indentations make it look like a jelly mould from Mrs Beeton. Murillo's celebrated *St Anthony of Padua with the Infant Christ* has miraculously taken to the air like the Holy House of Loreto to migrate from its proper home in Seville Cathedral. For all the apparent exoticism of a quintessentially Andalusian theme, the disposition of the figural groups is based upon the language of classical art. The small boy in the left foreground, the anomaly of whose Philip III costume is not at first obvious, has the graceful nobility of an aristocratic portrait by Van Dyck from his Genoa days, while the adults, clustered to the right of the altar, owe their existence as much to the Venetian votive tradition as to the iconography of an Adoration of the Shepherds. The 'Genoese' boy appears as a gate-crasher at the party, but he is kitted out in this anomalous way because he too, like the Murillo altarpiece, comes from Seville: he is one of the dancing boys, the *Seises*, or choristers whose twice-yearly dances with castanets and plumed hats in front of the high altar of Seville Cathedral, on the Feasts of the Immaculate Conception and Corpus Christi, was for the English what the carnival had been for the grand

15 J.F. Lewis, *The Celebration of Mass in a Moorish Chapel in Cordova Cathedral*

tourist in Venice. But even then Lewis's inspiration had nothing to do with Murillo, still less with Islam, but rather, betrays a pose lifted from Van Dyck's *Franchi Family* (National Gallery, London), acquired in 1824/25 by Lord Berwick – ironically, a picture which Lewis had almost certainly studied before he ever set foot in Spain. Perhaps Lewis may have taken filled artists' notebooks to Spain: reminiscences of how to do it in Flemish and Italian so as to inoculate himself from the idiosyncrasies of the Spanish School.

At the British Institution and Royal Academy, 'Spanish' themes were not frequent but, then, still less were the visits British artists made to Spain between 1820 and 1870. British painters were rarely able to rid themselves of an Italian way of looking at Spanish art, and narratives of Spain were usually Italian. This was because painters had been involved for so long with the Grand Tour, and there had never been a Grand Tour of Spain. Still more importantly, there was no narrative painting of the Spanish Golden Age upon which a Victorian artist wishing to exploit Iberian subject matter could base his work. Velázquez had never been a storyteller.

By 1838 Wilkie had finished his intense engagement with Spain. By contrast, Lewis had continued to paint Spanish subjects after his return to England in 1833. He had created something of a flurry with his *Sketches and Drawings of the Alhambra made during a Residence in Granada in the Years 1833-4* (1835) and *Sketches of Spain and Spanish Character* (1836). The taste for Spain Lewis was ready to exploit: many of his Spanish themes have a clear reference to Murillo. Indeed Murillo sometimes becomes the subject itself, as was to be the case twenty years later with the work of the Aberdonian interpreter of Spain, John Phillip.

Murillo Painting the Virgin in a Franciscan Monastery (1838) is one of the most ambitious tributes to a famous Spanish master by Lewis (Figure 16). Murillo stands on a step toward the back of a chapel while behind can be seen some of his most famous pictures, including the *St Thomas of Villanueva distributing Alms* which hung in the Monastery of the Caridad in Seville. Here Murillo looks like Murillo, as we know his appearance from existing self-portraits, though the conception of the artist poised in meditation in front of a giant canvas is clearly taken by Lewis from the way in which Velázquez had chosen to depict himself in *Las Meninas*. Lewis has worked hard to get this picture right but – as with Wilkie's own excursions into Spanish painting – it is a failure. It becomes painfully clear why Lewis would abandon his most ambitious of all Spanish narrative pictures, *The Proclamation of Don Carlos*. In *Murillo Painting the Virgin*, the separation of the two main groups by a step breaks the rhythm, while in order to emphasise the centrality of Murillo himself, there is an empty corridor in the middle. This represents a failure of organisation rather than a caesura. Although there are nearly twenty figures, the whole ensemble is comatose. Seated monks, heads in hands, look like disconso-

16 J.F. Lewis, *Murillo Painting the Virgin in a Franciscan Monastery*

late holiday-makers waiting for a delayed flight to Alicante.

Lewis had more ambition than Roberts and promised to surpass even Wilkie as a narrator of the Golden Age. However, like Wilkie, he was unable to master the challenge of multi-figure narrative. He continued to work up Spanish themes after returning to England, but never produced a major Spanish history piece. This was something of a tragedy since three out of what is known to have been at least four wonderful studies survive for his long-considered epic, *The Proclamation of Don Carlos*.[32] The trouble was that Lewis could never get beyond the spirited vignette – beyond, that is, exciting passages which clearly led to dead ends. However, in the process of making what has been described as 'a valiant effort to recast the water colour exhibition piece as a proper vehicle for the dramatic reportage of contemporary history', Lewis has taken something which had nothing to do with Spanish art as his starting point.[33] Perhaps it was partly because Lewis had had no direct experience of the savage horror of the Carlist Wars that he turned to Rubens as he attempted the grand manner for the depiction of what was like all civil wars, markedly nasty, brutish and long. It has been suggested that Lewis based his design for *Don Carlos* on *St Bavo receiving the monastic habit* which the National Gallery in London had received in 1831. But even Rubens, famously himself never daunted by a project however ambitious, could not give Lewis the confidence he needed to see his project through. Instead, Lewis assuaged vicariously something of his frustration about being unable to accomplish the elevated genre of narrative. In the vaults of the Royal Scottish Academy, are seventeen miniature copies in water colour by Lewis after Velázquez.[34] Almost forgotten since they were presented by the painter himself to the Academy in 1853, their colours glow like polyanthus. Lewis was proud of them. Writing to Stirling asking if he would be good enough to present a copy of his *Annals* to the Royal Scottish Academy, he referred to his copies and to their joint passion for Velázquez:

> Accept my thanks for y^r most kind note, as well as for the promise of your most interesting book on Spain and Spanish Art:
>
> The Scottish Academy I am sure will rejoice in its acquisition as they will I am sure recognise your goodness in so promptly acceding to their wishes as expressed by myself.
>
> Perhaps when you give orders for its transmission to Edinburgh, you will kindly cause it to be addressed to D.O. Hill Esq., Sec^r to the Royal Scottish Academy.
>
> ... the trustees [of the National Gallery] have also made a glorious acquisition in the Aquilan Velasquez: This is as it should be – who I wonder has the beautiful sketch of Murillo's *San Tomas de Bonaventura* the picture of which is in Seville? It was most perfect, as was the man in black with the dog.
>
> I am here possibly for the summer, but have only left London lately; the S. Academy have possessed themselves of all my Spanish copies and in fact are

doing great things for the education of the people – and I think that when you know and see the efforts which they are making here to put art on its proper footing you will be much interested in their endeavours.³⁵

High Victorian painters changed emphasis. Now there was much less concern with architecture – ample figures observed at closer quarters fill out the canvas, while there is a greater focus on gourds and oranges, black-eyed girls and hidalgos. Social exchange is freighted with ambivalence. If the trademark of Roberts and Lewis had been the doe-eyed supplicant in black mantilla, now the rustle of the black cassock can be heard in so many stories of questionable taste by the artists John Phillip, Edwin Long and Alfred Elmore. These represented a trio who were the main suppliers of Hispanic themes to the Victorian collector. Their repertoire at large, however, was not such as to suggest that they would offer a very profound analysis of Spanish mores. Elmore's most famous picture, *On the Brink*, says it all. Here a respectable but impoverished Victorian mother hovers outside a gambling den while she is being propositioned. A melancholy end is predictable. She needs the money. Long's themes were even more louche. His titles included *Ready for the Bath* and *Love's Labours Lost*. The innocent spectator might be forgiven for assuming the latter to have been an edifying scene from Shakespeare. Not at all. It turned out to be four teenage Egyptian adolescent girls, three of whom are bare-breasted. But distance lends respectability: delicious creatures are offered up for the viewer or voyeur within an archaeological reconstruction of a pharian temple. As a consequence of the painter's bogus reconstruction of a supposedly 'authentic' setting, the girls become untouchable. Here, history painting is made to be at once powerfully arousing and assertively prohibitive. As for Phillip, titles such as *El Cigarillo: Taking a Quiet Whiff* hardly induce much confidence in his powers as an interpreter of Hispanic culture.

Many pictures with Spanish themes were exhibited at The Royal Academy, particularly in the 1850s. This was partly due to the flood of great Spanish art which was to be seen in the London sale rooms from 1848 onward. But it also had a direct connection with the appearance of so many Victorian histories of Spain and its empire dating from the publication of Prescott's *Ferdinand and Isabella* in 1837.

In 1846 Millais, aged merely seventeen, exhibited at the Academy for the first time. His offering carried the ambitious title *Pizarro seizing the Inca of Peru*. A rabid monk flourishes a crucifix with which he appears to be encouraging much energetic killing. Here Millais was riding on mounting anti-Catholic hysteria, but his picture was also a timely response to the new interest taken in the history of the Americas provoked by Prescott's *Conquest of Mexico* (1843) and the imminent publication of his next transatlantic epic, the *Conquest of Peru* (1847).

Millais was a friend of Stirling, who maintained close ties with some of the leading London artists. He became a prodigiously successful painter, becoming baronet and President of the Royal Academy. For his diploma piece – that was to say, the work an artist had to produce on election to the Academy – Millais offered up one of his many daughters as a Habsburg princess. Millais's *A Souvenir of Velázquez* (1868) is evidently a pastiche of Velázquez' inimitable technical magic. However, although this was in a very obvious sense a homage to the Spanish artist, it was also a ploy on the part of Millais to justify himself to his critics. Recently he had abandoned a minute and particular style, consistent with an erstwhile sympathy for the Pre-Raphaelite Brotherhood, in favour of a much rougher and more rapid assault on his canvas. His critics, and there were many, deplored this since they saw the change as facile, something induced by the need to pay for too many children. For his part, Millais thought that if he could identify a much revered Old Master – and he chose Velázquez – with this shift in style, that would counter some of the hostility with which his new way of painting had been greeted. In other words, Velázquez was recruited less upon his own merits than for what he could do to help Millais himself out of a tight corner in the studio.[36]

Millais, the most successful of the High Victorian painters, had his reservations about Spain. He was yet another eminent Victorian who never set foot in the country, and he was impatient with if not contemptuous of those who went on about what a wonderful inspiration Velázquez was for the young artist. But he always had an eye for the main chance and, whenever there was something to exploit, there he would be with brush at the ready. For the Royal Academy Exhibition of 1857 he had produced *Escape of a Heretic 1559* (Figure 17). The picture had been inspired by hospitality enjoyed at Keir, the Stirling seat near Dunblane in Scotland. But Millais had been summoned on his wife Effie's account as much as his own. Effie, erstwhile spouse of Ruskin, had researched in Venice for Stirling, working in the mornings in the Marciana and the Frari while her husband was writing *Stones of Venice*. From Venice, Effie would transcribe bundles of *relazione* for the study at Keir. These still lie in the Stirling archive: tied in Effie's favourite violet ribbon and unopened since Stirling put them away. Ten years later, John and Effie Millais, as guests, inspected the Keir library for those books on the Inquisition which Stirling had used for *The Cloister Life of Charles V* (1852).[37] They also admired the superb prints in what then was the best private collection of Spanish graphic art in Britain.

Millais's *Heretic* was the fruit of that visit, a return to a similar theme which Millais had painted five years earlier: *A Huguenot on St Bartholomew's Day Refusing to Shield Himself from Danger by Wearing the Roman Catholic Badge*. That had been exhibited at the Royal Academy in 1852. The *Heretic*, like the *Huguenot*, is a variation on the theme of love endangered by religion. In the former, a pretty but very

17 Sir John Everett Millais Bt, *The Escape of a Heretic*, 1559

English girl, pink as a milkmaid and hardly pubescent, has just been released from the custody of a monk who kneels in the background, bound and gagged. Her liberator looks like a chorister so incongruously youthful is he. He helps her into a cloak to hide the *sambenito*, or penitential garment. This uniform for death – an infernal football strip in red and yellow, with a logo of devils roasting in hell – the condemned wore on their way to the pyre. There is a certain irony about all this melodrama which hovers precariously over the abyss of the absurd. The juxtaposition of the lovers, the sudden appearance of the tousle-haired boy come to free a schoolgirl, offers a sixth-form *Perseus and Andromeda*. In the context of the oeuvre, the *Heretic* is less a starting point than a re-affirmation of the kind of anti-Catholic imagery often produced – whether out of inner conviction or with an eye to outward success, we cannot be certain. Response to the *Heretic* was mixed: it came in for much criticism, not least from John Ruskin who described it, with a welcome if unusual degree of economy, as '[a]t once coarse and ghastly in fancy, exaggerated and obscure in action'. Ruskin was hardly inclined to give the painter a fair chance – after all, Millais had run off with his wife. Former humiliation, however, would have been compounded by outrage if Ruskin had got an inkling of what remains a suspicion. With this picture, Millais allowed everyone to believe it to have been based on a real historical happening. It has been suggested that the episode illustrated by Millais was nothing more than an ingenious fake, a much inflated and embroidered account from *Documentos relativos a los Procesos por la Inquisición de Valladolid*. Millais was not beneath such things: in the same year he had exhibited *A Dream of the Past: Sir Isumbras at the Ford*. For that, poetry was supplied – or more properly, invented. In truth the source, alleged to have been taken from a medieval ballad, had in fact been written by Millais's friend Tom Taylor. Taylor was hugely versatile even by Victorian standards, sometime Fellow of Trinity College, Cambridge; art critic; popular playwright; editor of *Punch*; and evidently an ingenious hoaxer.

What might be termed the high-Victorian penchant for Spanish double entendre seems to have been provoked by Wilkie's *The Confessional* (Figure 18). This small unpleasant work of 1833 is an early example of what would become that Victorian paradigm between precision and uncertainty, an ambiguity concealed within an external shell of painful exactitude. Wilkie adopted the format of St Jerome in his Cell: the lion is replaced by a bible, but there is the skull and hour glass which accompany St Jerome like dismantled heraldic devices. An antique monk whose profile is a conflation of Raphael's *Julius II* and the Escorial Titian of *St Jerome*, much admired by the painter when in Spain, bows his head to listen to the confession of a much younger man who is a regular. Everything suggests the penitent is finding his vocation a desperate struggle. The intense concentration of the confessor, shaggy head immobile as marble, suggests the worst: this tortured young man, cruel lips parted in revelation, lizard-like features preternaturally but coldly sensual, has clearly committed a mortal sin, the exact nature of which expands in enormity to fit the imagination. The painting is a triumphant insult to that

18 Sir David Wilkie, *The Confessional*

aspect of Catholicism which crowds at the Royal Academy most hated and despised. Wilkie's *Confessional* stands as one of the great expressions of anti-Catholicism in Victorian England.

Phillip was the most successful purveyor of Spanish fantasies and, like his more famous contemporary Millais, often inspired by William Stirling. Apprenticed to a house painter, like Roberts before him, Phillip had first gone to Spain in 1851 to escape his wife, the sister of the lunatic painter Richard Dadd, with whom she shared a marked streak of mental instability. Phillip had then made a second visit in 1856. At first Ruskin had had doubts about Phillip and, although even as late as this juncture still regarded his work as 'slightly vulgar', gradually started to see merit in a painter whose bright and brassy pictures went down easily enough with the public. The high priest of Victorian taste came to recognise the painter's increasing feeling for Mediterranean light and a new ability to capture the mood of his Spanish subjects. Whatever Ruskin's strictures, the fact was that Phillip sustained a steady and increasingly serious commitment to Spanish art. His *Kate Nickleby* (1867), painted in the year of his death, suggests that he was moving ever closer to Velázquez, though perhaps he was seeing things in borrowed light since he had acquired for himself that famous pioneer study in Velázquez appreciation, Whistler's *At the Piano* (1858–9), a decisive gesture for the appreciation of the Spanish artist by English-speaking painters.

One of the most Spanish of 'Spanish' Phillip's creations was *The Early Career of Murillo – 1634* (Figure 19). It was first exhibited with a passage from the *Annals* inscribed beneath. It was an ambitious work by an artist whose painting *La Gloria*, acquired by the National Gallery of Scotland in 1897, would prove to be the most expensive purchase the gallery would make since the foundation of the institution in 1851. Why was Phillip evidently popular in his time but largely forgotten today?[38] In the *Murillo* the viewer certainly gets his money's worth: there is a multitude of figures painted with great technical skill. The picture illustrates the title – a clearly recognisable boy Murillo stands in profile at far left. The young artist's innate nobility of mind is suggested by his relaxed but elegant posture. He awaits with dignity the verdict of two passing monks who scrutinise a small canvas which would reveal a head of the Madonna could it be seen. Had Phillip confined himself to figures on the left that would have made a good picture. But he felt compelled to spoil a good story with the gratuitous pursuit of the picturesque and the wearisome insertion of the cliché, like most British artists set upon inventing Spain. The entire right-hand side is dispensable, merely emasculating the impact made by the treatment of Murillo and his interrogators. A *morisca*, muscular baby at her shoulder, takes an illicit peek at the canvas – her unlettered presence but obvious awe being reference to the claims derived from Palomino of how Murillo, the populist, was loved by the whole community of Seville. But she is too obviously a *beaux arts* figure, her ambitious *contraposto* descending from the females in frescos by Raphael in the Vatican. She is altogether too eye-catching as she distracts attention from Murillo, exiled to the far left of the picture. Beyond her and to the right, is a medley of figures who merely represent local colour. There is an immense still-life in the right foreground which, in its superabundance, might well have been a separate picture. Behind and in the middle ground are three figures who have nothing to do with the story but are present to affirm British preconceptions of Spain. Staring out of this sweaty market-

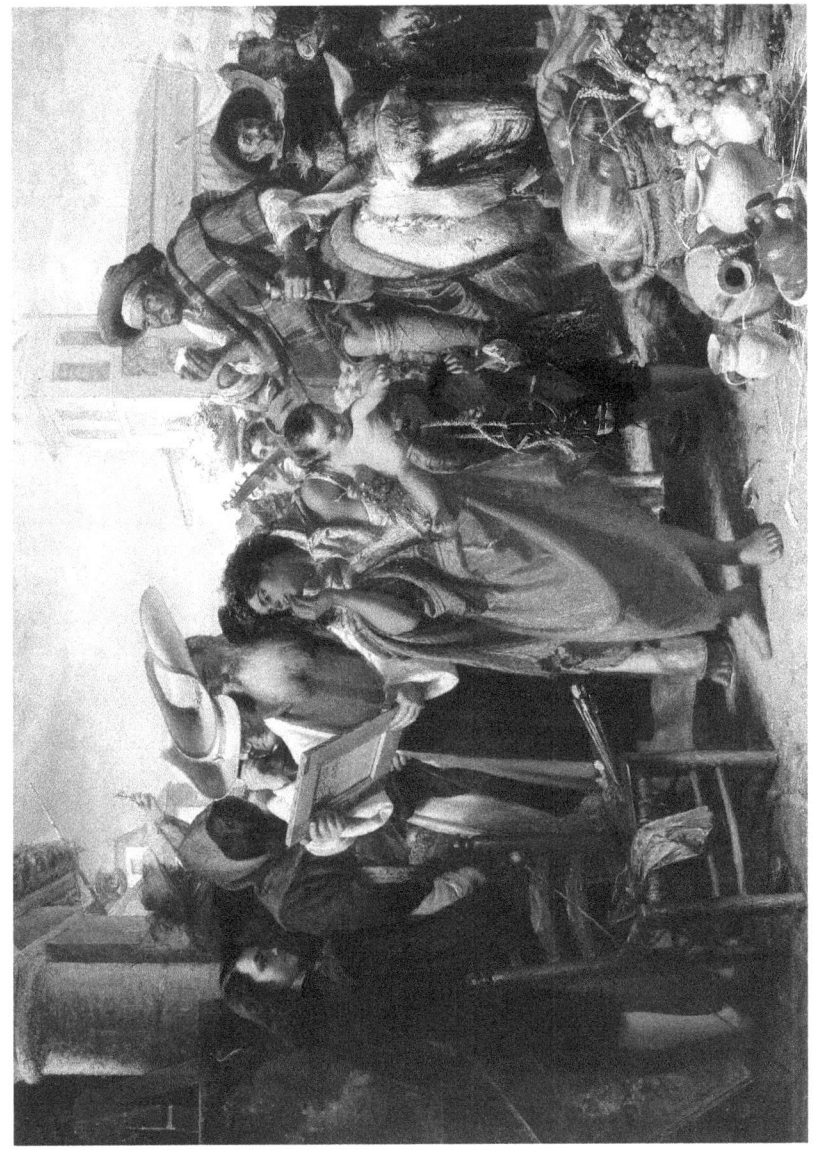

19 John Phillip, *The Early Career of Murillo*, 1634

day crowd is the disembodied head of a pretty Spanish woman whose dancing, alluring eyes are partially shaded by a basket of food on her head. She is a remote relation of those Sapphic ladies on the Erechtheum, comic because there is the suggestion of come-hither. Unfortunately this is not possible; a path is blocked by a simian figure whose bulk thrusts itself forward at an angle of 45° from the back of the donkey. Wrapped in a Spanish plaid, this hirsute being grasps a flask of wine in one hand and bread in the other. His expression is unfortunate: his look suggests he has broken a molar on his crust. Phillip has wholly abandoned any attempt to integrate the group; the man stares vacantly over the top of the group clustered around Murillo. But then, he is primitive and he is colourful and that is all that mattered, for this was what the British wanted from Spain. To the right is a resounding cliché. A grovelling man deferentially plucks off his hat to proffer documents to a Spanish aristocrat who, stiff with pride, passes without deigning to acknowledge an unctuous supplicant. That supercilious head was a detail appropriate for the label on a box of Havanas, but never the Academy.

Although the facture of *Murillo* has something of the glacé Holman Hunt, it is not all slickness and finish. Indeed as a recent exhibition has revealed, technically Phillip was extremely accomplished – versatile, adventurous and open to new ways of applying paint. He died in 1867, just fifty, and as he was just modifying his palette in the light of his admiration for the young Whistler, one of whose pictures he had recently acquired for his own collection. Much thought went into the contrivance of the *Murillo* which was rapturously received. It is therefore of some interest to see how 'Spanish' this image really is. Actually not at all. There is nothing about the way Phillip has applied paint which has the faintest reference to Murillo, nor indeed to any other Spanish master. Murillo certainly looks like Murillo; anyone with the slightest notion of Spanish art would have had no problem in knowing that this was an anecdote from the life of the painter, without having had to read either the label or the quotation from Stirling which inspired the whole thing. There is, too, one figure at least who might be regarded as a tribute to Zurbarán, the painter of monks. Unfortunately in this case the cowled regular is merely a prop. He stands motionless beside Murillo, still and sinister, breaking up the integrity of the narrative, and with no business to be there. But like the peasant on the donkey, he gets in as a concession to an attempted 'Spanishness'. Essentially this is a picture which expresses the notion Delacroix entertained that the coming of the railways would spell the end of guitars and castanets. Phillip has no more grasped the essence of Spanish painting than had Wilkie some thirty years before. What Phillip does accomplish, however, is to conceal beneath an Italian way of doing things one of the most original ideas in the history of Western painting.

There is something of an irony that the lay-out of the *Murillo*, to the extent that it is Spanish at all, was inspired by Velázquez, not the man to whom the picture ostensibly pays tribute. The concept of the monks examining a canvas which is withheld from the spectator is taken from *Las Meninas*. In broad terms too, the siting of the group left of centre and at an angle to the canvas front, is mapped out much along the same lines. A contour running from the sun hat of the snow-bearded monk down to the *morisca* and up again to the peasant on the donkey, before finally descending to the cornucopia of spilled fruits, describes the silhouette of the servants to the right of *Las Meninas*.

Phillip certainly admired that iconic work by Velázquez. A celebrated 1864 pair of views of Phillip in his studio, by John Ballantyne, shows in one of them Phillip's own full-scale copy of a section of *Las Meninas* on the back wall.[39] It is suspended above a tortoise-shell and ebony cabinet as if it were an *Assumption* over an altar. Phillip worshipped the original, though in fact it has been suggested that Velázquez haunts that whole interior by Ballantyne as if the seventeenth-century artist were a tutelary spirit.[40] While that most famous of Golden Age paintings *Las Meninas* was in some sense an abiding presence in Phillip's creative life, as with Wilkie twenty years before, the 'Spanishness' of Phillip's vision as we see it in his *The Early Career of Murillo* is adulterated: figures as densely interwoven as Romans on a sarcophagus have more in common with Mantegna's *Triumphs of Caesar* than with any narrative ever made for Philip IV.

In 1856, Alfred Elmore exhibited *The Emperor Charles V at the Convent of Yuste* at the Royal Academy (Figure 20). It was a case of word before image as always with things Spanish. The writers Blanco White and Byron had first opened the eyes of the artists Roberts and Lewis to the suggestiveness of Spain, so twenty years later painters continued to see the country through literature – by then, through the borrowed light of monumental Victorian histories. *Charles V at Yuste*, rather more moving and with greater narrative integrity than the Phillip *Murillo*, is also Italian in important respects. The gout-ridden emperor is slumped resignedly in a velvet chair with his feet impressed deeply into a cushion to ease the gout. Tonsured monks and velvet servants offer not Spanish pictures but favourite Titians, *The Empress* and *La Gloria*. As with *The Early Career of Murillo* so here, there is a confluence of sources: the *Last Supper* and the *Feast in the House of Levi*. A macaw perched on the back of the Emperor's chair might be intoning the word 'Veronese', since it was that painter rather than any representative of the Spanish school who provided inspiration.

Monks were a certain winner with the gallery-going public, but still more suggestive was the parish priest whose engagement with the world allowed all sorts of thoughts to spring up. Phillip was particularly adept at making an anecdote out of the cassock, and it was only after the death of the artist in 1867 that at last, British visions of the quotidian in Spain

20 Alfred Elmore, *The Emperor Charles V at the Convent of Yuste*

gave way to serious engagement between painter and painter. Whistler, Sargent and Lavery were the first to come to terms with Velázquez. With the new generation it was all to do with *how* painters painted, not *what* they painted. Before then Phillip had been hard at work with themes like *La Lotería Nacional*. To do justice to this subject, in 1860/61 he began the pair *Buying the Tickets* and *Reading the Numbers* (Figures 21 and 22).

They are anti-clerical pictures which contrast sharply with two images Phillip had painted in 1847 and 1849, images which – though conceived at an interval – the artist also came to see as paired. This earlier duet represented another country, another religion but, most revealingly, quite another attitude to peasant religion than Phillip would come to offer about Spain. The first of this earlier pair was entitled *Presbyterian Catechising*, the second, *Baptism in Scotland*. *Catechising* has elements of Hogarth and thus, though reverential, not without humour. Two years later, and with the *Baptism*, it became an altogether different matter. Silver light washes over an etherealised couple whose polished beauty suggests the incorruptibility of Calvinism. These humble folk stand with heads bowed before a minister whose venerable character is suggested by a crop of hair which falls over his collar as he sprinkles water over a baby. The mother adorned in a lemon and white dress is positively Blakean in her porcelain-like innocence, and in this beautifully painted picture there is not the slightest hint of subversion as there is in its pair. It was works such as these which made Phillip so dear to Queen Victoria.

There is a marked contrast between all this, set in a cotter's humble abode in Victorian Aberdeenshire, and the worldly hypocrisy of Phillip's vision of Catholicism played out in the fetid and dusty streets of Seville. The Spanish pictures were begun in 1860/61, well over a decade after his Scottish stories. That partly accounts for the radically different facture between the pairs. Nevertheless there is a coarseness in the application of paint in the *Lotería Nacional* pair, a trace of mockery in the rendering of the Spanish physiognomy, suggesting that Phillip sustained a belief in the racial superiority of the Celt to that of the Andalusian. This is reinforced by his deeply unpleasant picture *The Evil Eye* (1858). Here the artist, prosperous in hat and suit, drawing on a cheroot but also drawing an adolescent girl, observes her crouching behind a sun shield. The picture is shot through with menace and subdued violence. The more predatory *flâneur* would have much enjoyed *The Evil Eye*, which might have reminded him of picking up girls for under-age sex.

La Lotería Nacional: Buying the Tickets and *Reading the Numbers* suggest the credulous devotion of the Spanish peasantry for a priestly caste which does not merit the respect, let alone the idolatrous adulation, which the spectator witnesses. In *Buying the Tickets*, a parish priest walks out of the right-hand side of the canvas, back turned and oblivious to a small girl who kisses the hem of his cassock. He is unmindful because he is carefully inserting his ticket into his breviary where is to be found the

21 John Phillip, *Buying the Tickets*

22 John Phillip, *Reading the Numbers*

office of the day. *Reading the Numbers* also reveals a shepherd neglecting his flock: the same priest is seen in three-quarter profile intently studying numbers in the blinding sun while, in front, violence brews. To the right, a man in eye-catching ethnic costume appears to be flirting with a pretty woman unaware that her erstwhile partner, to the left of the priest with his back turned, sees it all. Perhaps here there is a misalliance in the making, a suggestion that those sections of society which should provide an exemplary moral lead are precisely the rotten core of the apple: the clergy and the prosperous Sevillian middle class. The adulterer is evidently of a higher social caste than the woman whose lover is becoming violently aware that he is about to be betrayed. The soon to be cuckolded man is placed at the left-hand margin of the canvas, peeling fruit for a smiling boy who, glancing up, has his left thumb cocked in the direction of the adulterous couple. The wronged partner uses a stiletto to operate on the orange. But his sinister sideways glance suggests that the weapon will shortly be applied to his rival. It is an essay on the deadly sins of avarice and lust couched in characteristically melodramatic terms, with predictable if sporadic lapses in taste on the part of the painter. But *La Lotería* was a success. The pair perfectly fitted the Victorian appetite for candied hypocrisy, a suggestive but enjoyable story of assignation with the tension of an imminent dénouement.

What, then, are we to make of British ways of picturing Spain? There was a limited range of subject matter, but such as there was allowed artists to meet the expectations of their public as they all traded in a limited stock of familiar archetypes: the beautiful Andalusian woman who was either morbidly religious or sparklingly coquettish. Whether describing interiors of buildings or *fiestas* outside, no one could be said to have understood Spain. There was neither a Viollet-le-Duc nor a Ruskin at the service of Spain. Gayangos and Jones collaborated on a scholarly production dedicated to the wonders of the Alhambra. But although that took its honourable place in a great tradition of the British architectural folios, to describe the Alhambra as Spain is like saying that the Acropolis is Greece or the Taj Mahal India. Artists came to Spain knowing what they were looking for and they extracted a partial view of its cultural heritage. It was one selected on the basis of what a British public could make sense of. The invention of Spain was a confirmation of prejudice, never a broadening of the mind.

Notes

1 Wilkie to William Collins, Madrid, 9 May 1828, in Allan Cunningham, *The Life of Sir David Wilkie*, 3 vols (London: John Murray, 1843), 2, p. 524.
2 Wilkie to Perry Nursey, 21 October 1821, in Tromans, *Wilkie and Spain*, p. 139.
3 This is the principal argument of Tromans's *Wilkie and Spain*.
4 R.A.M. Stevenson, *The Art of Velasquez* (London: George Bell and Sons, 1895).

5 Ibid., p. 18.
6 See Michel Foucault, 'Las Meninas', in his *The Order of Things* (London: Tavistock, 1974), Chapter 1, pp. 3–16 [First English translation of *Les Mots et les choses* (Paris: Gallimard, 1966)].
7 Madrid, 29 October 1827, in Cunningham, *Wilkie*, 2, p. 486.
8 Xanthe Brooke, 'A Masterpiece in Waiting: The Response to Las Meninas in Nineteenth-Century Britain', in Suzanne L. Stratton-Pruitt (ed.), *Velázquez's Las Meninas* (Cambridge: Cambridge University Press, 2003). Lawrence had stated back in 1810 that '[I] am more and more convinced that Spanish art will disappoint us'.
9 Lawrence to Wilkie, London, 27 November 1827, in Cunningham, *Wilkie*, p. 479.
10 Tromans, *Wilkie and Spain*, p. 276.
11 Ibid., p. 186.
12 Frank Hall Standish to David Roberts, Duxbury Park, 22 June 1838, NLS Acc. Ms. 11760 (unfoliated).
13 Sir David Wilkie to Frank Hall Standish, 14 November 1838, NLS Acc. Ms.11760 (unfoliated).
14 William Macpherson Brackenbury, British Consulate, Cádiz, 19 July 1833, NLS Acc. Ms.12158 (unfoliated).
15 Villaamil to David Roberts, London, 27 August 1841, NLS Acc. Ms. 8729 (unfoliated).
16 Raquejo, 'Arab Cathedrals', pp. 559–60.
17 *The Tourist in Spain: Andalusia By Thomas Roscoe Illustrated From Drawings by David Roberts*, London, 1836, p. xi.
18 Peterborough to Sarah, Duchess of Marlborough, 'From on board *The Resolution* in Alicante Road', 4 September 1706, BL Add. Ms. 61458, fol. 223.
19 R.Graham Moir to Stirling, Fonda de la Reina, Seville, Saturday 30 March [1850], MLG T-SK 29/5/250.
20 NLS Mf. Ms. 378 (unfoliated).
21 Idem. (from Literary Gazette New Publications *Illustrations to Jennings' Landscape Annual* 1835 *Granada, with the palace of the Alhambra*).
22 Owen Jones, *The Grammar of Ornament* (London: Day and Son, 1856), p. 66.
23 Brinsley Ford, *Richard Ford in Spain* (London:Wildenstein, 1974), pp. 24–6.
24 Quoted in James Ballantine, *The Life of David Roberts, R.A.* (Edinburgh: Adam and Charles Black, 1866), p. 77.
25 Thomas Roscoe, *The Tourist In Spain and Morocco* (London: Robert Jennings and Co., 1838), pp. 71–3.
26 Thomas Roscoe, *The Tourist in Spain, Andalusia* (London: Robert Jennings and Co., 1836), pp. 122–3.
27 Jennifer Melville, *Phillip of Spain: The Life and Art of John Phillip 1817–1867* (Aberdeen City Council, 2005), p. 64 and Plate 45, p. 67.
28 Roscoe, *Tourist in Spain and Morocco*, pp. 71–3.
29 Ibid.
30 NLS Mf. Ms. 378 (unfoliated).
31 See the work of Joseph Pennell, Muirhead Bone, Arthur Melville, Sidney Tushingham, E.S.Lumsden, W.D. Macleod, Ian Strang, Dora Carrington and David Bomberg.
32 Artist's Sale, 5 May 1877, Lots 298–301.
33 Nicholas Tromans, 'J.F. Lewis's Carlist War Subjects', *Burlington Magazine* (November 1997), pp. 760–5.
34 John Sweetman, 'John Frederick Lewis and the Royal Scottish Academy 1: The Spanish Connection', *Burlington Magazine* (May 2005), pp. 310–16.
35 J.F. Lewis to Stirling, 15 May [1853], 2 Great Stuart Street, Edinburgh, MLG T-SK 29/28/39.
36 Ibid. Brooke, pp. 61–5.
37 Millais to Stirling, 'Perth 10 Decr. [1]860', MLG T-SK 29/10/151: 'Dear Mr Stirling, I propose running over to see you for a couple of hours on Monday morning, as I want to

look at your woodcuts in your large book of costume. Do not answer if it is convenient. I am painting a picture about the beginning of the sixteenth century which obliges me to refer to prints of the time. Yours very truly, John Everett Millais'.
38 Phillip has recently been the subject of an exhibition in his home town, Aberdeen. See Jennifer Melville, *Phillip of Spain: The Life and Art of John Phillip 1817–1867* (Aberdeen City Council, 2005). The catalogue should serve to attract the attention to the artist which he abundantly deserves.
39 The pair to the picture with Phillip's copy of *Las Meninas* shows Phillip at an easel upon which is his own *The Early Career of Murillo* at a very early stage.
40 Ibid., Brooke, pp. 59–60.

Select bibliography

Ballantine, James, *The Life of David Roberts, R.A.* (Edinburgh: Adam and Charles Black, 1866)
Borrow, George, *The Bible in Spain* (London: John Murray, 1879)
Brooke, Xanthe and Cherry, Peter, *Murillo: Scenes of Childhood* (Dulwich Picture Gallery, 2001)
Bullen, Roger and Strong, Felicity, *Prime Minister's Papers Series: Palmerston: 1: Private Correspondence with Sir George Villiers (afterwards fourth earl of Clarendon) as Minister to Spain 1833–37* (London: Royal Commission on Historical Manuscripts, 1985)
Campbell, R.H. and Skinner, A.S. (eds): *An Enquiry into the Causes of the Wealth of Nations*, 2 vols (Oxford: Clarendon, 1976)
Davies, E., *The Life of Bartolome E Murillo* (London: Bensley and Son, 1819)
Doblado, Don Leucadio (Blanco White), *Letters from Spain* (London: Henry Colburn, 1822)
Ford, Richard, *A Handbook for Travellers in Spain, and Readers at Home*, 2 vols (London: John Murray, 1845)
Froude, James Anthony, *History of England*, 12 vols (London: 1856–1870)
Glendinning, Nigel, 'Goya and England in the Nineteenth Century', *Burlington* Magazine, January 1964
——, Harris, Enriqueta and Russell, Francis, 'Lord Grantham and the Taste for Velázquez: 'The Electric Eel of the Day', *Burlington Magazine*, October, 1999
Harris, Enriqueta, 'Las Meninas at Kingston Lacy', *Burlington Magazine*, February, 1990
Heide, Claudia, *The Many Lives of Pascual de Gayangos*, Edinburgh Ph.D., March 2005
Kagan, Richard L. (ed.), *Spain in America: The Origins of Hispanism in the United States* (Urbana and Chicago: University of Illinois Press, 2002)
Kenyon, John, *The History Men* (London: Weidenfeld & Nicolson, 1983)

Kirk, John Foster (ed.), *The Complete Works of William Hickling Prescott*, 12 vols (London: Gibbings and Co., 1896)

Lacambre, Geneviève and Tinterow, Gary (eds), *Manet Velázquez: La manière espagnole au XIXe siècle* (Paris and New York, 2002–2003)

Lipschutz, Ilse Hempel, *Spanish Painting and the French Romantics* (Cambridge MA: Harvard University Press, 1972)

Machin, G.I.T., *The Catholic Question in English Politics* (Oxford: Clarendon Press, 1964)

MacLarnon, Kathleen, 'William Bankes and His Collection of Spanish Paintings at Kingston Lacy', *Burlington Magazine*, February 1990

Melville, Jennifer, *Phillip of Spain: The Life and Art of John Phillip 1817–1867* (Aberdeen City Council, 2005)

Motley, J.L., *The Rise of the Dutch Republic: A History*, 3 vols (London: J. Chapman, 1856)

Murphy, Martin, *Blanco White: Self-Banished Spaniard* (New Haven, CT and London: Yale University Press, 1989)

Norman, Edward, *The English Catholic Church in the Nineteenth Century* (Oxford: Clarendon Press, 1984)

Roberts, David, *Picturesque Sketches in Spain* (London: Robert Jennings and Co., 1837)

Robertson, Ian, *Los Curiosos Impertinentes: Viajeros Ingleses por España 1760-1855* (Madrid: Editora Nacional, 1976)

——, *Richard Ford 1796–1858: Hispanophile, Connoisseur and Critic* (Wymondham: Michael Russell 2004)

Smitten, J. (ed.), *The Works of William Robertson*, 12 vols (London: Routledge and Bristol: Thoemmes, 1996)

Southey, Robert, *History of the Peninsular War*, 3 vols (London: John Murray, 1823–32)

Stirling, William, *Annals of the Artists of Spain*, 3 vols (London: John Ollivier, 1848)

Stratton-Pruitt, Suzanne L. (ed.), *Velázquez's Las Meninas* (Cambridge: Cambridge University Press, 2003)

Street, G.E., *Some Account of Gothic Architecture in Spain* (London: John Murray, 1865)

Sweetman, John, 'John Frederick Lewis and the Royal Scottish Academy 1: The Spanish Connection', *Burlington Magazine*, May 2005

Temperley, Harold, *The Foreign Policy of Canning 1822–1827: England, the Neo-Holy Alliance and the New World* (London: G. Bell and Sons Ltd, 1925)

Thom, John Hamilton (ed.), *The Life of the Rev. Joseph Blanco: with portions of his correspondence*, 3 vols (London: J.Chapman, 1845)

Tromans, Nicholas, 'Wilkie and Spain', University of Birmingham, Ph.D., 1995

Ward, Wilfrid, *The Life and Times of Cardinal Wiseman* (London and New York: Longmans, Green and Co., 1897)

Watson, Robert, *The History of the Reign of Philip the Second, King of Spain*, 2 vols (London: printed for W. Strahan and T. Cadell; and J. Balfour and W. Creech, Edinburgh, 1777)

Wiseman, Nicholas, His Eminence Cardinal Wiseman, *Essays on Various Subjects in Three Volumes*, 3 vols (London: C. Dolman, 1853)

Index

'n.' after a page number indicates the number of a note on that page

Acton, Lord, 79
  catholic controversialist, 80–1, 87
  criticism of Pius IX, 80
  library, 80
  Gladstone, 80
  'Golden Age', 80
  History of Liberty, 80
  Home and Foreign Review, 81
  Wiseman, uneasy relationship with, 81
  Ximenéz, Cardinal, review of biography, 80
Alhambra, 83, 198, 181, 193, 200–1
America and Spain, 18, 98–103, 178
  American authors on, xi, 99, 102, 111, 138
  colonies, 15–18, 25–6, 34
art (Spanish), 120
  azulejos, 151
  British perceptions of, 148, 152
  churches, xi, 72, 81–7, 120–1
  decree against export, 173
  see also Madrid
  paintings in London, 165
  patrimony, 171
  portraits and portraiture, 122, 130, 185
  sculpture, 86, 130–1
  see also under individual Spanish artists

Bankes, William John (1786–1855)
  despises El Greco, 163
  fanciful attributions of, 180
  at Kingston Lacy, 162
  Juanes and, 162
  percipient collector of Spanish painting, 162
  travels in Spain, 162
Bankes, Sir Ralph (d.1677), collects Murillo, 158
Bonapartism, ix, 40–2, 61–3
Borrow, George
  Alhambra, 83
  Bible in Spain, The, 38, 83, 89
  Cobbett, William, 70
  Ford, Richard, 39
    opinion of Borrow, 83, 109–10
  geography of Spain and, 89
  in León, admiration for cathedral, 83
  Murillo, admiration for, 83
  Peninsular War, 38
  Seville, Alcázar, 83
  Spain, catholicism in
    admiration for, 83
    priests, 68
  temperament, 70
  in Valladolid, 109
  witnesses public execution, 68
  Zincali, The, 109
Boyd, Edward, 46–9
Brackenbury, John Macpherson, 192, 194
British Legion, The, in Spain, 50–8
Brown, Archibald, collector of Spanish painting in Lima, 176–7
Byron, Lord, xi, 162, 197, 221

Calatrava, José Maria, 171–2
Canning, George
  Commons, oratory in, 44–5
  European powers, 42–4
  as pragmatist, 44–5
  Spain, colonies of, 44–5
    foreign policy in relation to, 43–4
Cano, Alonso
  Angel of the Passion, The, 166
  drawings by, 181
  Judgement of Solomon, The, 176
  pictures belonging to Standish, 180
  Virgin and St Joseph, 169
Caravaggio, confusion with Spanish painters, 160, 163
Carlist Wars, ix, 49–57, 158, 170, 212
Carlyle, Thomas, 45–7, 70, 125, 184
Catholicism in England, ix
  Catholic Emancipation, 61, 65, 70
  civil liberties, 65, 70
  Cobbett and, 70
  divisions within, 59–60, 79–81
  Dublin Review, The, 76
  Elizabeth I and, 70–1
  Gordon Riots, 60
  Infallibility as divisive between, 59–60
  Lord John Russell and, 73
  loyalty of, 71
  popular literature against, 71
  prejudice against, 6, 61, 64
  Recusants, 109
  relationship with Anglicanism, 59
  see also Southey, Robert
  Spain and, x, 59–87, 110, 203
  Tories, 61
  treasonable nature of, 64
  see also Wiseman, Nicholas; White, Joseph Blanco
Catholicism in Spain, 64, 83, 109
  monasteries, 165–73
  regulars, decline of, 65–6
Chambers, Sir William, 4, 123
Charles I (Stuart), 13, 155–7
Charles V, x, 3, 5, 7–18, 94, 138–9, 148
Cintra, Convention of, 33–7, 53
cities (Spanish), 7–8, 11, 15

Clarendon, Edward Hyde, 1st earl of, 12, 97, 173
Cobbett, William
  Borrow, compared with, 70
  eccentricities of, 70
  Elizabeth I (*Gloriana*), criticism of, 70–1
  English Catholics, 71
  Mary Tudor, admiration for, 70
  Philip II, admiration for, 70
  Protestant Reformation, The, 70
  radicalism of, 39, 70
  Weekly Political Register, 39
  William of Orange, 70
Cole, Sir Henry, 147–8, 151–2
Coleridge, Samuel Taylor, 31, 45–6, 63, 69
colonies (Spanish), 5, 17–21, 41–2
Coningham, William, 132–3
  attacks National Gallery about purchase of Zurbarán, 132–3
constitutions in Spain and South America, 11, 29–32, 41–2, 108
Crescenzi, Giovanni Battista, 156–7
Cristinos, 52–4
Crusades, 5, 10–12, 54

Disraeli, Benjamin, xi, 50, 121, 146
  Stirling Maxwell and, 97
Dutch, 20, 25, 34, 112
  art in Spain, 126
  in Seville, 126
  struggle with Spain, 112

Eastlake, Sir Charles, 129–30
  indifference to Spanish art, 130–2, 147
  influence on Layard, 147
  Madrazo brothers and, 149
  views on Velázquez's *Christ at the Column*, 149
Eastlake, Lady, friendship with Layard, 147, 150
Eden, Sir William
  collection of Spanish pictures at Windlestone, 165
  dedicatee of *Handbook*, 165
  describes Valladolid, 120–1

ecclesiastical buildings (Spanish), v, 72, 83, 120–1
economy of Spain, 23, 36, 42
El Greco, 163
  Adoration of the Shepherds, 141
  recognition in Britain, 139
  reputation in Spain, 139–40
  Stirling on, 140–1, 164
Elmore, Alfred
  Emperor Charles V at Yuste, The, 94, 221
  On the Brink, 213
Escazena, José Maria, 153 n.24, 172, 193
Escorial, 13, 26, 98, 104, 117, 125, 149–50, 157, 171–2, 182–3
Evans, General, Sir George de Lacy, 48–57
  historical romance about, 48
exiles in London from Spain, 41, 46, 63, 125

Ferdinand VII, king of Spain, 29–30, 41–3, 46–7, 49, 52, 125, 143, 158, 162
Ferdinand and Isabella, 7, 125, 201
  tombs, 201–3
Finden, Edward and William, *Byron's Beauties*, 197
Ford, Richard
  acerbity of, 69
  Alhambra, 165
    description of by, 200
  anti-Gallicanism, 37, 96, 164
  Apsley House collection, 164
  art criticism , influence of, 120, 125
  Borrow, cultivation of, 39, 83, 109–10
  Cajés, Eugenio, 184
  Carlist Wars, 56
  compared with Froude, 110
  Cook, Samuel, 143–4
  Froude, 110
  Goya, dislike of paintings by, 169
  Handbook for Travellers in Spain, A, 134–5, 137
    cancellation of, 170
    dedicatee of, 165
    revision of, 129, 149
    success of, 68, 125
  Head, Sir Edmund, 142
  Layard, Sir Henry, revisions of *Handbook*, 129, 149
  Lewis, J.F., 197
  Murray, John, 142, 149
  sexual liaisons of, 197
  Spain
    authority on paintings, 178
    buys art in, 166
    character of Spaniards, 170
    collector of, 178
    condescension of towards, 206
    drawings owned by, 180
    proposed visit to, 132
    writings on art, 120, 125
  Stirling, xi, 97, 134–5, 142
    as art critic compared with, 184
    Ford as agent for, 183
  Street's criticism of, 85
  Torrijos, General, 47
  travel writer, gifts as, 36
  Unchangeable Character of All Wars in Spain, On the, 56
  Velázquez, 136–7
  Wellington, duke of, 161–4
  Williams, Don Julián, 180–1
  Zurbarán, 129, 133, 162
    owns *S. Serapion*, 180
France, 3, 8, 23, 29, 31, 35, 37–46, 96, 164
Francis I of France, 8–9, 90, 96–7
Froude, James Anthony
  Alva, duke of, 111
  Catholic priesthood, 110
  Elizabeth I, attitudes towards, 106–7
  Henry VIII, 114
  as historian, xi, 92, 107
  Lytton Strachey, 108
  Mary Tudor, attitudes towards, 108–9
  methodology, 101
    criticism of his, 107
  morality, 101
  Motley, J.L. and, 113–14
  Newman, John Henry, 110
  the novel and, 106
  at Oxford, 105

Oxford Movement, 106, 111
personal life of, 106–7
Philip II, 108–11
public life, 105, 107–8
religious faith, 106, 111
reputation, 108
Spain, 106–7
  Catholicism in, 110
as story teller, 108, 114
William Cecil and, 107

Gautier, Théophile, 121, 132, 141, 164, 198
Gayangos, Pascual de
  Cortes, 12
  Don Carlos, 138
  influence of, on historians, 98
  Jones, Owen, collaboration with, 200, 226
  Prescott, W.H., 138
  Simancas, 138
  Titian, 138
  Yuste, 118 n.8
Gibbon, Edward, 1, 3, 5–6, 10, 89
Gladstone
  admirer of Acton, 80–1
  authority on architecture, 81
  Law Courts, competition with, 81
  obituary of Blanco White, 62
  Stirling, 81
  Street, 81
  unity of politics and religion, 59
Goya
  Attack on the Coach, 168
  Count Floridablanca and Goya, 168
  daughter, 168
  Desastres de la Guerra, Los, 53
  as etcher, 122, 129
  Ford, dislike of work, 183
  Grantham, 122–4
  Holland, collects, 168
  Layard, comments on, 149
  Rembrandt, compared to, 149
  Stirling, most discerning British collector of, 183
  Velázquez, copies, 149, 163, 168
  Villiers, collects, 167–8, 183
Grantham, Thomas Robinson, 2nd baron
  as ambassador in Spain, 13
  architecture, 123
  Escorial, presents picture to, 125, 171
  Goya, 122–4
  Pelham Henry, 122–5, 163
  Robertson, William, 13
  Spanish archives, 13–14
  sympathy for Spain, 13
  visitors to Madrid, 121–2
  Velázquez, projected life of, 122
  Villiers, George, contrasted to, 171
  Waddilove and, 13
Great Britain
  British attitudes towards Spain, x–xiii, 3, 9, 11–12, 15–16, 18, 25, 40–2, 64, 82, 116–17, 125, 170–1, 180, 190, 206, 213–15, 221, 226
  Carlist wars divide politics in, 49
  commitment to Spain, 47, 53, 56
  import of pictures from Spain and colonies to, 164
  intervention in Spain, 46
  life for British in Madrid, 121
  national debt compared with Spain, 24–5
  politics compared with Spain, 29
  prejudices against Spain, v, 48
  sex in Spain, 197
  taxes compared with Spain, 23
  the Union, and Spain, 8

Head, Sir Edmund, 142, 198
Henry VIII, 9, 90, 106, 114
Herrera, Francisco, 172, 178
histories of Spain, influence on pictorial imagery, 214
Holland, Henry Vassall Fox, 3rd Baron Holland
  Auckland, Lord, 32
  Charles James Fox, 32
  Goya, 168
  Holland House, 41
  Jovellanos, 31–2
  Lady Holland, 41
  liberales, 32
  Lord John Russell and, 30, 121
  patron of the arts, 31, 167–9

Index

political philosophy of, x
Spanish refugees, 41, 125
travels in Spain, 30–3, 72, 159
Villiers, Edward, earl of Clarendon, 167–9
White, Blanco, 63–8
Wiseman, 72

images of Spain, 189–226
Inquisition, the, 6, 80–1, 100–1, 110
Ireland
   catholicism in, compared with Anglicanism, 79
   Spain and, 74
Irving, Washington, xi
   portrait of 'Columbus', 138
   Prescott, influence on, 102
   subject of painting by Wilkie, 98, 195
Isabella of Castile, 7, 100, 116–17, 131
Isabella II and Carlism, 11, 30, 49, 202
Islam, 4, 10, 12, 102, 164, 197, 200

Jacobinism, ix, 31, 46, 164
Johnson, Samuel, x, 6, 7
Jones, George, images of the Peninsular War, 161
Jones, Inigo
   Crescenzi and, 156–7
   Escorial, 157
   quarrel with Jonson, 156–7
Jones, Owen
   Alhambra, 198
   Ecclesiological Movement, 200
   collaboration with Gayangos, 200, 226
   Goury and, 198
   influence on Morris, 199–200
Jonson, Ben, *To Inigo, Marquess Would Be, a Corollary*, 156

Keene, Sir Benjamin, ambassador to Spain, sympathy for country, 113, 125, 160
Kingston Lacy (Dorset), Spanish pictures at, 162–3, 180

Landor, Walter Savage, in Spain, 56, 147
Lawrence, Sir Thomas, 144, 190, 227 n.8
Layard, Sir Austen Henry, 114, 129
   archaeologist in Iraq, 146
   azulejos, 151
   Charles V, coffin of, 148
   Cole, Sir Henry, 147–8, 152
   as collector, 147
   controversy about, 146–7
   creator of taste for, 151–2
   Crowe and Cavalcaselle, 149
   description of, 146
   Eastlake, Sir Charles, appreciation of, 147
   Eastlake, Lady, friendship with, 147–8
   Goya, 149
   Layard, Lady, 147
   Madrid, ambassador in, 145–52
   Morelli, 149–51
   politician, 146
   revisions of Ford's *Handbook*, 129
   Spain, historian of art in, 148–51
   St Paul's Cathedral (London), 151–2
   Titian, 149–50
   Velázquez, fascination for, 149–51
   in Venice, 147
   Zurbarán, 129
Lewis, John Frederick
   Alhambra, 181, 201
   Andalucía, 197
   Byron, illustrates, 197
   Celebration of Mass in a Moorish Chapel in Cordova Cathedral, The, 208–10
   Fords, guest of, in Seville, 197, 208
   imagery, suggestiveness of, 213
   Islam, 197
   Murillo Painting the Virgin in a Franciscan Monastery, 210–12
   Picturesque Sketches in Spain, 201
   Proclamation of Don Carlos, The, 212
   Roberts, 206–8, 212, 221
   Rubens, 212
   in Spain
      copies of Velázquez, 197, 210

ethnicity, 197
  interest in art, 197, 210
  Murillo, 210–12
  Prado, copies in, 197
  Spanish subjects painted in
    England, 210
  *Sketches and Drawings of the
    Alhambra*, 211
  *Sketches of Spain and Spanish
    Character*, 210
  Stirling, corresponds with, 212
  Van Dyck, 210
liberalism in Spain, 29–32, 41, 43,
    48–9, 52, 69
Lima, 176–7
literature (Spanish), 65, 103, 168
  holdings of in Britain, 125
  relationship with Spanish history, xi
London, Spanish paintings in, 165,
    183
Long, Edwin, *Agua Santa*, 204, 213
Louis-Philippe
  admiration of Standish for, 179
  Baron Taylor, 164, 172, 179
  collection, sale of, 132, 164
  deposed, 165
  Musée espagnol, Le, xi, 132, 164,
    179
Low Countries and Spain, 110–11

Macpherson-Grant, John, 143–4, 174,
    194
Madrid
  Armería real, 14
  British in, 121
  Charles I in, 155–7
  dangers of, 158
  Gautier in, 121
  manuscripts in, 13–14
  Morelli in, 150
  Paris, compared with, 36
  Prado, paintings in, 142
  Palacio Real, 123
  School of, 142
    copyists of in, 156
    export of, 164
  Velázquez in, 149
Manchester, 1857
  Art Treasures Exhibition, 142, 177

manuscripts in Spain, 13, 138
Martineau, Hariet, 71–2
Melbourne, Viscount, approached
    about Spanish pictures, 179–82
Mengs, Anton Rafael, 13, 122–4
Millais, Sir John
  anti-Catholicism, exploits, 213–15
  Escape of a Heretic, 214–15
  friendship with Stirling, 214 n.37,
    217
  *Huguenot on St Bartholomew's Day,
    A*, 214
  Justice, 139
  Pizarro seizing the Inca of Peru, 213
  Ruskin, 216
  Souvenir of Velazquez, A, 214
  wife, 214
monasteries in Spain, dissolution,
    165–73
Morelli, Giovanni
  art historian, influence as, 150
  friendship with Layard, 149–51
Moriscoes, 102
Morris, William
  influence of Street on, 84
  Owen Jones, 200
  at Oxford, 84
  quarrels with Street, 86
  the SPAB and, 84
Moya, 176
Murillo
  Adoration of the Shepherds, 176–7
  affinity with Dutch and Flemish
    artists, 126
  Borrow, admiration for, 83
  British collections of, 159
  British merchants and, 158–9
  British responses to, 127
  Caridad, Seville, 181
  compared with Herrera, 178
  compared with Ribera, 177
  Death of Santa Clara, 126
  differentiation of styles, 165–6
  drawings, and use of, 127, 180–2
  etchings, 180
  export, 153 n.24
  'fancy pictures', 126
  first British biographer, 126
  Ford on, 142

fruit boys, 176
Hertford, Lord, 177
Immaculate Conception, 176
Invitation to a Game of Argolla, 127
Jacob's Ladder, 136
Lewis, J.F., 210–12
Nöel-Paton on, 178
novice compared with, 196
Phillip, John 'Spanish', 218–21
popular reputation of in Spain, 218
reputation in Britain, 121, 125–6
Roberts, 196
in Russia, 136
St Anthony of Padua with the Infant Christ, 161, 208
St Elizabeth of Hungary, figure of, 127
St José y Niño, 169
St Thomas of Villanueva giving Alms, 126
San Tomas de Bonaventura, 212
Samuel Cook and, 143
Self-Portrait, 160, 181
Southern and, 175
'Spanish van Dyck', 126–7, 159
Spring as a Flower Girl, 127
Standish, 179–80, 182
style, diversity of, 179
tableaux depicting paintings by, 189
Taylor, baron, 182
uncharacteristic Spanish painter, 127, 137
Walpole, Robert, 160
White, Blanco, 69
Williams, Julián, 181–2
Wiseman admires, 76
Wordsworth, compared to, 127
Zurbarán, compared with, 132, 134
Musée espagnol, Le, see Louis-Philippe

Napier, Charles, historian of Peninsular War, 37, 161
Napier of Merchiston, Francis, 10th Lord
  book on Neapolitan painting, 135–6
  diplomatic career, 134
  friend and critic of Stirling, 134–5
  Ribera and, 134–5

Newman, John Henry
  Catholic revival, attitude to, 75–6
  ecclesiastical architecture, 78
  Froude, friendship with, 105–6
  White, friendship with, 69–75
  Wiseman, contrast with, 75

Palmerston, Lord, 49–50, 56, 81, 135, 167
  the Basques and, 56
  tries to buy Escorial pictures for The National Gallery, 171–3
Peel, Sir Robert
  Catholicism, 59
  Wilkie, 189–91
Pelham, Henry, 2nd earl of Chichester, travels in Spain, 122–5
Peninsular War, 37–9, 96, 162
Peru, 18, 176–7, 213
Phillip, John 'Spanish'
  admiration for Velázquez, 218, 221
  Agua Bendita – a Church Scene, 204
  Baptism in Scotland, 223
  Buying the Tickets, 223
  compared with Elmore as interpreter of Spain, 221
  Early Career of Murillo, The – 1634, 218–21
  El Cigarillo: Taking a Quiet Whiff, 213
  Kate Nickleby, 218
  latent eroticism in paintings, 204, 222
  Meninas, Las, 221
  Presbyterian Cathecism, 223
  Queen Victoria, admiration for, 223
  Reading the Numbers, 223
  Ruskin comments on, 218
  Spain, anti-clericalism, 223
    condescension towards, 206, 223
    fantasies about, 204, 217, 222
    religious observance in compared with Scottish practice, 223
    superficial interpretation of, 213
    visits, 217
Ponz, Antonio, 123–4, 166
Popes and Papacy, 64, 78, 109
  Innocent X, portrait of, 164
  Pius IX, 59, 76, 80, 96

portraiture in Spain, 137–8
poverty in Spain, 16–17, 22, 117
Prescott, William Hickling,
  America and, 98–104, 117
  American Civil War, affect on as writer, 99–100
  as an 'American' interpreter of Spain, 102
  attitudes to Charles V, 98–9, 101–2
  bigotry of Spain, 99
  character and actions of Philip, 11, 100–2, 114
  Columbus, 138
  composition of *Philip II*, 98
  fall of Granada, 102
  Ferdinand and Isabella, 97, 100, 103, 138, 214
  Gayangos, 138
  influence of Stirling Maxwell on, 91, 98–9, 103, 114, 138–9
  Inquisition, 100–1
  Isabella of Castile, 100, 116–17
  Lepanto, 100
  literary output, 98
  methodology compared with Froude, 101, 102–3
  Moriscoes, 103
  Motley, 111
  never in Spain, 23
  New England and, 98, 100–1
  pre-eminent nineteenth century interpreter of Spain, 97–8
  Ranke, influence of on, 104
  revision of Robertson's *Charles V*, 89–90, 98
  Simancas, 98, 104
  Spanish Armada, 117
  Washington Irving, 102
primitivism in Spain, 50, 53–4, 198, 206, 220–3
Protestantism and Spain, 95, 99, 117
Pugin, A. W., 66, 78–9

religious practices in Spain, 10, 196, 204–8
Ribera
  Adoration of the Shepherds, 176
  Raising of Lazarus, 176
  research on, 134–5

Roberts, David
  Alhambra, 181, 193, 201
  Andalucia, 198
  Annuals, illustrator of, 194–6
  Beckford, 203
  Brackenbury, 194
  as connoisseur of Spanish art, 175
  criticism of in *The Literary Gazette*, 203
  Edinburgh, early life in, 203, 217
  Ferdinand and Isabella, tomb of, 201–3
  Lewis, J.F., compared to, 206–8, 212, 221
  literary influences on, 194
  motives as painter, 193–4
  Murillo and, 196
  paintings, nature of, 194
  patrons of, 194
  poetry, illustrator of, 179, 192
  Roscoe, 194
  Seville cathedral, 203–4
  Southern, 175
  Spain and
    creates popular image of catholicism, 193–4
    ecclesiastical interiors, 197, 203–4
    ways of seeing country, 203–4, 206
  Standish, 179–81, 192
  success of Spanish subjects, 193–4
  suggestiveness of imagery, 196–7, 204
  worship as theatre, 208
Robertson, William
  bigotry, 6
  Blair, 15
  catholicism, 6
  Charles V, funeral of, 93
  Crusades, 11
  Edinburgh life, 1–3
  Edinburgh University, 2
  Gibbon, 1, 5
  Grantham, 13–14
  Hanoverians, 7
  History of America, 14
  History of India, 14–15
  History of Scotland, 3
  Jesuits, 19

Life of Charles V, 5–28
  methodology, 12–13
  nationalism, 8–9
  Presbyterians, 6
  Prescott, 89–91, 98
  publications, 3
  reputation of, 6, 89
  Robinson, 15
  Samuel Johnson, x
  slavery, 6
  Smith, 15–16, 19, 90
  Stewart, 3–5
Rubens, 137, 175, 212
Ruskin, John
  Dennistoun, compared with, 134
  Millais, 216
  Phillip, 218
  Spain and, xi, 207
  Venice, 214
  wife, 214
Russell, Lord John
  battle of Vitoria, 30
  catholics' hostility to, 73
  Constitution of Cádiz, 31
  interest in *liberales*, 30
  visits Spain, 121
Russia, interest in Spanish art, 171–2, 188

Scotland
  attitudes to Spain, 3
  Carlistas compared with Highlanders, 53
  Church of, 3
  cities in, 8
  History of Scotland and definition of nationhood, 6
  international significance of, 1
  Johnson's hostility to, x
  religious life in, 6, 223
  Union, history before, 7
Serafín, García de la Huerta
  dealer in Madrid, 14
  reputation of, 169, 173
Seven Years War, 4, 9, 16, 18, 25
Seville, Caridad, 127, 181, 210
  cathedral, 72
  church of Holy Cross, 66–7
  church of S. Filippo Neri, 66–7

Smith, Adam
  alcabala, 22–6
  Britain and Spain compared, 19
  British colonies, 25–6
  Casa de Contratación, 21
  colonies and Spain, 19
  decline of Spain, 3
  economy of Spain, 12, 16–17, 19, 22, 24–5
  history, stimulates interest in of Spain, 19
  Holland, 20
  investment in Spain, 101
  judiciary in Spain, 23–4
  knowledge of Spain, 22–3
  monopolies in Spain, 20–1
  Robertson, relations with, 16
  Seven Years War, 25
  specie and Spain, 21–2, 25
  taxes in Spain, 22–6
  Wealth of Nations, The, and Spain, 16, 26
Soult, Marshal, collector of Spanish art, 133, 164, 181, 188
Southern, Henry
  art agent for Villiers, 169–73
  Bentham, 166
  co-editor of *The Westminster Review*, 166
  dealings with Serafín, 169, 173
  friendship with Villiers, 166–7
  promotion, 167
  secretary to Villiers, 166
  Spain
    admiration for painting of, 169
    speculation in pictures, 174–7
Southey, Robert
  Catholic Emancipation, 65
  composition of, 39
  English Catholics
    prejudice against, 64
    as treasonable, 64
  church and state, relations between, 64
  Cintra, Convention of, 33
  gitano, 196
  History of the Peninsular War:
    admiration for, 41
  Iberia, attitudes to, 33, 37

Peninsular War
  benefits for Britain, 38
  greatest conflict in history, 37
  morality of, 40
political allegiance, change of, 69
Spain and
  Britain benefits from commitment to, 40
  Britain learns from experiences in, 40
  British prejudices against, 39
  criticism of British attitudes towards, 37
  emotional bond with, 53
  familiarity with history by working people in, 38
  mutual crisis in Britain and, 40
  primitivism of, 53, 85
  reciprocity with Britain, 40
  Spain as pre-lapsarian, 40
  Spanish literature, mastery of, 65
  special relationship between Britain and, 41
  Torres Vedras, 39–40
  Wellington, duke of, 37
  White, Blanco, 63–4, 69
  Wordsworth, 33, 37
Southwark, St George's, 66
Sterling, John, 45–9
Stewart, Dugald, 2–4
Stirling Maxwell, Sir William
  Annals of the Artists of Spain, emphasis on patronage and collecting in, 131–2
  anti-Gallicanism, 96
  bust of, 9
  Cloister Life of Charles V, xi, 91–6, 116, 215
  Disraeli, 97
  Ford, influence of, 110
  Froude, 110
  Gayangos, 98
  Gladstone, 81
  historical evidence, attitude to, 14
  Law Courts, competition for, 81
  Motley, 114–16
  Prescott and, 91, 98–9, 103, 114, 138–9
  Roberston, 93

Spain, attitudes to, 72
  Catholicism in, 79
  painters in, 85
  Street, 85
  Yuste, offered to, 93
Street, George Edmund
  architecture, social history of, 85–6
    Spanish, xi, 82–7
    texture in, 86
  architectural practice, 84
  Brick and Marble in the Middle Ages, 81
  Ecclesiological Movement, 83
  Ford, 85
  Gladstone, 81
  handcrafts, 84
  Law Courts, Strand, 81–2
  medieval buildings, 85–6
  Morris, 84
  Oswestry, 84
  partisanship of, xi, 81–2, 102
  restoration of buildings, 84
  Ruskin, 85
  Society for the Protection of Ancient Buildings, The, 84
  Some Account of Gothic Architecture in Spain, xi, 81–3
  Southwell Minster, 86
  travels of, 86
  versatility of, 81
Swinburne, Henry, 123

Taylor, Baron Isidore
  competes with British collectors, 164, 172
  Murillo *Self-Portrait*, 181–2
  tensions with Louis-Philippe, 179
  tensions with Standish, 181–2
Times, The, 47, 56, 114
  controversy about Zurbarán in, 133
Torrijos, General, 46–8
Travellers to Spain, 121–5
Trevor, Richard, bishop of Durham, 128–9

Valladolid, 98, 109, 120, 131, 201, 216
Van Dyck, Anthony
  J.F. Lewis, 208

Index   242

Spanish artists and, xii, 126–7, 158
Velázquez and, 137, 158
Wilkie and, 189
Vega, Father Teodomiro, 66–8
Velázquez
  Angels appearing to the Shepherds,
    188
  art journalism about, 189
  Bankes, 162–3
  Barrachos, Los, 188
  bodégon, 188
  bodegones, 163
  Bolthasar Carlos, 188
  buyer of art, 132
  Caravaggio, 160, 163
  Charles I, 155–7
  Child eating a pastry, 188
  Christ at the Column, 149
  compared with El Greco, 141
  compared with Rubens, 137
  compared with other Spanish
    painters, 137
  compared with Van Dyck, 137, 158
  copies, 124
  del Mazo, 137, 163
  drawings by, 181
  English art, influence on, 189–90
  Ford on, 144, 164
  Goya, 149
  Grantham, 122–4, 157
  Justi on, 149, 189
  Lady at Lace, The, 178
  landscape by, 143
  Lawrence, 190
  Manchester, exhibited at, 177
  manuscript by, on Titian, 150–1
  misconceptions about, 136–7,
    162–3, 189
  Morelli, 150–1
  Nöel-Paton, 177
  paintings by difficult to see, 158
  Philip IV Hunting, 136
  portrait of Charles I, 136
    self-portrait of, 143
    status of, 164
  as pupil of Herrera, 172
  Rokeby Venus, 144
  as Sevillian artist, 163
  Standish, 180

Stevenson, R.A.M., 189–90
Stirling Maxwell, 139
Victorians and, 139, 157–8, 168
views of Layard on, 149–51
Water carrier of Seville, The, 160
Whistler, 193
  At the Piano, 218
Wilkie, 188–90
Williams, 189
Williams-Standish collection, 181

Villamil, Jenaro Pérez, 173, 192–3
Villiers, George, 4th earl of Clarendon
  as collector of Spanish painting,
    167–71
  unscrupulous methods, 171–3
  commissions artists in Spain, 173
  contrast with Grantham, 171
  Escorial, tries to buy paintings, 171,
    182
  Evans, opinions about, 50–2
  Grove, The, (country house), 167,
    174
  Hollands, the, 168–9
  interest in Goya, 168–9, 183
  Melbourne, 180
  Palmerston, dealing with, 171–2
  sexual liaisons, 167
  Southern, friendship with, 166–7,
    174–5
  Spain, attitudes to, 170, 173
  Standish collection, 179
  Williams collection, 173

Waddilove, Robert, chaplain to British
    embassy, Madrid and
    ethnographic collections in
    Madrid, 13
  Grantham and, 13
  paintings, buyer of in Madrid, 123
  research assistant to Robertson, 13
  translator of Ponz, 13
  tutor to Pelham, 123
Walpole, Sir Robert, Spanish pictures,
    160
Wellesley, Sir Henry, 162
Wellington, Arthur Wellesley, 1st duke
    of
  Apsley House, 159, 161

Bankes, Sir John, 162
British army, 49, 51
Carlist Wars, 51–2
Catholic Emancipation, x, 61
Evans, 51
Ford, 96, 164
Great Reform Bill, 31
patron of the arts, 161
pictures owned by, 159, 163–4
political views of, 44
reputation of, 38, 40, 51
Spanish Church, 65
statue of, 162
Torres Vedras, 39–40
views on France, ix
White, Joseph Blanco
Bonapartism, 63
Catholic Emancipation, attitudes to, 66
as catholic priest, 62–3
Doblado's Letters from Spain (1822), 66
Evidences Against Catholicism (1825), 68
Examination of Blanco by White, An, 62
Holland House, 63
journalist, 63, 66
Life by myself, A (1845) 62, 66
Newman, 69
Oxford University, 68
political thinker, 66
prejudices of, 66
Roberts, David, influence on, 194, 221
secret service agent, 64
in Seville, 62
sonnet by, 63
Southey, 64, 68
Spain
 influence in Britain on attitudes to, 65, 69
 character of, 69
 poverty in, 66
 sensationalist account of Catholicism in, 32–3
temperament, 62–3, 69
Vega, Father, 67–8
Wiseman family, 62

Wilkie, Sir David
Confessional, The, 217
contrived historicism of, Sir Robert Peel and, 190–1
Defence of Saragossa, 34
Standish, 192
in Spain, 188–92
Velázquez and, 192, 210, 220
William of Orange, compared favourably with Philip, 11, 112
Williams, Don Julián
character of, 181
conspires with Villiers, 172–3
dishonesty, 181
generosity of, 181
Louis-Philippe, 181
misattributions by, 189
Murillo drawings, 180
Roberts, 194
Standish, 181–2
Taylor, 182
Villamil, 193
Wiseman, Nicholas, x
Acton, 81
apology, 73–4
appearance, 75
art critic, 72
birth, 59
Browning, characterises in poem (*Bishop Blougram's Apology* (1855)), 76
Canova, friendship with, 76
Cardinal's Appeal, The, 73–4
cartoon of, 77
crisis for catholic hierarchy, 73–5
Dickens, friendship with, 73
Dublin Review, The, 72, 76–8
Essays on Various Subjects, 76
family, 62
Father Faber, 75
fine arts, 72
From out of the Flaminian Gate, 73
history, attitude to, 76
Holland family, 72
Ireland, 79
Nazarenes, 76
Newman, contrast to, 75, 78–9
O'Connell, Daniel, 72
Pius VII, 76

public reputation of, 76
Pugin, 78–9
Punch, 76
religious ministry, 73, 78–9
Seville, 72
   church of the Holy Cross, 76
   as 'St Nicholas of Seville', 76
Spain and, 73–5, 76
   distinction of its saints, 78
Stirling Maxwell, 79
Street, G.E., 81
Westminster, as archbishop of, 74
White, Joseph, 62
women, Spanish, reputation of, 167
Wordsworth, William
   anti-Gallicanism, 36
   Convention of Cintra, 33–4, 37
   Ford, compared to, 36
   France, 34–6
   Holland, Lord, 49
   Lyrical Ballads, 127
   Madrid, compared with Paris, 36, 54
      lack of industrialisation in, 36
   Southey, 37–41, 69
   Spain
      appeal of, 34
      Britain reflected in, 35
      commitment to, 37
      conservatism, 34
      history of, 34, 33–4
      lack of industrialisation in, 36
      national minorities in Britain compared to, 53
      primitivism, 196
      religion in, 35
      virtues of, 37

We Are Seven, 27
Wren, Sir Christopher, 4, 52

Zurbarán
   acquisition by Richard Trevor, 128–9
   Apotheosis of St Thomas Aquinas, The, 129
   Bankes, William John, 162
   Bishop Auckland, paintings at, 128, 162
   Christ in the Temple, 177
   Circumcision, 176
   Coningham, William, 129
   controversy about in *The Times*, 129
   ethnicity, 128
   fanaticism of, 133
   Ford, equivocal about, 129
   Jacob and the Twelve Tribes, 128
   Layard on, 129
   London, sales in London of, 165
   Mary, Joseph and Christ, 176
   Mendez, Benjamin, 128
   paintings as Jewish icons, 128
   piety of, 133
   poet of Spanish religiosity, 133, 220
   redolent of Spain, 132
   St Jerome, 176
   St Francis in Meditation, 132
   St Serapion, 133, 189
   Standish, significance of holding, 180–2
   Velázquez, colouring compared to, 144
   Williams, paintings owned by, 180–2

EU authorised representative for GPSR:
Easy Access System Europe, Mustamäe tee 50,
10621 Tallinn, Estonia
gpsr.requests@easproject.com

www.ingramcontent.com/pod-product-compliance
Ingram Content Group UK Ltd.
Pitfield, Milton Keynes, MK11 3LW, UK
UKHW021836140426
5217IPUK00021B/1479